THE LOYAL, TRUE, AND BRAVE

THE LOYAL, TRUE, AND BRAVE

AMERICA'S CIVIL WAR SOLDIERS

Edited by
STEVEN E. WOODWORTH

A Scholarly Resources Inc. Imprint
Wilmington, Delaware

© 2002 by Scholarly Resources Inc.
All rights reserved
First published 2002
Printed and bound in the United States of America

Scholarly Resources Inc.
104 Greenhill Avenue
Wilmington, DE 19805-1897
www.scholarly.com

Library of Congress Cataloging-in-Publication Data

The loyal, true, and brave : America's Civil War soldiers / edited
by Steven E. Woodworth.
    p. cm.
    ISBN 0-8420-2930-3 (alk. paper) — ISBN 0-8420-2931-1
(pbk. : alk. paper)
    1. United States. Army—History—Civil War, 1861–1865.
2. Confederate States of America. Army—History. 3. Soldiers—
United States—Social conditions—19th century. 4. Soldiers—
Confederate States of America—Social conditions. 5. United
States. Army—Military life—History—19th century.
6. Confederate States of America. Army—Military life.
7. United States—History—Civil War, 1861–1865—Social
aspects. I. Woodworth, Steven E.

E607 .L69 2002
973.7'42—dc21   2001054151

We will welcome to our number
All the loyal, true, and brave,
Shouting the battle cry of Freedom.
And although he may be poor, not a man shall be a slave,
Shouting the battle cry of Freedom.

—George F. Root
"The Battle Cry of Freedom" (1863)

Acknowledgments

It is a pleasure to acknowledge the kind assistance of those whose help has made this book possible. Matthew R. Hershey of Scholarly Resources both suggested the original concept and served as a diligent editor in pushing me to produce the best possible manuscript. Professors Earl J. Hess, of Lincoln Memorial University, and Daniel Sutherland, of the University of Arkansas, both took time out from their busy schedules of research and writing to read a draft of my manuscript and offer valuable suggestions for its improvement.

Finding the primary sources for inclusion in this book entailed visits to a number of manuscript repositories in various parts of the country. In those institutions I enjoyed the kind assistance of many librarians and archivists. I would like to thank the staff of the Manuscript Reading Room of the Library of Congress, the Illinois State Historical Library, the Indiana Historical Society, and especially Richard Sommers, David Keough, Pamela Cheney, and James Baughman of the U.S. Army Military History Institute archives.

About the Editor

Steven E. Woodworth received a B.A. in history from Southern Illinois University and a Ph.D. from Rice University. He is currently associate professor of history at Texas Christian University in Fort Worth. Woodworth is the author of numerous books on the Civil War, including *Jefferson Davis and His Generals: The Failure of Confederate Command in the West* (1990); *While God Is Marching On: The Religious World of Civil War Soldiers* (2001); and *A Scythe of Fire: The Civil War Story of the Eighth Georgia Regiment* (2002).

Contents

Introduction

In his November 1863 address dedicating a cemetery for the Union soldiers slain in the recent battle of Gettysburg, Abraham Lincoln modestly opined, "The world will little note nor long remember what we say here, but," he continued, "it can never forget what they did here." As in many of his statements, Lincoln has proved accurate as the years have gone by. The courage, perseverance, and dedication of the Civil War soldiers—coupled with their disarming humanness—has lent an enduring attraction to their story. Generation after generation of Americans has turned in fascination to the varied and colorful experiences of those three million men who, in the words of Oliver Wendell Holmes Jr., had their hearts "touched with fire."

The way in which the soldiers' story has been told has changed over the years, as passing generations have each brought to it their own interests and questions. The decades immediately following the conflict saw the soldiers' story narrated by the men themselves, as many of them wrote memoirs of their service, emphasizing those aspects of the war—and their part in it—that they believed were most important. The soldiers were often self-effacing, but they stressed the transcendent nature of the cause for which they fought.

The mid-twentieth century saw the rise of a different genre of writing about the common soldiers of the Civil War. Epitomized by the work of Bell Irvin Wiley, this school stressed the humanness and the ordinary, unheroic nature of the soldiers and their service. Ideological concerns were played down. In the late twentieth century, there were additional shifts in historiography. If Wiley's era found heroism vaguely embarrassing, then the post-1960s scholarly world found it flatly incomprehensible and assumed that it could not exist. Soldiers came to be seen not as heroes—even quiet, unassuming heroes—but rather as victims, behavioral specimens tossed to and fro and driven about by various social forces acting upon them. This approach appears most starkly in Gerald

Linderman's 1987 book, *Embattled Courage*, which argues that by mid war the soldiers had become completely disillusioned with the ideals brought with them to the conflict.

Meanwhile, and almost simultaneously, a different school of thought, seen in the work of James McPherson and Earl Hess, continues to maintain that amid all the inglorious and disillusioning experiences of war, the soldiers nevertheless persevered, overcame, and maintained the basic values and ideals that had led them to enlist in the first place. And through all of the interpretations and reinterpretations, the soldiers' own story remains the focus of the entire study. Changing genres of historical writing may come and go, but the world "can never forget what they did."

The purpose of this book is not to present new research about the Civil War soldiers but to present to readers—whether formal or informal students of the war—the sum of the research that has already been done. I have not set out to make a new contribution to the historical debate but rather to present a synopsis of that debate to those approaching it for the first time or seeking to see it anew through a broad overview. My method has been to select brief excerpts from some of the numerous books that have been written about the soldiers and to present these with brief introductions and as much explanation as seemed necessary. For those who have not already done so, this book is meant to be an invitation and a challenge to delve deeper into the literature of the Civil War soldier, exploring in full the works here excerpted and seeking others as well.

The chapters that follow deal with various aspects of the soldiers' experience. Some of these areas have been the subjects of debate among historians, particularly the issue of the nature of courage, discussed in Chapter Three. I have tried to give readers a vivid sense of those debates. In other areas there has been less disagreement, and my presentation of those matters has been simply descriptive. The courage, fortitude, and resilience of the Civil War soldiers in the most appalling circumstances still challenge our admiration more than a century after their deeds. Their story is well worth reading and studying.

CHAPTER ONE

Joining the Army

Nowhere is the difference between Civil War soldiers and their modern-day counterparts more striking than in the way they became soldiers in the first place. Today's soldiers enlist in a relatively bureaucratic army that whisks the new recruits away to training depots to be drilled into the interchangeable human parts that are then distributed throughout the huge organization. Civil War soldiers, by contrast, signed up along with their friends in their local community and in a hometown company that would keep those friends together. The company would later take on a formal designation (a letter) within a formally numbered regiment, but it would still be at heart a band of men and boys with home-grown names meant to sound military—the Raymond Fencibles, Rockford Zouaves, Rome Light Infantry, Tioga Mountaineers, and hundreds of others.

Civil War soldiers received scant training. A regiment was lucky to have among its officers a few who had experience in the regular army or who had served (generally in equally ill-trained volunteer regiments) in the Mexican War or Seminole Wars. Often the colonel was the only one with such experience and sometimes even the regimental commander might be as green as any of his recruits. To make matters worse, the nineteenth-century American militia system, under which the Civil War regiments were organized, provided that officers all the way up to the rank of colonel should be elected by their troops. This system was detrimental in several ways. First, there was no reason to expect the green recruits, innocent of all knowledge of war or military ways, to select the best qualified men to lead them. On the contrary, the new volunteers seemed prone to vote for the least qualified men, perhaps because they could identify with them. West Point graduate and colonel of the 41st Ohio

1

William B. Hazen remarked that among the newly elected officers, "as a rule, fitness was found to vary inversely with rank."[1]

Second, while a given company was in the process of forming, before its formal elections were held its temporary officers dared not attempt to impose military discipline for fear of irritating their soldiers and ruining their chances to have their rank confirmed. Even after the officers were elected, the pernicious effect continued as the new leaders, only recently elevated from among their comrades by those same comrades' votes, often lacked the respect needed to enforce discipline. In short, many factors combined to make the transition of midnineteenth-century American youth into soldiers slow, inefficient, and never fully complete.

This chapter deals with the process by which the young men of the Civil War generation entered the army and received such early training as their particular regiments could provide before meeting the shock of battle. As you read, consider the process of transformation from civilian to soldier and also consider what motivations might have prompted young men to enlist in the Civil War armies. Looking back a quarter-century later, how did they feel about those motivations?

Wimer Bedford Helps Raise a Company[2]

The process by which young Illinoisan Wimer Bedford became an army officer is a good example of the strange, almost haphazard, way in which various prominent or influential men endeavored to enlist troops in their own companies and thus move up to officer status. A man who successfully enlisted a company—about 100 officers and men—could usually count on a captain's commission. As Bedford's experience demonstrates, the process of raising a company could sometimes be almost farcical, with rival would-be captains striving to lure recruits away from each other to advance their own dreams of glory.

The first writers to tell the story of the common soldiers were the soldiers themselves. While the historians of that era focused on the deeds of great leaders, the men who had seen what one of them would call "the rough side of war" began the task of describing for a younger generation the part of history they had lived. Bedford wrote this memoir for his own children in the early 1890s.

My dear Daughter:

As you have frequently requested me to write you about some of the incidents of my life and experience in the Union Army during the Rebellion of 1861–1865, I will endeavor, in a rough way, from memory, to obey the request. I have a very poor memory for dates, and many incidents have also escaped that treacherous memory.

At the opening of the war in 1861, when troops were being raised by the several states for what was called "Thirty days' service," I was residing in Illinois, and occupied the position of Route Mail Agent along the line of the Illinois Central Railroad between Centralia and Cairo, making my home alternately at either place.

At Centralia some four companies had been raised for the United States service and were in readiness to be called upon by the Government. In my leisure time I had been making visits to Springfield with a view to obtaining some kind of a position with the army, but without success for two reasons, first, as I felt that I might possibly not be able to fill a place properly, should one by chance be given me; and secondly, as I had very little influence with those in authority to obtain what I should like, if I could fulfill the duties. I determined to secure the aid of some one or more of my friends at Centralia in the effort to get up a company of infantry.

Finally Mr. Joseph Cormack, who was a conductor on the road, at my earnest entreaty sought for and obtained a commission from the Governor of Illinois as Captain of Illinois Volunteers with permission to raise a company. He and I both made the effort; but as the town had been by this time pretty well drained of material by the four companies already raised, we met with but little success there, securing only a few recruits.

However, one of these recruits seemed to be an enterprising fellow; and as Captain Cormack had been ordered to report with his company (should he succeed in raising one) at Anna in Union County—a station on the Illinois Central Railroad where was raising a regiment afterwards known as the 18th Illinois Infantry, Col. Lawler commanding—Capt. Cormack sent this recruit, dubbing him Sergeant, with power to get all the other recruits he could, and held them at the headquarters of this regiment, where Capt. Cormack had been assigned company quarters.

The Sergeant soon reported to us that he had several men in camp ready to be mustered in, and both the Captain and I went down there to do what we could to augment our force.

In the meantime a company of men had been raised in southern Illinois; and they were now resting in the woods outside of our camp, waiting and hoping for the word from Springfield to be permitted to join the same regiment. The leader of this company was inclined to a too free use of liquor; and, leaving his men in the evening in order to apply at our camp for rations for them, he forgot his duty to his men and used the time in getting drunk, while they passed that night hungry in the woods.

Now U. S. Grant, afterwards the great conqueror of the Rebellion and President of the United States, had been sent down from Springfield by Gov. Yates to muster in our regiment as soon as its complement of men should be full. Capt. Cormack had his commission but did not have his company, and here was a collection of about sixty men outside who wanted our places. Grant had politely informed Capt. Cormack that his duty compelled him to admit men who were ready and willing to enlist; and in case he could not report a full company, or at least sixty men, by the following day, he must let these others take our places,—hence we should be left out.

I heard of this outside company just about the time their leader forsook them to go on a spree, and immediately sent our Sergeant to invite them up to get some breakfast with our mess: we had very comfortable quarters and plenty to eat. They accepted my invitation. Then these strangers, who had come hungry to eat with us, also accepted an offer to share our sleeping quarters: and by these means I got forty new members in our company; for they in turn forsook the leader whose appetite for liquor induced him to leave them hungry and without care at a very critical moment. Consequently, within the time allowed my Captain, our company was large enough to be admitted into the regiment; and we became "Company D" thereof.

Before being admitted as Company D of the 18th Ills. [*sic*] Vols., and preparatory thereto, as we had only one regularly appointed officer—our Captain—it was necessary to fill the other positions, viz.—1st and 2nd Lieutenants, Orderly Sergeant, Sergeants, Corporals, &c. So I called the company together, marched them to a secluded and beautiful grove of timber nearby, first passed around the segars (probably as an act of diplomacy), made them a little speech in which I stated the necessity of full organization before our muster in; and we proceeded with our election of officers. I was fortunate enough to be elected First Lieutenant, and felt very proud thereat. I took upon myself the duty of drilling the company: in fact the Captain left nearly everything to me in regard to the government and discipline of the men. I worked with them industriously, and was rewarded by the acknowledgment of the entire regiment, a little later on, that ours was the best drilled and disciplined company in the command.

Soon the regiment was ordered southward to a point called Mound City, about seven miles above Cairo. Here we were quartered very comfortably indeed. Our Colonel—Lawler— had been in the Mexican War. He was an Irishman, anxious for distinction, and therefore wanted to get to the front as soon as possible. General McClernand commanded the District of Cairo. He was our Colonel's friend, I believe, an old schoolboy friend, and the Colonel urging our muster into the Three Years Service, we soon became regularly a portion of the U.S. Volunteer troops.

John C. Reed Goes to War[3]

A Princeton-educated lawyer, John Reed was the son of a Georgia planter. He enlisted from Greene County in what became Company I of the 8th Georgia Regiment. He served throughout the war, was wounded at Gettysburg, and rose from the rank of lieutenant to captain. In 1888 he wrote a reminiscence of his experiences in the Confederate army. He intended to have this manuscript printed, and even wrote a note to the prospective publisher suggesting that it be entitled either "From First Manassas to Appomattox, in the Line" or "Four Years a Confederate Line Officer." Although interesting and well written, it was not published and instead found a home in the Alabama Department of Archives and History. It is a good example of what Confederate soldiers a generation later had to say about their wartime service.

In the brief passage that follows, Reed describes leaving home, traveling to Virginia, and being incorporated with nine other companies from elsewhere in Georgia into the 8th Georgia Regiment. The men's lack of uniform appearance was typical of Confederate troops.

The day of the departure of the company, June 3, 1861, had come. That morning I shaved, vowing to a companion that I should never shave again until the south had achieved her independence; and I have not broken my vow. The mothers, wives, sisters, aunts, and male relatives of the company assembled in Greensboro [Georgia], and the grief of the discerning old and triumphing joy of the unseeing young broke out stronger and stronger until our train arrived. But I should not prolong this part of my narrative. I need only say that the girls and young women waved handkerchiefs wildly at us until we had reached Harper's Ferry [Virginia], where we were mustered into the service of the Confederate States, as company I, of the 8th Georgia, [Col. Francis] Bartow being colonel. . . . The Savannah boys, Bartow's own company, with their perfect drill, neat uniforms, and city ease and polish—to use a backwoods saying—took the shine off of all the other companies. Savannah, Atlanta, and Macon each furnished a company, Rome—or more correctly Floyd county—three, Meriwether, Pulaski, Oglethorpe and Greene counties each one—the regiment consisting of ten in all. Every company had a uniform conspicuously different from that of the rest—homespun being largely present even then. None of the officers but a few from the cities had respectable side-arms, and though their dress was somewhat more pretentious than the men's it was actually a burlesque of what it should have been. I never did get a decent sword or a Confederate uniform. As a whole, we were in appearance fantastic citizens playing soldiers. We never acquired any holiday gloss and show, but we did soon learn to march and fight.

W. R. Eddington Remembers His Enlistment[4]

Although W. R. Eddington waited until 1862 to join the army, the process had changed very little. The confusion had diminished somewhat, but there was still a distinctly local flavor to the recruiting. For Eddington, recruiting meant riding the train to nearby Gillespie, Illinois, "where they was making up a Company for the war." The authorities' lack of preparation for receiving recruits is demonstrated by Eddington's having to sleep in a boxcar loaded with wheat, and the continued lack of training appears in the fact that having been issued Sibley tents, Eddington and his friends had to hunt up a soldier from another regiment to show them how to set one up. Like the other authors of firsthand accounts in this chapter, Eddington wrote in the late nineteenth century. Note his eagerness, almost desperation, to get in the war, even to the point of deceiving the mustering officer.

I wanted to enlist in the army but my Mother [a widow] was not willing and, as I was not of age, I could not get in without her consent so I waited until the second year, when President Lincoln issued a Proclamation calling for 600,000 more men. The war had been going bad for the Union up to that time so my Mother told me if I still wanted to go in the army I might do so.

Early on the morning of August 7, 1862, I with 4 of the neighbor boys left our homes and went to Bunker Hill, Illinois, and took a train for Gillespie, Illinois, where they was making up a Company for the war. There we signed the roll for a three year enlistment in the U.S. Army. We slept that night in a box car loaded with wheat. The next morning they put us on a train and headed us toward Springfield. They then took us out to Camp Butler, 7 miles east of Springfield. We got sibley tents [developed by Henry Hopkins Sibley and inspired by the teepees of the Plains Indians] the same day. They were big round tents with a hole in the top to let the smoke out. They were about 8 feet high and was supposed to hold about 15 men each. We had to get a man from another Regiment to show us how to put them up. That night we slept in our tents, our heads to the outside, our feet toward the center, on the ground without blankets.

The next day we drew blankets and uniforms. Then we was sent out to clear off a place to drill and parade. Then we were sent out to drill 5 hours each day and dress parade in the evening. This parade is for the purpose of seeing by the officers if every man has his uniform clean and his buttons and equipments bright and shiny and to hear what Regimental Orders are to be given for the next day.

On the 8th day of September, 1862, we were drawn up in two ranks about three steps apart and inspected by the mustering officer to see if we were fit for the service and to put us into the U.S.

service. I was the first man to be examined. After he had gone all over me carefully he started for the next man but turned around and came back to me again and said, "How are your eyes?" I told him I could not see anything but the light with my right eye. He said, you step to the rear. I stept back behind the rank and he went on inspecting the others and while he was doing that I walked back to the other end of the rank and stept up in the line again on the left, and when he came to me the second time he went all over me again. He said, you will do, you will pass. He never asked about my eyes. So he mustered us into the U.S. Service for 3 years or during the war. That meant if the war closed before three years was up we would be sent home when the war closed.

We drew our guns and stayed at Camp Butler drilling until about Oct. 20th when they put us on cars. My first guard duty, while we were at Camp Butler, was guarding a large covered wooden R[ail]R[oad] Bridge which spans the Sangamon River at this point, to see that no one crossed there unless they had a permit from Commanding Officer of Camp Butler and also to prevent anyone from trying to set it on fire.

Abner R. Small on Enlistment and Motivation[5]

Abner Small, an officer in the 16th Maine Regiment, was an early and thoughtful commentator on the Union soldier. Here he addresses the motives that led hundreds of thousands—eventually more than two million—of his fellow Northerners to enlist. This passage is revealing in two ways.

First, it reminds us that the motives that lead young men to enlist may differ widely among individuals and from the actual cause of the war. This war was about the future of slavery and the survival of the republican form of government, but Small and many of his comrades enlisted out of a desire to experience adventure or to prove their manhood. As Small surmised, the same was true for many Southern young men as well. It is important to remember, therefore, that the soldiers' motivations do not necessarily tell us why the war happened or what it was about.

Second, Small describes in this passage an almost universal characteristic of young manhood, not only in this conflict but in others as well. That characteristic is the tendency to view oneself as invulnerable. Enlisting for adventure and excitement would have little appeal to young men who believed that they would shortly be killed or maimed, and courage comes easier to those who can convince themselves that it is only "the other guy" who will suffer.

It can safely be asserted that a very large number of men volunteered to "go for a soldier" from motives of patriotism; but ambition, love of adventure, personal courage, and lack of other employment gave the largest numbers to our army, and, I doubt not, to the rebel army, too. There ever was, there ever will be, a fascination in danger that appeals to youth, that calls men to arms at the beat of a drum. Yet no soldier desires—not even to save his country—to be torn in pieces by a shell, made a disfigured and hopeless cripple. A man of sense is not built that way. He simply takes his chances, always believing that as an individual he is immune. It is the buoyancy of youth, the hopefulness of his nature, that makes the man with a gun cheery and light-hearted as he locks step with fate, with death. It is a part of his temperament, his philosophy, to be a humorous optimist, to laugh in the face of peril. To him, it is always the man in the next rank who is to be the victim.

William N. Tyler and the Making of Horse Soldiers[6]
William Tyler left rural Boone County, Illinois, to enlist in the 9th Illinois Cavalry. A country boy, Tyler knew a thing or two about horses, but as he and many other Northern boys were about to learn, that was a far cry from knowing how to be a good cavalryman. Moreover, their mounts in the army were a breed apart from the placid plow horses that they had known back home. In this selection, Tyler gives an account of one of the regiment's early training sessions in the fall of 1861.

The next move after we had drawn our spurs and saddles was when Colonel Brackett ordered the bugle to sound the call to fall in for drill. The whole regiment was on hand with horses all saddled and bridled for a drill. You must remember that our horses were well fed and in the best condition, full of life and spirit. It was all some of us could do to make them keep their place in the ranks.

"Now," said the Colonel, "when I tell you to mount you must put your left foot in the stirrup and grasp the reins and the mane with your left hand, and at the word 'mount,' all mount together."

"Mount" was the command.

Well, we did make the effort to all mount together but you should have seen them; the horses started off in every direction, pell mell over the field; some [men] were dragged along on the ground with their feet in the stirrups, while others were on their horses all right, but the harder the horses ran, the harder they stuck in their spurs; one poor fellow let go all hold and grabbed the head and mane; stirrups flew in every direction and he went straight for the center of the barn; just as the horse got within four feet of the stable, it came to a sudden halt, but the rider went on with a crash through the side of the barn; he could not have made a cleaner hole if he had been shot out of a cannon. I must say he came out pretty lucky; of course he was bruised and stiff legged for a day or two but that was all. Some of the men got hurt very severely but it did not take long for us to find out that [astride] we had to keep our toes in and our heels out.

Bell I. Wiley on Southern Enlistment[7]

As the nineteenth century gave way to the twentieth and the new century advanced, the last of the old soldiers followed the 620,000 of their comrades who never came back from the war. By midcentury the remaining men who had worn the blue, the gray, or the butternut had made the final river crossing. The task of telling their story fell to professional historians who now began to pore over not only the memoirs the soldiers had written since the war but also over the letters and diaries produced in prodigious amounts during the conflict. More than that of any other Civil War historian, Bell Wiley's name is associated with the common soldier. His two books, *The Life of Johnny Reb* and *The Life of Billy Yank*, set the standard for historians who would later follow in Wiley's footsteps by seeking to write straightforward accounts of what a soldier's life was like during the Civil War.[8] In this passage Wiley gives an overview of recruitment in the Southern armies at the outset of the war.

Hatred for the North received a tremendous boost from the prevailing agitation in favor of secession. The fire-eating element, made up largely of country editors, preachers, lawyers, and politicians-on-the-make, was the most vocal and eloquent. Recrimination and name-calling in private conversation, in public meeting, in editorial columns, from the professor's desk and country pulpit, produced a tide of emotion in the early months of 1861 that reached all sections and all classes. . . . [Their spirit] contributed greatly to the wave of volunteering which swept over the South during the first year of conflict.

It would be misleading . . . to give the impression that all who took up arms in 1861 were moved by hatred of Yankees, or that all who expressed hostility felt any considerable depth of antipathy. Later events proved the contrary. The dominant urge of many volunteers was the desire for adventure. War, with its offering of travel to far places, of intimate association with large numbers of other men, of the glory and excitement of battle, was an alluring prospect to farmers who in peace spent long lonely hours between plow handles, to mechanics who worked day in and day out at cluttered benches, to storekeepers who through endless months measured jeans cloth or weighed sowbelly, to teachers who labored year after year with indifferent success to drill the rudiments of knowledge into unwilling heads, and to sons of planters who dallied with the classics in halls of learning.

Long before Virginia seceded restless boys at the state university and at Washington College raised the Confederate flag on their respective campuses. At the University of Mississippi a company was recruited on the campus, and the faculty advanced the date of examinations so that students could be off to the war. The Centenary College faculty assembled on October 7, 1861, for the purpose of opening the fall session, but "there being no college students and few preparatory students," the dispensers of learning had to go home. Opposite the minutes of this futile session in the faculty record book the secretary splashed in bold script diagonally across the page this entry: "Students have all gone to war. College suspended: and God help the right.". . .

There was also a large group of those who volunteered not from any great enthusiasm, but simply because enlistment was the prevailing vogue. Scions of leading families rode about the country organizing companies for their command, thus adding the weight of social position to that of patriotism. Community belles offered their smiles and praise to men who joined the ranks of "our brave soldiers," but turned with the coolest disdain from those who were reluctant to come forward in the defense of Southern womanhood. In some communities young men who hesitated to volunteer received packages containing petticoats, or were seized by boisterous mobs and thrown into ponds. Thousands of persons indifferent to enlistment, and many who were downright opposed to it, were swept into the ranks in 1861 by the force of articulate popular pressure.

Henry M. Stanley, famous after the war as the searcher for [David] Livingstone in Africa, is a case in point. Of English birth and only recently established in this country, he was temporarily living in Arkansas at the outbreak of war. He volunteered simply to follow the example of his acquaintances, and to avoid social ostracism. After fighting bravely at Shiloh he was captured. When offered release from prison in return for Federal service, he joined the Yankees and fought for some time against his erstwhile comrades. And he evidently suffered no qualms of conscience for his turncoating.

Men so indifferent as Stanley, however, formed only a small minority of the Confederate volunteers. And even those, once they had "joined up," shared in most cases the prevailing desire to come to blows with the Yankees, and that quickly. Almost everyone seemed to think that the war would be decided by a battle or two in Virginia or Kentucky; it was necessary, therefore, to get to the fight with dispatch or run the risk of not making it at all.

Bell I. Wiley on Northern Enlistment[9]

Paralleling his discussion of Confederate recruitment, Wiley, in this excerpt from *The Life of Billy Yank*, deals with the same process on the Northern side. What differences can you perceive in the motivations and expectations of Northern and Southern soldiers? In what way did Southern action become a spur to Northern enlistment?

The South's attack on Fort Sumter fell like a thunderclap on the country north of Dixie. True, there had been talk of war, especially since the secession of the cotton states and the organization of the Southern Confederacy, but the agitators, consisting mainly of politicians, journalists, preachers and reformers, many of whom were on the make, were relatively few. A substantial portion of the population still hoped for a peaceful solution of the sectional crisis even after Jeff Davis set up his rival government.

Fort Sumter changed all this. The flag had been affronted. Men wearing the American uniform had been forced by hostile fire to surrender a Federal fort and march out in acknowledged defeat.

And with that humiliating incident peaceable secession lost all respectability. The die was cast.

Lincoln's request for troops was in a sense an anticlimax. The roar of cannon at Charleston, like the crash of bombs eighty years later at Pearl Harbor, was the country's call to arms.

During most of the war the raising of troops was a slow and painful process. But in the weeks following Fort Sumter the opposite was true. From Lake Superior to the Ohio, from Maine to Minnesota, and even from far-off California men rushed to arms with camp-meeting fervor. "Everybody eagerly asks everybody else if he's going to enlist," wrote a Detroit reporter on April 19, and the same might have been said of almost any other town or city in the North.

The tremendous surge of patriotism manifested itself in various ways. In Bangor, Maine, schoolgirls pounced on a boy who came among them wearing a palmetto flag [the flag of South Carolina] and destroyed the despised emblem. At Pembroke, Maine, a lawyer of alleged Southern sympathies was threatened with a ducking in a river, and at Dexter, Maine, a group of volunteers "rode a Mr. Augustus Brown . . . on a rail for . . . saying that he hoped every one of them would be shot." Elsewhere Southern sympathizers, real or imagined, were pelted with rotten eggs or otherwise put in their places. And if traitors could not be found, patriots full of excitement and liquor often fell to fighting among themselves. . . .

The women were the most spirited of patriots. Usually their activities consisted of displaying flags, singing martial songs, raising funds and making clothing for the volunteers. But occasionally they chose more aggressive roles. The ladies of Skowhegan, Maine, for example, on a Saturday afternoon in April rolled out the village artillery piece and treated their neighbors to "a salute of thirty-four guns."

For males the order of the day was volunteering, and the fever extended to all ages and classes. At Shenango, Pennsylvania, the young boys organized a "company," elected a thirteen-year-old captain and held weekly drills in the schoolyard to the accompaniment of a dinner-bucket drum corps. And in Belfast, Maine, thirty-odd veterans of the War of 1812 responded to Lincoln's initial call by forming themselves into a company and tendering their services to the state.

Nowhere was the war spirit more rampant than in the classrooms. At Bowdoin College the students on hearing of Sumter's fall rang the chapel bell, displayed the national colors, defiantly waved a skull-and-crossbones banner and shortly began daily drills on the campus. In Oxford, Ohio, Ozra J. Dodds, a senior in the college, rose in the chapel and proposed organization of a University Rifle Company. Within a few minutes 160 students and local boys signed up for service in what was to become Company B, Twentieth Ohio Volunteers. Girls of the neighboring female college, not to be outdone, set themselves to making red shirts, flannel underclothing and a flag for the volunteers.

From the University of Wisconsin a student wrote his parents on April 20: "Madison is in a great state of military excitement. The fever has penetrated the University walls. Seven of the boys have enlisted in the Governor's Guards." Four days later he reported the dismissal of his geometry class "to see the soldiers off." At the University of Michigan five companies were organized within a fortnight of Sumter's surrender.

Reid Mitchell on Flag Presentations[10]

Usually after a few days or weeks in an improvised military camp in the neighborhood of their own hometown, the soldiers prepared to leave for the fighting front. They did so as companies, each of which was closely linked to its community by ties of family and friendship. When a community sent off its company, it formally presented to the men a company flag, usually handsewn by a committee of local ladies. Such flags were almost never carried in battle, where flags were limited to two official ones per regiment. However, the company flag was a material prop in the ceremony by which a community gave its blessing to the departing soldiers and the soldiers promised, through their commanding officer, to uphold their hometown's honor.

In his 1988 book *Civil War Soldiers*, historian Reid Mitchell explored aspects of the character and motivation of the soldiers, emphasizing themes such as family and community, duty and honor, faith and patriotism—all considered not so much as enduring virtues but rather as manifestations of the quaint and curious values of a particular time and place—in this case, the United States of the Victorian era. Mitchell's was part of the new genre of Civil War soldier books that tended almost to deconstruct the men's image of devotion to the causes for which they fought. Such scholars had a point, but overall the trend went too far and presented a jaundiced and highly inaccurate view of the Civil War generation, recast in the image of post-1960s America. Mitchell's work, however, is perhaps the most balanced of the lot and the least guilty of such exaggerations. Here is how he describes the flag-presentation ceremony and its meaning to the soldiers.

When Americans North and South raised regiments for the army and sent them to war, they saw the soldiers off with almost identical ritual and celebration. The population at large wanted their soldiers to believe they represented all of them. The soldiers of 1861, after all, were volunteers—independent and rational citizens freely choosing to defend American ideals. In a sense, the soldiers' reputation would become the home folks' reputation as well. Nothing made this clearer than the ritual of flag presentation observed North and South. Customarily, particularly in the early stages of the war the ladies of the community would get together to sew a flag for their boys, which would be presented to the hometown company in a public ceremony.

This ceremony became stereotyped early in the war—a speech given by a leading citizen, a reply by the company commander, and perhaps a picnic or banquet. Confederate Col. C. R. Hanleiter's acceptance address is typical of the genre. "Their defense of this Flag—the insignia of our Nationality [*sic*], and the contribution of warm hearts devoted to the cause of our section," the colonel proclaimed, "shall attest how well the 'Jo [*sic*] Thompson Artillery' acquit themselves in the momentous struggle." He promised those who made the flag that it would "be cherished by us as one of the most sacred mementoes of *Home*; and when it waves over far distant fields, it will remind us of the loved ones left behind." The men of the regiment would "plant this Flag on the field of carnage" and maintain its honor always.

Hanleiter's address reveals something of the significance of this often repeated ritual. The flag itself was the emblem of the community that sent companies and regiments into the field. These units were almost always composed of men from a single town or county; in a very real sense they represented their communities. Their flags linked them to their homes.

Furthermore, the flags tied the soldiers to an element of society they had left behind when they marched to war. The flag, made by the women of the community, was something to be protected much as they thought their wives and mothers should be protected. If the men left their communities to protect their homes, as many of them insisted they did, they brought something of their homes with them into battle. The flag was the physical tie between the home life they had left and fought for and the war into which they were plunged. In Civil War battles the importance of advancing one's flag and defending it from capture—and, conversely, capturing enemy flags—indicates a devotion to flags far beyond what military rationality might seem to demand.

Finally, the importance of the individual flag, presented to them by their friends and families, takes on additional meaning when one considers how often men's patriotism was expressed not in terms of political discourse but simply in terms of the flag. Many a Northern soldier said he went to war to fight for the flag, the emblem of a nation. Philip A. Lantzy announced his enlistment to his parents by saying, "I am Gone to Fight for the Stars and Stripes of the Union. . . . I think it is gods will that the Rebels Should be made [to] come under our Stars and stripes." Whatever these men were fighting for seems to have been better expressed in material symbols than in reasoned discourse.

Reid Mitchell on Military Discipline[11]

Mitchell also wrote on the soldiers' reactions to the experience of coming under military discipline. The degree of regimentation in the camps of the Civil War armies might seem lax to modern-day enlistees who are introduced to military life in boot camp. However, nineteenth-century Americans were thorough individualists for whom the ways of even the volunteer army were a considerable shock. Mitchell here writes about the ways in which Civil War soldiers found this regimentation disturbing.

Americans found military regimentation hard to accept. North or South, the soldier of the 1860s was most likely an independent farmer or a farmer's son. His work had been regulated by the weather, the cycle of the growing year, and the remote but all-important authority of the market. The authority immediately over him was personal—not the "feudal" authority of the planter, but the patriarchal rule of a father or an older brother who bossed him until such time as he could set up his own farm, and whose authority derived from his place in the family. Besides his relative freedom from discipline in the workplace, the volunteer had been brought up in a political culture that celebrated personal autonomy and democracy. In the North, of course, the Republican Party was based largely on the defense of free labor and free men; and in the South the Democratic Party, with its sometimes paranoid denunciations of corruption and with its thoroughly egalitarian rhetoric, outlived the commercially oriented Whig Party. Finally, American political thinkers had always viewed the military with suspicion; a Confederate soldier could still use eighteenth-century terminology and refer to an officer as a member of the old "standing army."

If regimentation was difficult for most Americans of the 1860s to bear, it was particularly onerous for a Southern white man. For him, subordination and regulation were not simply abstractions in a republican demonology. He had seen them during his life—perhaps every day. The rules and restrictions of the army reminded the Confederate of the humiliation of slavery and of the degraded position that blacks held in his society.

Southerners of all classes referred to military discipline as a form of slavery. Edwin Fay, a Louisiana soldier and perpetual grumbler, had not been in the Confederate army long when he decided, "No negro on Red River but has a happy time compared with that of a Confederate soldier." One regulation in particular drew the ire of Fay and other Confederates: when a soldier wanted to leave camp he had to obtain a pass. The spectacle of white men carrying passes drew the amused attention of at least one Southern slave and probably more. Sgt. C. E. Taylor wrote his father in July 1861 what a black in Corinth, Mississippi, said after he witnessed a guard demand to see Taylor's pass. "He said it was mighty hard for white folks now. He said he had quit carrying a pass and his master had just commenced to carry them." J. C. Owens summed up the resemblance between slavery and soldiering when he wrote, "I am tired of being bound up worse than a negro."

Northerners, too, could feel the comparison between the soldier and the slave. A soldier doing common labor might say he "worked like a nigger." Another soldier wrote from Virginia, "We keep very comfortable for soldiers. But it [is] nothing like white living." Allen Geer became homesick contemplating the difference in his life after enlisting: "yesterday a freeman—today a slave." The true difference between his slavery and that of slaves in the South was that his obedience was, in a sense, not coerced. "A Sense of duty and patriotism made me obedient to all the discipline."

Besides the image of the slaves, men used that of the machine to explain their position in the army. One war-weary Northern officer wrote his mother, "The interest I once took in [the] Military is almost gone. I do my duty like a machine that has so much in a day to do anyway." One veteran remembered that the doctor in the hospital looked upon his patients as "so many machines in need of repairs." He explained, "In War men are looked upon and considered as so many machines. Each machine is expected to perform a certain amount of service. If the machine becomes weakened or impaired by service, care is taken that it be mended and restored so that it may again do its duty. But if, in the arduous service and dangers to which it is exposed, the life or moving force is destroyed, then a trench and covering of earth hides the remains, and that is all. This, of course, looks very heartless, but War is relentless and cruel, and so long as War will last, and men will take up arms against one another, this State of things will continue." The machine and the slave were two metaphors for entities without wills of their own. The soldier was a third. But the machine goes beyond the slave and soldier: it is not even human.

Reid Mitchell on the Soldiers and Their Communities[12]

In *The Vacant Chair*, published in 1993, Mitchell continued his discussion of the common soldiers of the Civil War, looking specifically this time at those of the North. In the passage that follows, he discusses the ways in which Civil War armies were peculiarly community-oriented and how the home communities continued to exert powerful influences over the soldiers long after the latter had marched off to war.

In many ways American armies during the Civil War contravened normal military practice. The process by which men are turned into soldiers—one is tempted to say "reduced to soldiers"—involves removing them from the larger society. They wear distinctive dress, distinctive haircuts, submit to unusual drill, discipline, and ritual, are commanded by officers. They are literally regimented. Armies master people by subjecting them to unfamiliar environments and thus they become soldiers. Armies work by setting men apart.

To a large extent, Civil War armies succeeded in doing these things. The volunteers did become soldiers. But the transformation from civilian to soldier was rarely completed. One reason for this is that in some ways the company—the basic military unit—functioned as an extension of the soldier's home community. In most ways a soldier's company was the army for that soldier. . . . In 1861, a Union which went to war by creating a centralized army would have been unrecognizable to [the soldiers]. The local nature of the companies and regiments faithfully mirrored the body politic at large.

For new recruits, the army should be a terrifying institution; soldiering should be different from anything they have known before. Like all institutions, established armies have traditions of their own. A Scottish recruit coming to a British regiment or even an American teenager entering the cadet corps at West Point would find himself bound—and inspired—not only by formal discipline but by the powerful traditions, history, and myths of his new home. These traditions too play their role in transforming civilians into soldiers. But in most cases Civil War regiments had no such traditions. These were new regiments, making up their regimental traditions. . . .

Civil War companies were first and foremost military institutions, but they were not exempt from the culture of the nineteenth-century American volunteerism that produced them. Sometimes soldiers insisted that their company—their new home—serve other functions. They might form societies "for mutual improvement in cultivating the mind" or for debating important questions of the day, such as whether or not "education has more influence over the mind of man than money." Bible classes held in an Indiana regiment paid special attention to the conflicting claims of Calvinism and Arminianism [opposing Calvinist predestination]. Soldiers would donate money to buy their regiments libraries, organize Christian associations, or hold Sunday prayer meetings—all as if they had read Tocqueville. Companies of Union volunteers, then, behaved much as other American fraternal organizations. The average Civil War company began with all the discipline of a lodge of Elks. . . .

Officers rapidly became aware of the problem that the local nature of military units posed for discipline. In 1861 Major Charles S. Wainwright noted "how little snap men have generally." His regiment's officers, even though they were well thought of, could not "get fairly wakened up." "Their orders come out slow and drawling, then they wait patiently to see them half-obeyed in a laggard manner, instead of making the men jump to it sharp, as if each word of the order was a prod in their buttocks." He blamed this state of affairs in part on customary small-town indolence; he also blamed the process by which companies were organized—"the officers having raised their own men and known most of them in civil life.". . . Even soldiers themselves might identify this as a problem. When mismanagement by the quartermaster led to a shortage of rations in one regiment, one soldier, who a few weeks earlier had complained of strict discipline, attributed the inefficiency to the fact that affairs were run on a volunteer basis: "The officers have no dignity & the men no subordination."

The threat to discipline posed by the community came from other than just the soldiers themselves. The community kept in close touch with the companies it sent to war. Newspaper articles reported their exploits, homefolk sent and received letters, soldiers returned home on furloughs, and civilians even visited their friends and family in the army. The reinforcement of local values that this constant communication permitted could run counter to military values. When Captain John Pierson told his wife that his soldiers were probably writing home he was a tyrant, he was not alone. Officers usually planned to return to their communities when the war was over; the way they treated their neighbors and their neighbors' sons would be remembered. . . .

As unfamiliar as the military experience was to most northern soldiers, the presence of friends and even brothers, uncles, or cousins, the frequent communication with those at home, and the ad hoc nature of the volunteer army served to make it more familiar than is typical of armies. Small-town mores were an impediment to military discipline as classically understood. The constant reminders of home provided men with an alternate set of values and diminished the authority of their officers—men who were equally imbued with civilian values in any case. Yet at the same time small-town mores reduced soldiers' military efficiency, they also worked as the glue of this citizen army. If community values helped make the Union soldier a difficult one to command, they also helped make him as good a soldier as he turned out to be.

First, soldiers believed that they were fighting for their families and communities. The homefolk had sent them to war. Rallies, public meetings, exhortations from the press and pulpit had encouraged the teenagers and men of the North to enlist; . . . The question why parents and wives seemed so eager to sacrifice their menfolk is a troubling one, but it is clear that their influence helped persuade many men to volunteer. To be a good son, a good brother, a good husband and father, and to be a good citizen meant trying to be a good soldier.

The call of home could, of course, unravel a soldier's morale. Silas W. Browning confessed to his wife, "I have not shed tears but twice since I left Home & that was when I received your letters." . . . A preacher's sermon on "the dear ones at home" could start veterans crying. A New Jersey soldier claimed that in the trenches around Petersburg soldiers literally died from homesickness. But as long as soldiers were sure that those they most missed believed in them and the cause for which they fought, their love for home stimulated their support for the Union.

Second, soldiers knew that their behavior while in service was monitored by the folks back home. The army provided little escape from the prying eyes of small-town America. News of a man's conduct, moral and military, was too easily sent home. . . . And men took rumors and hometown opinion seriously. One soldier wrote his parents that he and "the other boys were amazed that you heard that we were guilty of unworthy conduct." Denying the story, he asked who was spreading it. On the other hand, soldiers were not particularly reluctant to spread rumors themselves. One mother who warned her son always to speak respectfully of his officers received a defiant answer: "I intend to write just as I think they deserve and tell the truth and nothing but the truth.". . .

Bravery was a virtue that would earn a soldier the respect of his community back home, not just his company, and cowardice its contempt. A man who skulked or ran faced not just ridicule from his comrades but a soiled reputation when he returned to civilian life. George Waterbury first tried to get put on the sick list and then deserted to avoid fighting in the Chancellorsville campaign; a fellow soldier sent the news back to Connecticut. When one captain dodged battle in 1862, a soldier under him broadcast his conduct: "He contrived to stumble, then gave out he was wounded in the knee, and called for a stretcher, was put on it, and carried a little ways when the carriers rested and the shells falling a little too thick for the Captain, he told them men to hurry up which they did not do, when up he jumped and beat the whole to the Hospital, after which we never saw him until we got upon this side of the Rappahannock."

Soldiers demanded courage of their officers in a way they rarely did of their fellow soldiers. Soldiers who had enlisted under the company commanders had a right to feel particularly betrayed if their captains proved cowardly. After all, the officer who formed a company among his friends and neighbors promised them either implicitly or explicitly—usually the latter, and in most grandiloquent fashion—to lead them into battle. James K. Newton wrote home that the reputation of his captain's bravery at Shiloh "was all a hoax." On the contrary, the captain had disappeared when the battle began. . . .

During combat, could men think of their reputations? The answer is probably yes. Men wrote home how they thought of their loved ones even in the cannon's mouth; men did die with the names of their beloved on their lips. The desire to live up to the expectations of those at home reinforced natural bravery and military discipline in helping determine men's conduct on the battlefield. Leander Stillwell remembered that when his regiment turned and ran in his first battle, he kept thinking, "What will they say about this at home?" Nonetheless, combat has its own compulsions. The good opinion of the folks back home was probably more important in men's decision to continue their service.

While courage in battle resulted from the moment's excitement, it took considerably more reassurance to stay in the army day after day, year after year. There were military compulsions; deserters could be shot. Many deserted successfully, however, and the so-called "bounty-jumpers" made a career of enlisting and deserting. The continual reassurance that those back home approved of one's service, a reassurance provided by letters—and painfully missed when letters did not come—was crucial to the soldiers. As long as the communities of the North supported the war effort, there would be northern soldiers in the ranks of the Union army.

Notes

1. Quoted in Gerald J. Prokopowicz, *All for the Regiment: The Army of the Ohio, 1861–1862* (Chapel Hill: University of North Carolina Press, 2001), 23.

2. Wimer Bedford Papers, Library of Congress (hereafter LC).

3. John C. Reed manuscript, Alabama Department of Archives and History, Montgomery, Alabama, pp. 2–3. Reprinted by permission of the Alabama Department of Archives and History.

4. W. R. Eddington Papers, Civil War Miscellaneous Collection, U.S. Army Military History Institute (hereafter USAMHI).

5. Abner R. Small, *The Road to Richmond: The Civil War Memoirs of Maj. Abner R. Small of the 16th Maine Vols., with His Diary as a Prisoner of War*, ed. Harold Adams Small (Berkeley: University of California Press, 1959), 186. © 1939 by The Regents of the University of California. Reprinted by permission of the University of California Press.

6. William N. Tyler, *The Dispatch Carrier* (Bernalillo, NM: Joel Beer & Gwendy MacMaster, 1992), 2–3.

7. Bell I. Wiley, *The Life of Johnny Reb: The Common Soldier of the Confederacy* (Baton Rouge: Louisiana State University Press, 1994; orig. pub. Indianapolis: Bobbs-Merrill, 1943), 17–19. © 1978 by Bell I. Wiley. Reprinted by permission of Louisiana State University Press.

8. Wiley, *The Life of Johnny Reb*; Bell I. Wiley, *The Life of Billy Yank: The Common Soldier of the Union* (Baton Rouge: Louisiana State University Press, 1994; orig. pub. Indianapolis: Bobbs-Merrill, 1941).

9. Wiley, *The Life of Billy Yank*, 17–19. © 1978 by Bell I. Wiley. Reprinted by permission of Louisiana State University Press.

10. Reid Mitchell, *Civil War Soldiers* (New York: Viking, 1988), 18–20. © 1988 by Reid Mitchell. Reprinted by permission of Viking Penguin, a division of Penguin Putnam.

11. Ibid., 57–59. © 1988 by Reid Mitchell. Reprinted by permission of Viking Penguin, a division of Penguin Putnam.

12. Reid Mitchell, *The Vacant Chair: The Northern Soldier Leaves Home* (New York: Oxford University Press, 1993), 21–28. © 1995 by Reid Mitchell. Reprinted by permission of Oxford University Press.

.

CHAPTER TWO

In Battle

C ivil War soldiers called it "seeing the elephant," a phrase that
evoked the greatest thrill of a boy's life growing up in rural
nineteenth-century America: seeing the elephant when the circus
came to town. For these boys who were becoming men, the dis-
tantly anticipated experience of combat was a big part of the thrill
of enlisting in the Civil War armies. By facing combat, they would
prove their mettle and their manhood. During the early days of the
war, when the armies were assembling and soldiers were learning
how to pitch their tents and, if cavalrymen, how to mount their
horses, many young men feared that the war might end before they
got their chance to see the fighting. Once they had experienced the
shock of battle, the soldiers subsequently expressed little eagerness
for combat. Still, combat was the common coin of war, and it would
be the business of the soldiers as long as the conflict lasted.

In reading the selections that follow, consider the common
soldier's perspective. How did his perception of a battle differ from
the view of the commanding general at his headquarters? Or from
the overview presented in a good modern history? What sense could
a man in the ranks make out of that part of a major battle that came
within his own experience? How would these perceptions affect his
frame of mind and his willingness to go on fighting? And how did
his own actions relate to his feelings in battle?

Rice C. Bull on Going into Battle[1]
In 1861, Rice Bull enlisted in the 123d New York Infantry and
served throughout the war in the Army of the Potomac, fighting in
some of the most famous and bloody clashes, including the May 1863
action at Chancellorsville, where he was badly wounded. In his memoirs he reflected about the fear of soldiers about to go into battle.
Once the men became experienced, they had to deal with fear each

time they approached combat. Yet new and untried soldiers also had to deal with their own doubts about how they would behave in battle. This inner struggle with doubts and fears meant that sometimes the most frightening part of the soldiers' existence was not the time of greatest physical danger.

There is nothing that tests men's nerves more than marching up to a line of battle that is already engaged; they know they are soon to take their place on the firing line. While making the advance they can see, hear, and think, but can do nothing to take their minds off the dreadful work they know is before them. Until their own battle line is formed and they are facing the front and firing, their nerves are almost at the breaking point; then the strain relaxes and the fear and nervousness pass away. As we neared the firing line the noise was deafening, the air filled with the fumes of burning powder; the lazy whining of bullets almost spent, the shot and shell from the enemy batteries tearing through the trees caused every head to duck as they passed over us. With all this tumult could be heard the shouts of our men and the yells of the enemy.

Abner R. Small on a Soldier's View of Battle[2]

In this passage, Abner Small, a major in the 16th Maine Regiment, comments on the confused nature of battle and how it was impossible for the common soldier to see or understand the larger strategic or even tactical picture.

Any member of a regiment, officer or private, can have but little knowledge of movements outside of his immediate command. In an engagement with the enemy he has his special duty to perform, and no time to look with a critical eye upon his comrade's conduct; he has all he can do to obey orders and keep from running—many failed even in this. Almost the first thought that comes home to a brave man is one of self-preservation, and the second, the safety of his honor, when pride comes in as a powerful auxiliary and, oftener than courage, keeps him to the front.

The idea that a soldier, whose duty it is to remain in the ranks and move in geometrical lines, has an opportunity to view a Gettysburg as he would a panorama, is absurd. After the first volley of musketry, he is a rare man who theorizes, or speculates on the action of his comrade, or of his regiment, much more on that of the commanding general, three miles distant. The inequalities of the ground, the wooded slopes and deep ravines, the fog, the dense smoke, and the apparent and often real confusion of troops moving in different directions under different orders, utterly preclude the possibility of a correct detailed observation of a battle of any magnitude.

John C. Reed and the 8th Georgia at First Bull Run[3]

Bull Run, or Manassas as the Rebels called it, fought in Virginia on July 21, 1861, was the first major battle of the Civil War. For both sides it was an introduction to the as-yet unimagined horrors of war. For none was this more true than for the soldiers themselves. Here John Reed, the young lawyer-planter from Greene County, Georgia, relates the experience of his own Company I, 8th Georgia. The confusion he describes was, to a certain degree, typical of Civil War combat as viewed from the ranks. It was particularly pronounced in this first battle. For the 8th Georgia there was an additional reason for confusion: its commander, the popular politician Francis Bartow, though charming, persuasive, fiery, and bold, had only vague ideas of tactics and led the regiment in disastrous blunders. The 8th Georgia was certainly not the last Civil War regiment to pay in blood for the leadership of a beloved but incompetent commander.

Interestingly, although the 8th suffered appalling casualties during the pine thicket phase of its fighting at Bull Run, it was an early stage of the battle, during which the regiment had to lie still under enemy shelling, that Reed described as "the most trying part of the day." It was a typical infantryman's response to the helplessness of undergoing bombardment without being able to return fire. Only when Reed was able to accomplish a specific objective was he able to conquer his fear of the incoming shells. Finally, like most officers, Reed tended to be optimistic when reporting on the performance of his men in battle, claiming that they were all taking careful aim while many of the enemy's shots went high.

We marched a few hundred yards, surmounting a hill [Henry Hill] that rose with a steady slope, and the shock was stunning when on the crest from which we caught a view of two miles beyond. We came, as it seemed to me, all at once, in the midst of the fight. Under orders we laid down a short distance to our rear of the Henry house. The Wise artillery [a Confederate battery] was just beyond the house, and it was firing rapidly. Hostile guns were replying, but they did not have the range; and the shot and shell were passing far overhead. This was the most trying part of the day. The projectiles sung and whizzed and exploded over us, around us, and a very few among us. One of the Macon Guards [Company C of the 8th Georgia] was killed here. I shrank from the accursed things for several minutes. Once I saw dust rising from the roof of the house, indicating that a shot had passed through it. Major Cooper directed a brush fence, dividing the regiment somewhere between the right of our company and the next, to be pulled down. I was lying ten or fifteen yards distant, and as another officer was nearer, I did not heed the command. It was repeated. I looked up, and to my shame saw that nobody had stirred. I forgot the hostile battery; and in a minute a dozen of our men had enlarged a passage to the major's satisfaction. This small affair was a great relief to me; and I think that with my springing up went the last of my nervousness that day. When I lay down again, I located the battery on the other side of the turnpike, and about three fourths of a mile off. A long range of woods ran around the further limit of the field, and out of a place in this, as it seemed, I could see the smoke puff. Then I distinguished the report, and I have forgotten how many seconds I made it between the two. In a short while after I had heard the report, here came the shot or shell. Then I saw a long line of the enemy, far towards our left; and it rejoiced me to see them scamper as some of the shot from the Wise artillery tore through their ranks. General [Barnard] Bee was fighting across the turnpike, as we could hear, not see. After we had stood the fire of the distant battery about half an hour, Bartow started with us to reinforce Bee. As we moved off, another man was struck down by a shell—killed, I think. We kept behind the rising ground, crossed the pike, went up a long steep red hill [Matthews Hill]. . . .

Just as we reached the corner of a square grove of oaks I descried the battery, and noted that [we] were nearer to it by half than when on the hill [Henry Hill]. It sent a few ineffectual shot at us; and passing on around the rear of the oaks, we turned up the other side; and when we got to a fence running off to our right on a projection of the front line of the oaks and leading to the famous pine thicket, we filed to the right, and proceeded along the fence. It was partially thrown down, and there was some small growth on each side, called in the south a hedgerow. As we turned away from the oaks a few men were wounded by Minie balls [rifle bullets] from the long fence, some three hundred yards off. . . .

Eight companies had passed on—the regiment was marching by the flank, with the right in front—and just as company I was turning from the woods, a shell from the battery, now hardly three hundred and fifty yards from us, knocked three men out of a file behind me. Some of company K were also wounded here by a shell. Shortly afterwards I heard canister shot fly through the bushes, the marks of which I found the next day. Bartow was leading us to the thicket about a hundred and twenty yards distant from the oaks. A fence on the side of the oaks we were leaving reached on the protected side about 250 yards to the front, where it intersected with what I call the long fence, which last extended several hundred yards to the right. The 4th Alabama were lying on the ground, to the right of the fence running from the oaks, and I saw them in this position loading and firing upon the long fence. At the point where we left the oaks this regiment was between us and that fence.

Now let me tell you of the latter and the thicket. It was evidently Bartow's design, or Bee's, that we should take advantage of the thicket in order to approach under its cover within good range of the long fence. The latter was about 125 yards from the front of the thicket, and our march was along the hedgerow to enter the rear of the thicket. We were foolishly carried over the last sixty yards of this route before and not behind the hedgerow, and a most galling fire was concentrated upon us from parts of three [Union] regiments. We made this last of the way on the run. I could hear the bullets zipping and zeeing among us like angry bees, and I knew that our men were falling fast. Two of our company were hit just here—George Heard, one of them, falling dead as we entered the thicket. This with the three wounded by the shell, made five. We slackened down to quick time, and I glanced up [at] the regiment and was struck with the good order in which the files were dressed. We were in sight of the battery, and in position to be raked from end to end, but its canister came too high. When we moved forward, the ground concealed us from the guns. Just as we resumed quick time I looked back at the perilous place we had just passed. Jesse Dalton, of company K, a man over sixty, against whom I had brought a suit for slander for Higgins, was coming over the ground running slowly and weakly. Thousands of bullets seemed to be striking up the dust around him, but he did not quicken his gait. He was too exhausted. I thought that he would run the gauntlet safely, but just as he got to the pines he received a serious wound. When I saw him fall I could not help thinking of the rule of law under which a personal action dies with the party. I said we had dressed our files. Bartow, quivering with rage, shouted, "By the left flank, march." That threw us in line, to the front.

Everybody understood that it was now our time; and there was a wild rush to the edge of the thicket. It was rectangular and contained about three acres, with a front of some 110 yards. We should have had at least three hundred yards. From the fence came a volley that roared more loudly than any I ever heard afterwards, but it seemed to do no hurt. Huddled up in some places seven or eight deep, and even more, our firing commenced. I observed three colors [flags] at regular intervals, just on the other side of the long fence. A dwelling was a little beyond it, and four out-houses were on its line, and some grain stacks besides. The dwelling and out-houses were opposite the left and right center of the regiment. The further side of the fence, the out-houses and stacks were lined with federals. An ice-house was a few yards nearer on our side of the fence, and just a trifle to the left of the projected left line of the thicket, and more federals were around it; and they extended in rather desultory order, in front, to a point not far to its right. To the left of the ice-house, in an oblique line towards the fence, by which the 4th Alabama were lying, another regiment took position, just after our fighting commenced, and its musketry was very destructive to companies K and I, as it approached somewhat to an enfilade and many of the men of these companies were pushed out into the open.

This last mentioned regiment fired buck and ball [that is, with smooth-bore muskets loaded with one .69 caliber musket ball and two or three buckshot each], as I discovered from the marks on the trees the next day, the other regiments fired Minie balls. Now, were we not in a pickle? The houses, the stacks, the fence, the line of the regiment on our left—all seemed a continually playing flash. The trees were becoming white all around us, from having the bark cut away, though I noted that numerous bullets were going too high and bringing down leaves. Many of our men were being wounded, and there were frequent cries of pain, "Oh, Lord!" becoming from that time on the ejaculation that I usually heard a man make when struck in battle. But the loading and firing kept up with eagerness. Jim Lewis, one of the company, came to me and told me goodbye. The brains and blood seemed to be running out of his forehead. I never expected to see him again, but the next day it appeared that the ball had gone around and not through the skull. I shall never forget how pale, stiff and thoroughly dead Gus Daniel, another one of the company, looked as I glanced down when I had stumbled over him. This was the first dead man I saw.

Our men were taking careful aim. McCall, a glorious fellow from New York State, our second sergeant . . . was shooting at the colors of the regiment on our left; and all of company K, and the left half of I, were aiming at that regiment. The weary and feeble were staying their muskets against the pines, and each man was selecting a mark. A federal in front of the thicket bravely rushed into an opening in the fence, where he raised his piece, but before it came to his shoulder it flew into the air and he fell. A second later I saw another adventurous man climbing an out-house, and down too he came. But we were under the concentrated fire of at least four regiments, and probably each was of fuller rank than ours. I was never afterwards in as hot a place. The men were so crowded as seriously to impede their work. Some few fired as many as fourteen rounds, but the most of them fired but seven or eight. And let me make you understand the peril of those few minutes. According to a count some of us made upon a careful study of the company rolls, the regiment carried into the action 490 officers and men. Of these 41 were killed, 159 wounded, and seventeen reported missing ten or twelve days afterwards. It is probable that most of the seventeen were wounded and captured. So out of 490 we lost 217—not very far from half. I think it was 39 or 40 of dead in the thicket that I counted a little before sun down, and they lay within less than half an acre of ground. In our company six were killed in the thicket; and thirteen severely wounded. Two of the latter died soon afterwards. Our total of officers and men in the company at the commencement of the action was sixty-four. . . .

As those who heard him told me the next day, Bartow vociferated to the captain of the Atlanta Grays [Company F], "We must get these men out of here." Several times he ordered us to fall back, but I was among those who did not hear. Nothing could be understood in the din to which our ears were so new. But some of the men at last, misunderstanding the order to fall back, began a disorderly retreat. On the right of the first platoon, close behind it, I was encouraging some of the men of our company to fire with more coolness, and I reminded them that the enemy's fire was slackening. The regiment furtherest to the left had disappeared—its smooth-bores probably being no match for the Mississippi rifles of company K—and the line before us looked thinner along the fence; and there was nobody standing on our side of it. Ransome, one of my men, lying on the ground, was keeping his musket quiet. He seemed very cool, and with much warmth I asked him why he had ceased to fire. He fired at once, began to load, and shouted to me that he had been obeying orders; and he rolled his eyes in such a manner that I glanced to the left and then to the right. Nearly everybody was going back at about quick time. Of course I could not stay. I carried off my squad very doggedly. Their sullenness increased mine. At every step they seemed on the point of rushing back, and some would turn and fire. . . .

Bartow's horse was killed in the thicket; and when I came to the fence dividing the pines from the wheat field, he was there dismounted, and ordering the colors to be planted near the fence. He was greatly excited, and he implored his men to rally. I went to him, and I thought his eye twinkled with pleasure as he saw that I was coming from the front. The last words that passed between him and me were my enquiring where he wished the line to form, to which he pointed with his arm along an open place running diagonally through the pines, and said, "Just there." I was nearly ready to sink in the ground at what I too hastily conceived was the disgrace of the regiment, for I did not then know that we had been ordered back. "Who is the officer that is leading off these men," said the colonel, hoarse with rage, stamping his feet, and shaking his fist in the direction of our poor fellows going across the wheat field. Jake Phinizy, 1st lieutenant of company K, made great efforts to bring the men back. I shouted from the fence, calling everyone by name that I saw. We got back a few. But balls began to come hotly from the right and the colonel commanded us to fall back. All organization was lost.

John M. Roberts and the 83d Indiana at
Chickasaw Bayou[4]

The December 29, 1862, battle of Chickasaw Bayou, near Vicksburg, Mississippi, was a debacle for Union arms, yet the experience of John Roberts of the 83d Indiana Regiment illustrates how much the common soldier's perception of battle was an individual matter. Roberts, a member of the 83d's color guard, was permitted to take part in active skirmishing against Confederate sharpshooters who were firing on the colors, or flag, and the rest of the color company (E) from across the bayou.

"Zouave fashion," mentioned by Roberts, refers to the units of Algerian soldiers in the French army, dressed in uniforms based on traditional North African garb. Later the Zouave regiments were made up of Frenchmen in the same colorful uniforms. The Zouaves emphasized rapid movement and open formation. One of their tactics to which Roberts referred involved the soldier lying on his back to load his rifle, then rolling over and rising up to shoot.

Colonel Robert's reference to Confederate president Jefferson Davis and the Mexican War had to do with the battle of Buena Vista, where a regiment of Indiana volunteers, along with other troops, was partially driven back. After the war, as sectional animosities built up within the United States, some Southerners liked to point to the Buena Vista incident as a demonstration of the alleged congenital cowardice of Hoosiers in particular and all Northerners in general. Davis, however, was not among those who made such taunts. He had been present at Buena Vista when a part of the Indiana regiment had rallied with his own 1st Mississippi Rifles to turn back a Mexican attack at a key moment of the battle. Still, the slightly garbled claim of Davis's disparagement was a good spur for Colonel Spooner to use on the Hoosiers of the 83d as they went into battle at Chickasaw Bayou.

Col. Spooner said, "Boys, Jeff Davis said in the Mexican War that Indiana soldiers were cowards. Remember your state. Forward."

Just as we struck the abatis [an obstacle usually of sharpened stakes] of fallen timber and Spanish moss the Rebels poured in a volley of musketry. I could see the Spanish moss quiver for 20 or 25 feet before me. Eleven bullet holes were made in our colors and one bullet cut our flag staff half in two, but every man sprang forward until we reached the bayou, having taken all the enemies prisoner that we found concealed in the timber. When we reached the water's edge we received another volley from the enemy's rifle pits across the bayou. We could see the heads and shoulders above the pits and thought it time to return fire. The order came, "Fire at will. Fire, and continue to fire as long as you can see a man's head above breast-works." I saw one poor Rebel jump up like a buck rabbit and fall back in the pit. I suppose he had been shot in the head and never knew what had hurt him. Another order came, "Pour it into them, boys, keep them down so our batteries can shell them." We had now got the fire on them and if a man's head came above their breast-works he received a bullet from a Union soldier that put him to sleep in his new-dug pit which answered the purpose of a grave.

By keeping up a continual fire we succeeded in keeping them down. Orders being to shoot at will, some of the boys had selected big cypress logs three or four feet thick as their breast-works. The enemy was kept down and only once in a while would a man raise his head above the breast-works to be shot down as soon as he popped up, so they concluded to keep quiet, except a few sharpshooters who came out of the fort and concealed themselves in a ravine.

This ravine led down to the water's edge with a heavy coat of underbrush along the bank. I hadn't taken any part in the battle as yet having orders to reserve our fire to protect the colors. I had been watching this squad of Rebels that had been firing, and every time I saw the blue smoke ascend there would be a man picked off in Co. E. I told Capt. Calvert what I had seen and where the Rebels were located. My orders prevented my shooting but he told me to let him have my gun and he fired into the clump of bushes which they returned by shooting at the colors. I told him that was an insult to our little squad and asked permission to return the fire. He said for me to take one-half the guard, which is six men, and advance to a big log on the bank and drive them out of their hiding place. We started but there was another danger we hadn't thought of. It was nearly fifty yards to the log through an open space and we had not got half the distance when we saw a man wearing a broad hat raise out of his rifle-pit and his ball came singing past my head, but we kept on and reached the log.

We saw the blue smoke again and another 83rd man fell for they were in close range and every shot told. We took aim at the bushes where the smoke came from and fired, and one shot was sufficient for we could see them running up the ravine like a gang of frightened turkeys. But my greatest danger wasn't over. The man in the pit had his gun reloaded by that time and had me spotted, I think. If I undertook to retreat he would get me as I went, so I loaded my gun and lay on my back, Zouave fashion, across the log so as to be ready if he was still there. I raised up, peeped over the log, saw him and we both fired, his bullet passed over my head this time. The third time his ball passed close enough that I felt it "tingle" my right ear. I saw that it depended on which could load first for the next round, as escape was impossible. I was first and got my gun sighted for his rifle pit, saw the bright muzzle of his gun come up first, kept my gun sighted and when his head and shoulders filled the sight of my gun I pulled the trigger. He didn't bother me any more and I don't know whether my ball struck him or not, but I saw his gun fall back in the pit. It had to be one of us, and it was the other one.

I was still in danger. My comrades had taken advantage of the time he was loading and gone back to the regiment and a cannon had taken the place of the other fellow's gun, only a little farther back. I placed myself behind the log to see what would come next—and it came, two heavy charges of grape shot. By this time the regiment had orders to lie down so our battery could shell them and here was another danger. They had cut their fuse too short and their shells were falling short, hitting the log near me. I took the Rebel side of the log for safety. The Rebels returned their fire by raising their guns and firing over the top of the log. Our men soon saw their mistake and cut their fuse longer and the artillery battle lasted an hour longer. I don't know which side got the best of it, but think the Yankees did as they kept up the firing the longest. When the firing ceased the 83rd was relieved by the 8th Missouri. We were still in close quarters for every Rebel in the rifle-pits raised up and fired as they saw us being relieved and bullets were flying as thick as ever. I soon overtook the regiment and the first man I saw was old Major Cravens, Lieut. Col. of the 83rd. He had on a long-tailed coat and like Absalom of old he was hanging, not by his hair but by his coat tail. He had jumped over a big log and the lining of his coat had fastened on a limb on the opposite side. It took but a moment to relieve him and the last time I talked with him he said he knew someone had loosed him but never knew who it was until I told him.

Johann Stuber Sees the Rough Side of Battle[5]

Another soldier in a different part of the same battle might have a completely different experience. Unlike John Roberts and the 83d Indiana, Johann Stuber and the regiment to which he belonged, the German-speaking 58th Ohio, were deeply involved in the disastrous Union defeat at Chickasaw Bayou. The Federal commanding general, William T. Sherman, hoped to take Vicksburg, but the terrain over which he had to attack funneled his troops into one small and completely impossible avenue of advance, where alert Confederate defenders killed or wounded 1,776 of them. After the battle, Sherman made a brief truce with the Rebels to retrieve his dead and withdraw his defeated army.

The 58th Ohio, a regiment of German immigrants, was among those that suffered heavy casualties in the attack. Johann Stuber recorded his reminiscences of the battle in German, and they are here translated.

On Monday, December 29, we were ordered in all haste to take up a position in another direction. There we stood until almost midday, while the artillery kept up a lively fire on the enemy position on the opposite hillside, to which the enemy made only a weak reply. It was obviously their intention to entice us into advancing over this dangerous field. No rifle fire was heard. We had to take up a position behind the artillery in order to gain cover.

Now heavy rifle fire broke out on our right. Soon we had to return to our position of this morning, namely, in front on the far left. General [Frank] Blair ordered his brigade to fix bayonets, because we had to make a charge on the enemy position. The signal for this charge was to be a general salvo of all the artillery along the whole line. As soon as this signal was given, the troops were to charge out of the woods with loud hurrahs and hasten through the low brush to the first breastwork, hence over the breastwork, across the field to the second breastwork, and so on. The three new Missouri regiments were to form the first line. If these troops should falter, the 58th had orders to drive them forward, or to fire on them.

After a short time came the artillery signal. The 58th Regiment started moving and, bellowing fiercely, stormed out of the woods into the depths of the swamp and underbrush. Scarcely had the foe seen us than they opened on us a murderous fire from several batteries, from the left, right, and center. The whole hill was a cloud of smoke, for at least three ranks of infantry could fire on us from their position on the hill without hurting their own troops, who stood about ten or twelve feet below them. So it came that our regiment advanced through the brush very slowly and in bad order. By the time we reached the first breastwork and tried to regroup there, the ranks were already substantially thinned. As we then rushed over the breastwork and across the muddy field beyond it, through a terrible hail of rifle balls, toward the second breastwork, we were ahead of the Missourians, who had lain down on the ground to take cover. Yet the rifle balls from the hill still hit them there.

That was a dreadful slaughter, too ghastly to describe, much less to understand or even to gain some idea of. The terrible screams of the wounded drowned out every command, as they writhed about in the mud with heartrending cries. Reaching the second earthwork, I glanced backward over the field and everything went black before my eyes. I heard the call "Retreat" and turned back myself, for the [Rebel] cavalry was coming from the flanks to cut off our retreat. I was constantly trying to stay with the regiment, but I could no longer get any glimpse of a flag. I could see no more officers nor was any regimental line to be found. All was a wild confusion without any leadership. I did not stop until I had the first breastwork behind me again. My hat was ripped from my head, and when I picked it up it hung in shreds. So too did my blanket, which I carried rolled up on my back on top of my knapsack. The first members of the 58th I met were wounded, and in response to my question about Colonel Difter I got the answer that he fell shot through the head at the second breastwork. Another of them said Colonel Difter had left his horse stuck in the mud back at the first breastwork and had continued with the regiment on foot as far as the second breast-work. There he had waited perhaps five minutes to give the men time to gather themselves. Then he had climbed onto the breast-work, swung his sword, and called, "Forward, 58th Ohio!" In this moment he received a shot in the head and toppled back over the breastworks at the feet of his soldiers. As the men were about to pick him up, the order to retreat was given, and whoever did not want to be captured had to get back as fast as he could. Only then the brigade on our right made its attack, but it too was soon in retreat.

About 100 yards away I saw a man now stumbling, now falling, trying to get out of the deep bushes into the cover of the forest. He looked like Lorenz Heitz, a comrade from Company A. I called to him with all my might to hurry. He seemed to hear me and, struggling to his feet, made a couple of steps before falling again and lying still. I called several more times, but he seemed not to hear. The musket balls were still buzzing among the trees or striking the ground, so it was questionable whether I could get to him without being hit, or whether I could bring him back to where I now lay. I considered briefly and then made a big rush and hurried toward the place where the man lay, but scarcely had I left my position than the balls came thick as hail around me. The Rebels, who had now advanced their lines, must have discovered me. I threw myself to the ground. When the shooting stopped, I jumped up and ran on, but the firing started immediately. I finally reached a hollow where I was protected from Rebel fire. When I reached the man, I saw to my disappointment that he was a complete stranger and he was dead. Now the outlook for me to get back into the cover of the woods was very critical. Only the prospect of a long and wearisome imprisonment moved me to run the risk of wounds or death and make my retreat as rapidly as possible. Again I flattened myself on the ground when the balls came too thick, and on the second rush I reached the edge of the forest unscathed.

Not far away another soldier had gotten to the woods about the same time I did. I looked around for him and recognized him at once as Carl Rudolf of Company A. I called to him and asked if he was wounded. He pointed to his leg. Immediately I hurried to him and at his wish used his pocket knife to cut open his boot, for his foot was already badly swollen. I hurried into the woods to get help and found an ambulance from another regiment. Through pleading and all manner of persuasion I got a man with a stretcher to go with me and get Rudolf. We had to carry him a good half mile through thick forest with underbrush and boulders—scarcely passable—to the place where a doctor examined him and explained that the leg must be amputated at the knee. Before he was lifted into the ambulance, he asked me to send word to his wife that he had been wounded. I wrote his address down, promised to write as soon as I could, and took my leave of him forever. Shortly thereafter I met about a dozen members of the 58th who were wounded, some lightly, some severely, and had managed to drag themselves this far. By their account, most of the regiment must have been dead, wounded, or captured.

I had to leave there because a cavalry cordon came through the woods to drive the scattered troops back together again. From there I came to a big farmhouse in the middle of a big field. A yellow flag [which in the Civil War indicated a hospital] flew from its roof. It was a hospital for the wounded. Scarcely had I reached the door of the house than I met Corporal Abbott of Company A coming out, having just had his left arm amputated. "There are more members of the 58th in there," he said to me before climbing into an ambulance. I found Corp. Gustav Koerner, his chin shattered by a bullet, and Friedrich Arkenberg, who had a wound in the lower body. Several others lay on the second and third floors. The house, the halls, the yard, even the attic was pressed full of wounded. I saw the doctors on the verandah with knives and saws working as diligently as butchers at the meat market. Shuddering, I turned away and went out into the grounds, where about a dozen blacks were engaged in digging graves. When I lifted the cover to see who lay there, a great heap of amputated arms and legs with ghastly pale shriveled skin stared back at me. After I had returned to the house, the doctors ordered all soldiers who could still walk to leave the house and go to the boats at the landing, about two miles away. I started walking there. The ambulances with their human freight rushed back and forth at top speed. Along the way I heard that a truce had been arranged and that [Gen. William T.] Sherman's army had 48 hours to vacate its position. So all our exertions, all our sacrifices of thousands of soldiers were purely wasted.

Henry O. Dwight Recalls the Battle of Raymond[6]

Another view of Civil War battle comes from the pen of Henry O. Dwight, a soldier in the 20th Ohio. Four and one-half months after the debacle at Chickasaw Bayou, Dwight and his regiment were part of Ulysses S. Grant's successful campaign against the fortress city of Vicksburg. On May 12, 1863, as the campaign unfolded across the Mississippi countryside, the 20th Ohio fought in the small but intense battle of Raymond. Dwight's account of the conflict, twenty-three years later, is particularly vivid.

As did many other firsthand chroniclers, Dwight describes the pervasive effects of black powder, the gunpowder of the 1860s, which produced choking clouds of heavy white smoke that smelled like rotten eggs and hung low on the battlefield among the fighting soldiers, drastically reducing visibility. It left a black residue everywhere it settled, including on the faces of the soldiers themselves, making them look, as Dwight put it, like "coalheavers." Another phenomenon on the field, observed by Dwight only in the enemy lines, was a fierce, adrenaline-driven battle-rage that could make men appear to be perfectly calm or even deliriously happy in the midst of a furious fight with comrades falling at their sides. Dwight also noted the sensation of being opposed by overwhelming enemy force while at the same time feeling neglected and even forgotten by one's own side. It was a common experience among soldiers in battle.

Somehow the will of a line to advance into enemy fire was not the sum of the courage of its members; rather, it was a group will to face danger—a reflection of the confidence that the men had in each other, in their leaders, and in their ability to defeat the enemy. Thus, Dwight describes a battle line wavering, starting forward, and swaying back to where it started and likens the movement to dry leaves swirled about by an autumn wind.

Dwight's story begins as his regiment is halted for rest near a small brook.

As we lay on the ground at the brook, taking our ease soldier fashion, the boys were grumbling, chatting, munching hard tack, or making fires to boil coffee in their tin cups. The other regiments of the brigade came up, an Indiana regiment going into line along the edge of the woods on our right and the 78th Ohio taking the place on our left, with the 68th near by. DeGolyer's battery of artillery, which always marched with us, stopped in the road near the skirmish line, and two of the guns were pointed down the road, in case any inquisitive chap should be coming from the other direction to see what we were about. Some of our boys sauntered off toward the road to try and find out what the cavalry had seen to put us to all the trouble of marching in line three mortal hours. The whole country was still with the stillness which you only see at nooning after a hard day's work in the fields. The grass where we lay was sweet with clover, and a few wild flowers showed their heads here and there. In the woods not very far away a mockingbird was singing. Near where I was an old dead tree had fallen over on to the big arms of one of its neighbors, and on one of its decaying branches a red squirrel popped up its head looking down at us along the brownish streak that marked his usual highway to the ground.

"Bang cr-r-r-r-r-r-ang! Bang cr-r-r-r-r-r-ang!" came two shells from the peaceable country in front, bursting over the heads of the groups in the road. There was a running to and fro, and almost immediately DeGolyer replied with his two guns to this sudden challenge of the enemy whose existence we had just been disputing. We all jumped, of course, every man feeling as he hadn't felt since the last time he was caught stealing apples. But we hadn't time to more than turn our heads when from out of the quiet woods on the other side of the brook there came a great yell of thousands of voices followed by such a crashing roar of musketry as one doesn't very often hear unless he has been prepared for it.

"Attention battalion, take arms, forward march," shouted Colonel [Manning F.] Force, and we all blessed him for knowing exactly what to do, and for doing it. As one man, the boys seized their guns—some were barefoot, for they were washing their feet in the brook; some had the coffee in their hands which the first scare had made them clutch from the fire, and some twenty or thirty were dead or wounded from that first volley. But quick as thought, all who could stand had taken their guns and had plunged through the brook. On the other side, not fifty yards distant, the enemy were crashing through the under brush in a magnificent line determined to carry all before them.

Two brigades of Texas troops had been watching our movements all the morning, and when we stopped for our nooning their pickets were not a hundred yards from our skirmish line. The moving of our main line to the edge of the woods without sending skirmishers on in front had given them their chance for a surprise. Three regiments had come quickly to the thicket in front of us, got all ready, and made their rush with seven or eight other regiments backing them up.

On our side our own brigade happened to be in line, but was not expecting any such unprovoked assault. What cavalry we had, had been sent off to the left to take a look at things toward the Big Black, where after all the chief danger seemed to be. DeGolyer's battery was watering its horses so near to the skirmish line that if the infantry was driven back an inch it would be captured by the swarming rebels long before help could be got from our other brigades, for the other two brigades of our division were scattered along the road, just where they happened to be when they received the order to halt for lunch.

At the first rush the rebel line far outflanked the Indiana regiment on our right and the whole regiment broke into inch bits, the boys making good time to the rear. This left the Johnnies a clear road to pass our flank, and they made good use of their chance, working well to our rear before long and putting bullets into the reserves of our line the best they knew how. At this moment the fate of the brigade, and certainly of our battery down there in the road, depended on the possibility of our holding those fellows at bay until the other brigades could be brought up.

When we rushed through the brook we found the enemy upon us, but we found also that the bank of the brook sloped off a bit with a kind of a bench at its further edge, which made a first rate shelter. So we dropped on the ground right there, and gave those Texans all the bullets we could cram into our Enfields [rifles] until our guns were hot enough to sizzle. The gray line paused, staggered back like a ship in collision which trembles in every timber from the shock. Then they too gave us volley after volley, always working up toward us, breasting our fire until they had come within twenty, or even fifteen paces. In one part of the line some of them came nearer than that, and had to be poked back with the bayonet.

It was the 7th Texas which had struck us, a regiment which had never been beaten in any fight. We soon found that they didn't scare worth a cent. They kept trying to pass through our fire, jumping up, pushing forward a step, and then falling back into the same place, just as you may see a lot of dead leaves in a gale of wind, eddying to and fro under a bank, often rising up as if to fly away, but never able to advance a peg. It was a question of life or death with us to hold them for we knew very well that we would go to Libby [a notorious Confederate prison]—those that were left of us—if we could not stand against the scorching fire which beat into our faces in that first hour.

Meanwhile the Johnnies sent in another regiment on our left to pick up DeGolyer's battery, as a kind of pastime like. But the battery had given back a little, for the sake of a better ground, and when the Johnnies tried to go there they got the fire of the 78th and 68th, besides as much canister as they could digest for one while. So they concluded that they would not take DeGolyer just then. General [John A.] Logan sent all his aides on a run down the road for the other brigades of the division, while he himself made a rush for the Indiana regiment which was falling back from our right and got the boys to face about and take position where they could pepper the Rebs who were firing into our flank and rear. General Logan knew that he had the whole corps behind him, and [Maj. Gen. James B.] McPherson was already on hand, sending back to [Brig. Gen. Marcellus] Crocker to hurry up his division; but he also knew that this sort of thing—the piling of ten rebel regiments on to three or four of his regiments—could not go on very long. So the other brigades seemed to him a terribly long time in getting up.

In the midst of all this anxiety one of the staff came back to General Logan from one of the wished for brigades and said: "General _____ will be here before very long. He says that he will start as soon as his men have finished their coffee."

Even in the hurry of that rough time this answer made General Logan stop and stare. His feelings were too deep for proper utterance. He only said, "Go tell General _____ that he isn't worth h___," and rode off to place the regiments of the First Brigade, which now began to come up.

The staff officer mounted his horse and galloped down the road. He is said to have given Logan's message word for word. I am sorry to say that I have not the papers to prove this statement, but it was believed by all the boys at the time, and if it was not true it ought to be.

All this time we were hanging on to the bank of the brook with those fellows pouring gunpowder smoke into our faces, and we answer back so fast that the worst game of football is nothing to the fatigue of it. As for the noise of that discussion between the 20th Ohio and the 7th Texas, a clap of thunder, a wicked roar with no separations between the bolts, and all the time the Johnnies made it hot for us in flank and rear as well as in front.

The Johnnies seemed rather to like it. We could see them tumble over pretty often, but those who were left didn't mind it. One officer not more than thirty feet from where I stood quietly loaded up an old meerschaum, lit a match, his pistol hanging from his wrist, and when he had got his pipe well agoing, he got hold of his pistol again and went on popping away at us as leisurely as if he had been shooting rats. Why that fellow didn't get shot I don't know. The fact is when you start to draw a bead on any chap in such a fight you have got to make up your mind mighty quick whom you'll shoot. There are so many on the other side that look as if they were just getting a bead on you that it takes a lot of nerve to stick to the one you first wanted to attend to. You generally feel like trying to kind of distribute your bullets so as to take in all who ought to be hit. So a good many get off who are near enough to be knocked over the first time.

We could not understand why somebody wasn't sent out to cover our flank in place of the Indiana fellows. It seemed as if we were forgotten. So when they sent us some ammunition it was like a gift from distant friends, and did us good like a reinforcement. It was quite as well that we did not know that the first of our two rear brigades had come up and had deployed on the right of the rallied Indianians, but that even then Logan found himself outnumbered two to one. The fellows on the right kept the Rebs from scooping us up, but could not get forward enough to cover our flank, and had to fight like everything to hold their own.

The brook bank protected us some. The leaves and twigs mowed from the bushes by the Texan bullets fell softly about us, but those fellows shot to hit and not to cut twigs about our ears. Captain Kaga got his collar bone and shoulder blade splintered and badly mixed. Johnny Stevenson wanted to be in his father's barn more than ever when a half inch of lead had ploughed a hole through his neck. One of the sergeants shouted to me as I stood beside him, but I could not hear. He was loading his gun, and he roared again in my ear, "They've got me this time sure, but I'm going to have one more pop at them." He took careful aim and fired, and fell backward into the brook, with a bright red hole in his shoulder. Then I understood what he meant. Company C lost its officers and was commanded at last by a high private named Canavan, who managed things like a West Pointer. Most of the men killed were shot through the head and never knew what hurt them.

Well, the short of it is, it was a pretty tough time that we had of it, lying there by the brook and digging our toes into the ground for fear that the mass of men in front would push us back over the bank after all. But every man held to his place, for every one felt as if there was a precipice behind and he would go down a thousand feet if he let go his hold on that bank.

At last the rear brigade of our division got up, and Logan sent them in on the right, where the Johnnies were again ready to make a flanking rush. Our fresh brigade went in with will and effect. They didn't wait for much ceremony, but just felt their front with a few sharp volleys to kind of get the temper of the chaps, and then they charged like men who had had their coffee. We heard their cheer, but we didn't hear the angry burst of musketry with which the Rebs replied to it, nor the noise made by our other brigade as it came up on to the line with us.

Pretty soon we found the Rebs in front of us were edging off a bit. Somehow we were not pressed so hard. The firing kept up, but the smoke did not puff into our mouths so much. More twigs and leaves were hit and fewer men. Then we began to hear the bullets for the first time. The Johnnies were farther away. Then there was nobody left to shoot and our own fire stopped. Now we could stand up and stretch our legs and rinse the charcoal and saltpetre [the components with sulfur of Civil War gunpowder] out of our mouths at the muddy brook. I looked at my watch. We had been at work on those Texans near two hours and a half, although I must say that after it was over it did not seem more than an hour.

We were a hard looking lot. The smoke had blackened our faces, our lips and our throats so far down that it took a week to get the last of it out. The most dandified officer in the regiment looked like a coalheaver.

But there was not time to be thinking about looks. "Attention battalion, forward march," came the order of Colonel Force again and away we went with a shout, over the ghastly pile of Texans who had been laid along their line by our fire. Shortly we came out into a big cornfield beyond the woods, and the first thing I saw on the ground was the meerschaum which the Rebel officer had smoked in the fight. It was still warm as it lay where it had dropped from his mouth when he ran, and I picked it up and took my turn at smoking it. In front of us was a bare ridge, and over this the Rebels were retiring in a bulging and shaky line, pelted by DeGolyer's best shrapnel and pestered by the rifle fire of our Third Brigade boys. The affair on the Raymond Road was over.

Gerald F. Linderman on Courage in Battle[7]

Among the post-Vietnam War generation of scholars to write on the Civil War is Gerald Linderman. Typical of historians of his era, Linderman tells of the courage of the soldiers in a detached way, as if the men in blue and gray were specimens under a microscope. His main argument is an elaborate theory about midnineteenth-century beliefs. Courage, he maintains, was a primary moral value to

Americans at the outset of the Civil War. In turn, it was tied to all
other positive values, so that a moral person was bound to have courage and an immoral one could not possibly be equally brave. Finally,
the moral, and therefore more courageous, side was certain to win
and to suffer fewer casualties in doing so.

In the passage that follows, Linderman argues that Civil War soldiers felt a need to prove their courage—and thus their inward moral
worth—in battle. Compare this passage to the actual soldiers' accounts.
To what extent do their stories bear out Linderman's thinking?

Few Civil War soldiers felt able simply to declare their courage. No man knew how he would behave in battle, Ulysses Grant's
aide, Horace Porter, insisted, so courage was never assured until it
had been put to trial. Critical to the soldier's Civil War was his
willingness to expose himself in a direct test of his mettle against
that of the enemy.

The requirement that courage be a fearless courage meant that
the soldier's feelings about what he was doing were as important as
his actions. Particularly admired—sometimes extravagantly—were
those who seemed to possess fearlessness as nature's gift, those so
oblivious to fear that it could not exist within the range of their
emotional reactions. Such men showed an absolute indifference
under fire; they were those ideal officers who were perfectly brave
without being aware that they were so. A Union artillery barrage
catching Confederates in the open sent them running for cover—
all but General Turner Ashby. He was, concluded an observer as
moved as the general was unmoved, "totally indifferent to the hellish fire raining all about him." Southern soldiers were convinced
that both Stonewall Jackson and J. E. B. Stuart ("he saw everything
in battle utterly undisturbed by the danger") lived with no consciousness of the feeling of fear. When in battle, such men appeared
to expose themselves recklessly, with no idea that they stood in danger of being killed. Long after others had abandoned uncommon
markings as a sure invitation to enemy bullets, Stuart continued to
wear in battle his distinctive slouch hat adorned with a long plume.
He was widely admired for what others took to be his constitutional insensibility to risk. Similarly, Jackson's "utter disregard of
danger" was one of the strongest elements of magnetism drawing
the Southern rank-and-file to him.

To the relief—and sometimes the alarm—of those many soldiers who felt such *sang-froid* was no part of their own natures, there was a wider path to courage. One could—indeed, would have to—test oneself in combat and, applying the powers of will, try to expel fear. Few could hope to achieve the insouciance of a Stonewall Jackson or the fearless courage of an Ashby or a Philip Kearny, but soldiers would at least so diminish their secret fear that they too would become capable of heroic action. Few felt that they would be able to join the company of courage's exemplars, but all knew it was essential to prove that they were not cowards—and that was itself a formidable task. . . . Hence few balked at submitting themselves to the test of battle.

Reduced to tactical terms, courage was preeminently the charge—the boldest actions were assumed to be those of offensive warfare—but there were many other situations to which the tenets of the test were no less applicable, trials of steadfastness as well as advance. In the first years of the war the rank-and-file held themselves to a strict standard, that of fighting "man fashion." They were expected to wait stoically through the tense and difficult period just prior to battle; to stand and receive enemy fire without replying to it (one of Lee's soldiers called this "the most trying duty of the soldier"); and to resist all urges to quicken their pace under fire, to dodge or duck shells, or to seek cover. (Within those assumptions men who at the war's outset had purchased body armor were ridiculed, but the issue became moot when breastplates were discovered to stop nothing except movement.)

Difficult as those tests were for enlisted men, the burden on officers was far heavier. While each of those in the ranks felt the necessity to prove himself to himself, to those comrades around him and to his family, the officer was compelled to do the same and, in addition, to impress his courage, less by stoic endurance than by positive demonstration, on all those he commanded. A Wisconsin colonel was convinced that "the men who carried the knapsacks never failed to place an officer just where he belonged, as to his intelligence and bravery. Even if [officers] said nothing, yet their instinctive and unconscious action in battle placed upon the officers the unavoidable brand of approval or disapproval." Not even the highest-ranking officers were exempt. "We knew the fighting generals and we respected them," a New York artilleryman said, "and we knew the cowards and despised them." Of 425 Confederate generals, seventy-seven were killed in the war.

For the officer, the arena was larger, the audience more numerous, the possibilities of courageous demonstration more varied, from the casual to the monumental. In his first battle Robert Burdette, whose Illinois regiment was bracketed by rifle and cannon fire, watched an officer ride down the line, stop to ask a soldier for a match, light his pipe, puff on it as he would relaxing before his hearth, and then ride forward to overtake his skirmishers: "How I admired his wonderful coolness!" A less "natural," more hortatory, but no less admired courage was that of Colonel Emerson Opdycke, who, caught in the rout at Chickamauga, was determined to hold ground vital to General George H. Thomas's stand against the onrushing Confederates. He sat on his horse at the crest of a hill and, though fully exposed to the enemy view, continued to point with his sword in the direction his regiments were to fire. Such a pose might today appear appropriate only to his posthumous equestrian statue, but to those who watched, Opdycke was "the very incarnation of soldierly bearing and manly courage."

That passages through the test should sometimes appear effortless or theatrical should not hide its essential characteristics. Its gravity was unquestioned. William Dame was a young, well-educated Southern gentleman whose artillery battery, the Richmond Howitzers, fought under Lee. A teamster—"a dreadful, dirty, snuffy, spectacled old Irishman," certainly no gentleman and not even a soldier—one day insisted on taking the pulses of William and his friends. He then announced the one soldier was excited, another was frightened, that a third "would do all right" in combat, and so on. Some of the judged were pleased, others hated the Irishman for his verdicts, but no one dared to refuse to submit to the test or to question its results. "Nobody can tell what a dreadful trial this simple thing was!"

Earl J. Hess on the Nature of Battle[8]

Writing a decade after Linderman, historian Earl J. Hess's depiction of Civil War soldiers in battle is solidly grounded in firsthand accounts. Hess's work also has a central argument: that the soldiers ultimately proved equal to the moral and psychological demands of battle. First, however, he gives a vivid account of the chaos of combat. In the passage that follows, he describes what Civil War soldiers experienced on battlefields where their orderly formations and neat expectations quickly degenerated into disorder and a horrifying loss of control. This was illustrated in the way terrain features disrupted maneuvers and also in the way the violence of battle demolished even such apparently solid features as the great trees of the forest. Hand-to-hand combat represented the ultimate in disorder and loss of group control, and the soldiers dreaded it.

Battle was a comprehensive physical experience of the senses that surrounded the soldier with a lethal, chaotic environment. He had no control over that environment and often had great difficulty controlling his emotional response to it. Historian Eric J. Leed, in writing of World War I, described the soldier's perception of himself as an autonomous player in a world that could be manipulated. He was used to living this role in civilian life but found that in the trenches of the Western Front, those safe assumptions were no longer valid. The result could be a breakdown of something essential to morale.

The Civil War soldier never quite became entrapped in the kind of physical environment of combat that the unlucky veterans of World War I found themselves in, yet he and all soldiers in combat faced the same problem: how to deal with an environment over which he had little control. Chaos was the theme most consistently used by Northern soldiers in the descriptions of combat. On all levels—from the smoke-enshrouded vision of the individual to the confused movements of companies struggling through brush-entangled terrain—the soldier struggled against chaos and strove to create a coherent vision of battle.

Soldiers often found that combat wrecked the most reassuring element of order in military life: the linear tactical formations that were the foundation of movement on the battlefield. "It is astonishing how soon, and by what slight causes, regularity of formation and movement are lost in actual battle," mused David L. Thompson of the 9th New York. "Disintegration begins with the first shot. To the book-soldier all order seems destroyed, months of drill apparently going for nothing in a few minutes." Thompson admitted that the presence of the enemy was the most important factor in the breakdown of order in the ranks, but it was also caused by vegetation and the terrain. A clump of trees, for example, could cause one portion of a line to lag behind the rest, skewing the whole or even resulting in the line losing its direction and advancing to a point its commanders had not intended.

As Thompson indicated, the chaos of battle was not caused solely by the dangers of flying lead threatening frail bodies; it was also the result of the natural arena on which Civil War battles took place. The South occupied a vast geographic area with a variety of terrain and natural growth. Generally, about half the land on any given battlefield was covered with vegetation, ranging from open woods to thickets of scrub trees choked with dense brush and briars. Maps of several battlefields large and small—from Wilson's Creek, Pea Ridge, and Prairie Grove in the Trans-Mississippi; to Shiloh, Corinth, and Chickamauga in the west; to Second Bull Run, the Wilderness, and Five Forks in the east—show a mixture of open fields, choked thickets, and grand forests. Long battle lines typically spanned this mixture, part of them moving freely in the open and the rest struggling through jungle matting. Infantry units clawed their way through woods until they burst out into fields and then wormed their way once again through thick growth. Civil War field armies were so large that they could not fit onto the small farms and pastures of the South but sprawled across the landscape. Theodore Lyman, an aide on Major General George Meade's staff, commented on the difficulties of keeping the 5th Corps line straight during the early phases of the Petersburg campaign. It "was not straight or facing properly. That's a chronic trouble in lines in the woods. Indeed there are several chronic troubles. The divisions have lost connection; they cannot cover the ground designated, their wing is in the air, their skirmish line has lost its direction, etc., etc."

Vegetation had an enormous impact on Civil War tactics. It broke up formations, nullified the power of shock on the battlefield, and allowed firepower to dominate the action. This greatly intensified the problem of controlling the movements of individual regiments, brigades, and divisions. Lateral coordination broke down, leaving units unsupported on their flanks and commanders frustrated over the lack of control they could exercise over their own men. Vegetation severely limited visibility, thus reducing the range of rifle fire. Soldiers often had to wait until the enemy was seventy-five, forty, or even twenty yards away before catching glimpses of gray-clad figures. Heavy growth often nullified the effectiveness of artillery fire, for projectiles that hit trees lost considerable velocity and were deflected from their course. Most important, thick vegetation hid targets, and Civil War artillerymen could fire only at what they saw. It also made the cavalry even more irrelevant on the battlefield than it had already become due to the rifle musket. On open ground, cavalry was decimated by rifle fire when it attempted to launch mounted assaults against infantry; in brush-entangled terrain, cavalrymen had no chance to employ shock tactics against infantry.

Trees, bushes, and grasses of all kinds were such ever-present elements on the battlefield that they became unintended targets. Civil War battle had an enormous, awe-inspiring effect on vegetation, ripping the natural growth like a great reaping machine. Soldiers were nearly as astonished by this as by the destruction of human bodies. Lieutenant Colonel Alexander W. Raffen of the 19th Illinois looked with amazement at the field of Chickamauga several months after the battle. "The trees in some places are cut down so much by the artillery that it looks as if a tornado had swept over the field, all the trees and stumps are plugged all over with bullets; it is astonishing to think that any one could have come off safe without being hit." Such destruction led an Indiana soldier to remark of Shiloh, "Thare is some places that it Looks as if a mouse could not get threw alive."

Captain John William DeForest of the 12th Connecticut, an educated and highly literate observer of the military experience, was very sensitive to the sublimity of this part of battle. Industrialized warfare shattered the natural environment of the battlefield, representing in DeForest's mind the growing power of man over the wilderness. It was a power that he felt must be viewed with ambivalence. Observing the effect of Confederate artillery fire during a Federal assault on the defenses of Port Hudson, DeForest noted that "every minute or two some lordly tree, eighteen inches or two feet in diameter, flew asunder with a roar and toppled crashing to earth. For some minutes I admired without enjoying this sublime massacre of the monarchs of the forest."

Few soldiers could actually enjoy seeing nature destroyed, partly because it meant that the stable placement of natural objects around them was also destroyed. Their sense of disorder and the inability to control their immediate environment was heightened when they saw great trees shorn and splintered. It was physical proof that nothing, not even the "monarchs of the forest," could withstand combat unscathed. And it was not only the trees that suffered; astonishingly, even bushes, underbrush, and blades of grass were clipped as if by shears and scissors in the storm of rifle fire that swept the battlefield.

The most famous instance of nature suffering at the hands of soldiers engaged in combat occurred at Spotsylvania on May 12, 1864. In one of the most horrific battles of the war, massed Union and Confederate formations poured fire at each other all day long while locked into static positions on opposite sides of an earthen parapet. Late that night, an oak tree some twenty inches in diameter fell; its trunk had been so pared by the rain of rifle balls that it could no longer stand. In its fall, the oak knocked a South Carolina soldier unconscious and grazed several other men. For the soldiers, this tree came to symbolize the awesome destructive power of combat. The trunk was quickly cut up by Federals eager for a relic of the great battle, and the stump was removed to find its way many years later into the Smithsonian Institution's National Museum of American History.

It seemed rather odd to Northern soldiers that trees, bushes, and grass could become casualties of war. That is why so many of them commented on this aspect of combat. Indeed, considering the small size of field armies and the usually short duration of engagements in America's previous wars, the Civil War was the only conflict fought on American soil in which the natural environment was decimated by artillery and small-arms fire. The destruction of natural growth was yet another example of the bizarre chaos generated by battle. Nothing was safe from the lethal fire unleashed by massed formations of determined men.

Virtually no man was safe from that lethal fire either. One of the great untold stories of the Civil War was the tragic deaths of Union soldiers from what twentieth-century writers would call "friendly fire." The Union army made no attempt to determine how many of its members became victims at its own hand. Much of it was the result of poor artillery fire and faulty equipment. The ever-observant Theodore Lyman of Meade's staff noted the frequency of this occurrence: "Not a battle is fought that some of our men are not killed by shells exploding short and hitting our troops instead of the enemy's, beyond. Sometimes it is the fuse that is imperfect, sometimes the artillerists lose their heads and make wrong estimates of distance."

The majority of friendly casualties, however, resulted from small-arms fire. "A lot of Maine Conscripts fired into us the other day wounding several of the boys," complained William Ketcham of the 13th Indiana. Nervousness and lack of training led to the unintended deaths of thousands. Musing on the death of a "wicked profane boy" who nevertheless was a "good soldier" (he was struck in the back of the head by a Federal ball while standing picket duty), Thomas White Stephens of the 20th Indiana complained, "It is a shame that men can not keep cool in time of battle, but fire into one another." The religious Stephens took this philosophically, but many others were greatly embittered by such an unexpected loss of their comrades.

None of the green volunteers who flocked to the recruiting stations in 1861 could have guessed that battle would consume men in this fashion. As they came to know it, some of the glory went out of the sacrifice, and the soldier's awareness of the chaotic nature of battle increased. He had to be concerned not only with fire to the front but also with the potential of fire to the rear.

Beyond the disorder caused by tangled terrain and friendly fire, the ultimate chaos of combat occurred when soldiers engaged in hand-to-hand fighting. When soldiers were exchanging blows with clubbed muskets or lunging at each other with bayonets and swords, all order broke down. Officers found it impossible to direct or control their men, and soldiers found themselves surrounded on all sides by an enemy who was close enough to knock them down with their fists. Hand-to-hand combat created an environment of brute survival unequaled by any other form of battle.

Lieutenant Holman Melcher, commanding Company F, 20th Maine, took part in a classic example of personal combat during the battle of the Wilderness. His company had advanced too far into the thick scrub timber and had become separated from its regiment. He and seventeen men were forced to retreat through Confederate lines. They crept through the brush to within fifteen paces of the Rebels, then fired and rushed into the scattered Confederate line. Although most of the Confederates fled rather than engage his men, some accepted the challenge. After seeing one man pin a Rebel to the ground with a bayonet, Melcher swung his sword at the back of another Confederate who was about to fire his musket, but he was barely close enough to do any damage. "The point cut the scalp on the back of his head and split his coat all the way down the back. The blow hurt and startled him so much that he dropped his musket without firing, and surrendered." Melcher's little band made it safely back to the Union lines.

Melcher discovered what most soldiers knew: hand-to-hand combat was so confusing, so threatening, and so unpredictable that men seldom allowed themselves to be caught in it. An unusually reflective civilian, Sidney George Fisher, came to the same conclusion, and his thoughts were confirmed by a long conversation he had with a veteran of McClellan's Peninsula campaign. "I said it seemed to me that the most terrible thing in a battle must be a charge of bayonets, that a confused melee of furious men armed with such weapons, stabbing each other & fighting hand to hand in a mass of hundreds, was something shocking even to think of. He said it was so shocking that it very rarely happened that bayonets are crossed, one side or the other almost always giving way before meeting."

Fisher was unique, for few civilians realized that battle seldom involved close-range fighting. It was the most personalized form of warfare, and soldiers avoided it. To kill the enemy at a distance was safer and easier. Depersonalized combat represented the true nature of modern warfare, making the killing easier to do and to endure. "We hear a great deal about hand-to-hand fighting," complained Henry Otis Dwight of the 20th Ohio during the Atlanta campaign. "Gallant though it would be, and extremely pleasant to the sensation newspapers to have it to record, yet, unfortunately for gatherers of items, it is of very rare occurrence. . . . When men can kill one another at six hundred yards they generally would prefer to do it at that distance than to come down to two paces."

Notes

1. Rice C. Bull, *Soldiering: The Civil War Diary of Rice C. Bull, 123rd New York Volunteer Infantry*, ed. K. Jack Bauer (San Rafael, CA: Presidio Press, 1977), 116–17. © 1977 by the Presidio Press, Novato, California. Reprinted by permission of the Presidio Press.

2. Abner R. Small, *The Road to Richmond: The Civil War Memoirs of Maj. Abner R. Small of the 16th Maine Vols., with His Diary as a Prisoner of War*, ed. Harold Adams Small (Berkeley: University of California Press, 1959), 184. © 1939 by The Regents of the University of California. Reprinted by permission of the University of California Press.

3. John C. Reed Manuscript, Alabama Department of Archives and History, Montgomery, Alabama, pp. 16–24. Reprinted by permission of the Alabama De-

partment of Archives and History. Reed's one long paragraph has been divided for the reader.

4. From a handwritten manuscript written by John M. Roberts and entitled "A Pioneer's Story," Indiana Historical Society (hereafter HIS), SC 1744. Reprinted by permission of the IHS.

5. Johann Stuber, *Mein Tagebuch ueber die Erlebnisse im Revolutions-Kriege* (Cincinnati: S. Rosenthal & Co., 1896), 60–63 (trans. Steven E. Woodworth).

6. "A Soldier's Story: The Affair on the Raymond Road," *New York Daily Tribune*, November 21, 1886.

7. Gerald F. Linderman, *Embattled Courage: The Experience of Combat in the American Civil War* (New York: Free Press, 1987), 20–22. © 1987 by Gerald F. Linderman. Reprinted by permission of The Free Press, a Division of Simon & Schuster.

8. Earl J. Hess, *The Union Soldier in Battle: Enduring the Ordeal of Combat* (Lawrence: University Press of Kansas, 1997), 47–52. © 1997 by the University Press of Kansas. All rights reserved. Reprinted by permission of the University Press of Kansas.

CHAPTER THREE

On the Nature of Courage

No sooner was the war over than those who had seen the face of battle began to write about the meaning and nature of courage under fire. Was "courage" merely some animal instinct that propelled men into danger, or was it the whole constellation of motivations that led them to place duty ahead of their personal safety? What did it take to face the enemy? Why did some soldiers run away while others stayed and fought? What went through their minds while battle raged around them and death seemed imminent? Those who had not "seen the elephant" wanted to know the answers to these and other questions, and the first generation to write about the Civil War experience, the soldiers themselves, strove to tell them. They emphasized the confused nature of battle and the fact that it allowed very little opportunity for conscious reflection. In the heat of combat, instincts seemed to determine a man's behavior, and the origins of those instincts remained "deep mysteries" even to those in whom they operated. The real mental and spiritual battles were fought in anticipation of action rather than in the heat of combat, and there men had to wrestle with their fears. For God, country, comrades, family, and their own honor, the soldiers impelled themselves (or allowed themselves to be impelled) into chaos and horror and there coped as best they could. For that devotion, they were worthy of the thanks and honor of a grateful nation.

For a century after the war, little changed in the fundamental conception of what the men faced and how they faced it. American soldiers of the nation's other conflicts—the Spanish-American War, the World Wars, and, to some extent, Korea—were seen in similar terms by the public and honored for the act of will by which they went into harm's way. Then came the 1960s, the Vietnam War, and the beginning of a massive shift in the American worldview. As a war against communism, the Vietnam conflict was never popular with the radical wing of the American left, to which most academics, including professional historians, belong. As a war that the U.S. government deemed not worth winning, Vietnam gradually became unpopular with much of the rest of the population as well. Once again, American soldiers, mostly volunteers, went into battle for the same constellation of reasons that had motivated them in the nation's other wars, and they found courage in the same ways their forefathers had at Monmouth, Gettysburg, and Iwo Jima.[1] This time, however, they returned home to be greeted not with gratitude and honor but with hatred and scorn by a noisy minority who bitterly opposed the war and anyone connected with it.

Out of the bitterness of the anti-Vietnam War movement in America came new ways of thinking, a mindset in which all wars were evil on both sides, especially that of the United States, no war ever accomplished any worthy goal, and no soldier was ever ennobled by his sacrifice in battle. Followers of the new counterculture loathed the military and considered soldiers to be, at best, victims, who in turn victimized others. At the same time, abandoning the old belief in self-evident truths and "the laws of nature and of nature's God"—whether revealed by Him in the Bible or deduced from nature by man—many Americans, particularly in academia, began to assert that there was neither God, nor truth, nor any objective standard of right or wrong. There was no order or unity in the universe, but reality was fragmented, chaotic, and devoid of meaning. In the decades that followed, these views gradually began to color scholarly inquiry, creating an academic Zeitgeist, or spirit of the age, whose assumptions came to underlie many discussions that were not self-consciously philosophical.

The post-1960s Zeitgeist touched the study of Civil War soldiers particularly in regard to the nature of courage, and most directly in Gerald Linderman's 1987 book, *Embattled Courage.* Linderman argues that the soldiers went off to war with settled values in an orderly world. As discussed in the previous chapter, courage was, according to Linderman, chief among those values and indeed was woven into the fabric of all other fundamental moral attributes and values. War introduced the soldiers to reality, as Linderman sees it: a fragmented reality where no values are settled and all virtues are meaningless, especially courage. Survival and success, like everything else in the post-1960s, was a matter not of merit but of chance. The soldiers were helpless victims in the face of the irrational, impersonal, and inexorable forces of war. If they themselves said otherwise after the war, then, argues Linderman, they were not telling the truth. For him, as for much of the rest of the post-1960s generation, an orderly world of fixed values *must be* a fiction. In the concluding paragraph of his book he writes,

> To Bruce Catton, growing up in Benzonia, Michigan, in the first years of the new [twentieth] century, the veterans of the Civil War "seemed to speak for a certainty, for an assured viewpoint, for a standard of values that did not fluctuate" and for "the continuity of human experience." So did they speak to all Americans in 1900. Civil War veterans had become symbols of changelessness—but only by obliterating or amending an experience of combat so convulsive of their values that it had for a time cut the cord of experience.[2]

Linderman's radical assertions have not gone unchallenged. Historians James M. McPherson and Earl J. Hess have advanced well-researched arguments that the soldiers were not helpless victims of the chaos of war but rather overcame the horror of battle and the emotional stress demanded by courage and retained their basic view of the world. In this chapter are some of the soldiers' own thoughts on the nature of courage as well as passages from more recent participants in the historical debate.

Abner R. Small on the Nature of Courage[3]

The 16th Maine's Maj. Abner Small wrote his thoughts on the nature of courage in the Civil War soldiers. He believed, as did many who shared what Civil War veteran Oliver Wendell Holmes Jr. called "the incommunicable experience of war," that combat numbed the mind. Soldiers in battle, Small argued, acted on instinct, not on reason. Rational thoughts and inward struggles for courage came before or after the great clashes of armies, or on "the edge of a battle"— close enough to perceive the conflict but distant enough to remain painfully lucid.

Bravery and courage—these remain deep mysteries. In the heat and turmoil of a fight, the word "bravery" has no significance to the combatants; men are heroes or cowards in spite of themselves. All the demands of active service are for courage; but the real test comes before the battle—in the rear line, under fire, waiting. The true perspective of danger is observed and comprehended by the man attached to the edge of a battle—not in it, but near enough to feel its fierce pulsations and get an occasional shock of its power.

A young author [Stephen Crane], his boyish fancy stimulated by books, has written a story in which he takes a raw recruit into, through, and out of a battle and represents him with a brain fully alive to reason and revealing a cunning course of deception, all in a way apparently realistic, and intensely interesting, but only possible in an imaginative mind before a parlor grate.

That any man in my regiment, or in the army, analyzed his feelings and marked out any specific line of conduct while under fire, or even thought for five consecutive minutes of the past, present, or future, or measured out or acted upon any theoretical course of conduct irrespective of the arbitrary military law which held him in obedience, is absurd. Afterthoughts are in a sense real, and give a correct résumé of what might have been; but to put an endless and connected train of thought in the brain of a green soldier, so thoroughly scared—by his own admission—that is not accountable, and to set it in systematic motion which shall develop the "Red Badge of Courage," is sheer rot.

The bravest front, bolstered by pride and heroic resolution, will crumble in the presence of the agony of wounds. Wading through bloody fields and among the distorted dead bodies of comrades, dodging shells, and posing as a target to hissing bullets that whisper of eternity, is not conducive to continuity of action, much less of thought. The shock from a bursting shell will scatter a man's thoughts as the iron fragments will scatter the leaves overhead.

Thomas F. Galwey on Courage among His Fellow Soldiers[4]

An Irish-born soldier in the Army of the Potomac, Thomas Galwey took a rather cynical view of the soldiers' courage but one that nevertheless had some solid foundation. While new recruits might express an eagerness to fight, such feelings, as Galwey points out, were fairly rare. Veteran troops were particularly reluctant to return to the sort of slaughter they had witnessed in previous battles.

In all my experience I have never heard even the best soldiers growl for want of fighting. I know newspaper correspondents have often presented the army as spoiling for a fight, but they have been drawing largely on their imaginations. I have even seen retreats ordered where it was evident to all that a little more fighting would end in success, but I have seldom seen a man under those circumstances fail to obey the order with cheerfulness.

Poor human nature! It is not that men are wanting either in courage or patriotism; but each man has some private reasons of his own why he would escape danger of death or maiming if an honorable chance for doing so should offer. Malingering is the technical term among military men for shirking or evading work or any kind of military duty, and it is very prevalent. A few brave men do all the fighting and a few industrious ones all the work, whilst the rest go off behind clumps of bushes or into deep ravines and grow fat and save their bodies. They boil coffee, sleep, or play cards. It requires tact to get any labor at all out of them.

John W. De Forest on the Excitement of Battle[5]

An officer in the 12th Connecticut, John De Forest was a skillful writer who also later penned historical novels about the war. In his memoirs he commented insightfully on various aspects of the Civil War soldiers' lives.

In this brief passage, De Forest discusses his and his men's experiences and feelings on going into battle for the first time. How did they find the courage to march steadily toward the enemy? De Forest believed that it was partially the ignorance of the danger they faced, partially their adrenaline-induced state of excitement, and partially the assumption by virtually every man that he himself would not be hit.

In general, the terror of battle is not an abiding impression, but comes and goes like throbs of pain, and this is especially the case with veterans who have learned to know when there is pressing danger and when not; the moment a peril has passed they are as tranquil as if it had never come near. On the present occasion I was not as yet conscious of any emotion which could be called fear. I was still ignorant of the great horrors of battle, and buoyed up by the excitement of a rapid advance. A regiment of well-drilled greenhorns, if neatly brought into action, can charge as brilliantly as veterans. . . .

The Southern shots flew lower and lower. I said to myself, "They will hurt somebody soon." I did not duck or dodge, for I reflected that a missile would hit me about the time that I should hear it, and moreover I believed that all my men were watching me, whereas they were probably staring at the enemy. It cost me no great effort to keep my head up and move onward in good parade style. I had no twitching or trembling, I was not aware of any quickening of the pulse, in short, I was not scared. The Rebel gunners might hit me, but somehow I hoped not and thought not. It seemed to me perfectly natural that others should be killed and that I should escape. I have suffered more worry in subsequent engagements than I did in this first time under fire.

Rice C. Bull and a Comrade's Premonition[6]

A constant proximity to death placed a long-term strain on a man's courage. Sometimes a soldier who had faced death bravely on many battlefields failed the test when it was repeated one time too many. Sometimes the strain of overcoming fear gave veteran soldiers the sensation that they would be killed in the next fight, a feeling that sometimes plagued even the most experienced men. When such premonitions proved unfounded, they were soon forgotten, both by the soldier himself and by the comrade or two with whom he had shared his morbid thoughts. When, however, such a presentiment was realized, his comrades remembered the event vividly, as Rice Bull does in this passage.

I spread my blanket on the ground intending to get some sleep when Sergeant James Cummings of our Company came and sat down by me. Cummings was, I think, the finest soldier in our organization. A physical giant six feet four inches tall, well educated, a man of character, and a splendid soldier. He and I had formed a close friendship. I noticed he seemed melancholy and sad, the very opposite of his usual manner; and I asked him what was the trouble. He answered that for the last few days he had the feeling that he would not survive the next battle; he believed it would be soon and would not be surprised if it came this day. He said he had tried to shake it off but could not and now believed it was a warning to him. He told me that I was the only one he had spoken to, as he felt almost ashamed to say anything since we might think him cowardly, but he could not throw the feeling off. He said he had consecrated his life to his country's service and if it was necessary for him to die he would rather be killed in action than linger of disease in some hospital. He had strong religious convictions and had no fears in regard to death or the future life. I tried to convince him that it was foolish to give credence to such feelings, saying we all had such "warnings" at times but they never came true; and it was more than foolish to think of an early battle as it was then so quiet one could hardly imagine the enemy within fifty miles.

While we were talking the "fall-in" sounded and we took our place in line. . . . [The regiment went into action. The following passage relates the final stages of the engagement.]

My friend Cummings arose from a place near me. He had been quiet during all the excitement of the advance and attack and as far as I could see had not been worried; he had hardly spoken to me. Firing had nearly ended when he arose and placing the butt of his gun on the ground stood facing the front. I said, "Jim, you know there are orders not to fire, why do you stand and expose yourself." He answered, "I don't think there is any more danger in standing here than lying in the mud, I have had enough of that." He remained standing, leaning on his gun. I do not think it was more than a minute after I spoke to him that I heard a metallic sound, as though one had taken a hammer and hit a tree with it. Cummings's gun dropped from his hands and he and his gun struck the ground at the same time. A bullet had found its mark in his forehead, passing through his brain. We carried him back to the field hospital where he died before morning. In his death our Company lost its best soldier.

George H. Allen on the Hardening of the Soldiers[7]

Another effect of combat was a toughening or hardening of the men that also had an ugly side. Prolonged exposure to death all around them could make soldiers relatively immune to the shocks of fear that could afflict new recruits, but it could also make them callused to the point where they seemed to care little about the pain and suffering of others. George Allen here relates an incident from a late period of the conflict, when the Army of the Potomac, of which Allen was a part, had for months been locked in brutal trench warfare.

We [the 4th Rhode Island Regiment] had lost, up to this time, twenty-five men killed or wounded in twenty days, and all around us other regiments were suffering in like manner. By being accustomed to sights which would make other men's hearts sick to behold, our men soon became hard-hearted, and sometimes scarcely gave a pitying thought to those who were unfortunate enough to get hit. Men can get accustomed to everything, and the daily sight of blood and mangled bodies so blunted their finer sensibilities as almost to blot out all love, all sympathy from the heart, and to bring more into prominence the baser qualities of man, selfishness, greed, and revenge.

As an illustration of this condition I cite one case that came within my own observation.

One afternoon, two of the stretcher bearers brought out of the covered ways a man who had been fatally wounded, and setting down their stretcher near a small group of mounds, just above our camp on the hill, they began to dig his grave. From their actions I perceived the man was not yet dead, and went up to watch them. After digging a hole about a foot deep, they lit their pipes and sat down to smoke and talk over matters, and wait for him to die.

They betrayed not the least sense of emotion or feeling for the poor wretch who lay there before them, gasping in the agonies of death, and when he had breathed his last, roughly tipped him over into the hole, and covering him with a few shovels full of earth, picked up their stretcher and went back into the pits for the next one.

Such scenes were common, and few there were that were killed here that got more than a blanket for a coffin, or as much as a prayer over their burial. And yet all this lack of sympathy was without malice, and but the result of living night and day within the "valley of the shadow of death."

Gerald F. Linderman on the Unraveling of the Soldiers' Courage[8]

Modern historian Gerald Linderman advances the controversial argument that high casualty rates had, by the middle of the war, so eroded the soldiers' faith in the value of courage that the men experienced an overall sense of disillusionment. In this state, Linderman asserts, the soldiers were ready to question and reject not only the value of courage but also the entire value system of which he claims it was a part.

As Civil War battles revealed by degrees that bravery was no guarantor of victory, that rifled muskets and defensive works could thwart the most spirited charge, soldiers sensed the insufficiency of courage and began to move away from many of their initial convictions.

One of the first tenets to be discarded was the one holding that exceptional combat courage deserved special protection, even to the point of suspending efforts to kill the bravest of the enemy. Indeed, certain commanders had opposed such deference almost from the outset. Stonewall Jackson always urged special attention of another sort to the enemy's most courageous soldiers: ". . . Shoot the brave officers and the cowards will run away and take the men with them." . . . Jackson focused on the way courage bonded enemies, and he wanted no part of anything that might vitiate the combativeness of his troops. He also comprehended, as few did so early in the war, that to obliterate the most courageous of the foe was to demoralize those whose discipline drew on their example.

Other officers, without Jackson's relentless certainty in the matter, moved in his direction as the war went on. . . . That logic soon made targets of the enemy's color-bearers, soldiers whose courage had won them positions of honor as carriers of the regimental standards around which men might be inspired to charge or to rally. By the time of Fredericksburg, a Confederate officer was ordering his men, "Now, shoot down the colors," and by 1865 it had become acceptable practice to direct fire upon color-bearers even as they lay on the ground. . . . Often every member of the color guard, ordinarily one corporal from each of the regiment's ten companies, was shot down before the battle was over. Early in the war soldiers had coveted such positions. By 1863, though by then additional incentives were offered—in the 20th New York, exemption from guard and picket, company drills and roll call; duty of no more than three hours a day—few any longer volunteered. In such brusque ways, soldiers discovered that a war of attrition left less and less room for concessions to the enemy's courage.

A related casualty was the conviction that courageous behavior imparted battlefield protection. Experience taught the opposite. The cowards either remained at home or found ways to avoid battle; the bravest "went farthest and stand longest under fire"; the best died. In January 1863 General Frank Paxton of the Stonewall Brigade complained: "Out of the fifteen field officers elected last spring, five have been killed and six wounded. . . . In these losses are many whom we were always accustomed to regard as our best men." Three months later he again found it "sad, indeed, to think how many good men we have lost. Those upon whom we all looked as distinguished for purity of character as men, and for gallantry as soldiers, seem to have been the first victims." After thirty days of Wilderness combat, Colonel Theodore Lyman of Meade's staff deplored Grant's strategy: "[T]here has been too much assaulting, this campaign! . . . The best officers and men are liable, by their greater gallantry, to be first disabled."

Those in the ranks noted the phenomenon principally by its result: a decline in the quality of their leadership. John Haskell, an artillery commander in Lee's army, was bitter that those who took such care to protect their own lives, "the dodgers," by virtue of their seniority had been promoted to replace dead or disabled officers who had "taken no pains" to preserve their lives. By such routes soldiers moved far from their original conception of ostentatious courage as protection and assurance of victory to the realization that it was instead an invitation to death. A few might attempt to find a new virtue in that reality—Charles Russell, contemplating the death in battle of Robert Gould Shaw, decided that the best colonel of the best black regiment *had to die*, for "it was a sacrifice we owed"—but most simply felt its demoralization. . . .

As convictions about the potency and protectiveness of courage yielded to the suspicion that special courage had become the mark of death, another of the war's original precepts—that the courageous death was the good death; that it had about it some nobler quality reflected, for example, in the smiles of courageous dead and withheld from frowning cowardly dead—also failed the test of observation. As [Frank] Wilkeson's experiences in the Army of the Potomac taught him, "Almost every death on the battle-field is different." He knew a soldier who had died quickly and whose face had only then become "horribly distorted," suggesting to passersby a long agony that he had never experienced. The countenances of other dead had been "wreathed in smiles," allowing survivors to assure themselves that their comrades had died happy, but "I do not believe that the face of a dead soldier, lying on a battle-field, ever truthfully indicates the mental or physical anguish, or peacefulness of mind, which he suffered or enjoyed before his death. . . . It goes for nothing. One death was as painless as the other." Despondency sprang from that phrase "It goes for nothing," for the experience of war was teaching him, and so many others, that the rewards of courage were far less significant and the cost far higher than they had imagined and that the individual's powers of control were far feebler than they had supposed.

Doubt that the original equations were still valid sometimes arose in mundane fashion. A Massachusetts soldier noticed that those who persevered to complete arduous marches with the column were often "rewarded" by being placed on guard duty before the stragglers reached camp. [Charles Minor] Blackford, who like other Confederate cavalrymen was required to furnish his own mount, realized that if one were forthrightly courageous in battle, one's horse was more likely to be killed. From month to month replacements became more and more difficult and expensive to procure, and failure to find one resulted in reassignment to the infantry. "Such a penalty for gallantry was terribly demoralizing."

Though disconcerting, such challenges to the notion that courage permitted the soldier to control his life and death were pinpricks set beside the challenges presented by the failed charge. The rapidity with which great numbers of men were killed at Antietam and the ease with which they were cut down at Fredericksburg and Gettysburg produced gloomy reflection as soldiers contemplated a war that had inexplicably recast its actors as victims. Minds groped to comprehend why courage had failed to secure victory and in the face of such disastrous results began, hesitantly and diversely, to move away from conventional thought and language.

Lieutenant William Wood of the 19th Virginia was one of the 15,000 who made Pickett's charge. Prior to the attack he and his men were ordered to lie down, exposed both to a broiling sun and to the fire of Federal artillery batteries. (A Napoleon cannon could hurl a 12-pound ball a mile.) When they were brought to attention to begin the attack, some of the men immediately dropped of "seeming sunstroke," but for the charge itself Wood had only praise. It was a "splendid array" and a "beautiful line of battle." But it failed: "Down! Down! Go the boys." As he reached that spot of ground beyond which no Confederate could go, he suffered a sense of personal shame: "Stopping at the fence, I looked to the right and left and felt we were disgraced." The assault's failure bluntly told him that he and his comrades had not done enough, and yet he knew that they had done everything they had earlier been sure would carry the victory. The result was a paralyzing disbelief: "With one single exception I witnessed no cowardice, and yet we had not a skirmish line [still standing]." Courage should have conquered!

John Dooley also charged that day, with the 1st Virginia, but his reactions carried him beyond Wood. Those around him who survived the Union shelling, feeling the special impotence that comes to infantry who have no way to respond to a harrowing fire, were "frightened out of our wits." And then the charge: To Dooley it became simply that which opened the "work of death." "Volley after volley of crashing musket balls sweep through the line and mow us down like wheat before the scythe." Only thirty-five of his regiment's 155 men escaped bullets and shells, and Dooley, with his shattered thighs, was not one of them. "I tell you, there is no romance in making one of these charges," he concluded; "the enthusiasm of ardent breasts in many cases *ain't there*." He realized that the spirit of heroism no longer possessed the men; he mildly regretted its departure, but he had lost confidence that its presence would have reversed the outcome. He had not yet developed any clear vision of why failure came to such charges, but what emerged was a sense of his loss of control. His thoughts had turned from his performance to his survival: "Oh, if I could just come out of this charge safely how thankful *would I be*!" By such rough stages did soldier thought evolve. . . .

Forced to absorb the shocks of battle, to remodel combat behavior, to abandon many of the war's initial tenets, to bear discipline of an order intolerable not long before, to rationalize a warfare of destruction, and to come to terms with changes in their relationships with commanders, conscripts, and civilians, soldiers suffered a disillusionment more profound than historians have acknowledged—or the soldiers themselves would concede twenty-five years later. The intensification of ties with comrades and the maintenance of respect for enemy combatants were ultimately defensive reactions by soldiers who were alarmed that the war's experience was isolating them from those beyond battle and were turning for support to those who knew battle as they did. Neither, however, could offset the effects of their separation from the foundations of their prewar lives.

Disillusionment, here defined as the deeply depressive condition arising from the demolition of soldiers' conceptions of themselves and their performance in war—a void of disorientation, Robert

Wiebe has called it—is not an easy state of mind to detect or to verify in large groups. One must therefore rely on inferences from broad indications that general moods, transient earlier, became more intense and enduring and that soldiers testified to the gravity of those moods in new language, images, and conclusions regarding the war. The attempt to establish such disillusionment is meant to suggest not that it had an unrecognized military influence on the course of the war but rather that disregard of it in post-1865 considerations of the significance of the war would become a matter of great social consequence.

James M. McPherson on the Soldiers' Motivation[9]

Few would dispute the fact that the horror and carnage of battle were severe shocks to the Civil War soldiers and that they quickly dispelled soldiers' Currier and Ives mental images of what war would be like. Equally uncontroversial is the assertion that prolonged high casualty rates dulled a unit's fighting edge by removing many high-quality personnel through wounds and death and psychologically traumatizing those men who remained. What is open to debate in Linderman's depiction of the Civil War soldiers is his claim that this process produced widespread disillusionment and despair, what he calls "unraveling convictions."

In his Lincoln Prize-winning 1997 book, *For Cause and Comrades*, James McPherson maintains that such was not the case. Instead, his research showed that the Civil War soldiers underwent "little change in the values of honor and courage they brought into the war." As you read this excerpt, consider ways in which McPherson's picture of soldiers' motivations may differ from Linderman's one-dimensional emphasis on the importance of an abstract concept of "courage."

Some studies of combat motivation have found that the felt need of a soldier to prove himself in the eyes of his comrades is strongest in his first battle or two. After that the veteran believes he has done enough to demonstrate his courage, and subsequently his fear of death or a crippling wound sometimes overmasters his fear of showing fear. One study finds that same to be true for the Civil War, in which the seemingly endless carnage by 1863 supposedly eroded the Victorian notions of manhood, courage, and honor that soldiers had carried into the army.

Soldiers' letters offer some evidence for this interpretation. Reluctance to fight often characterized "short-timers" during their final weeks of enlistment—especially those Union soldiers whose three-year terms expired in 1864 and who had not reenlisted. "The 2nd R[hode] I[sland] has got but 4 days more and if they get into a fight I don't think they will last a minute," wrote a lieutenant in the 10th Massachusetts, another regiment in the same brigade, in June 1864. "It makes all the difference in the world with the men's courage. They do dread awfully to get hit just as their time is out." A private in the 3rd New York Cavalry with a good combat record confessed when he had only three weeks left of his enlistment that "I am what the Boys call 'playing off' " by pretending not to have recovered from an illness. "I have been sent for half a dozen times but so far have got out of going. . . . I am in hopes that it may last until my time is out." This psychology did not exist in the Confederate army because there was no such thing as a Confederate short-timer. The Richmond Congress required men whose enlistments expired to reenlist or be drafted.

A majority of Union soldiers served through the end of the war unless killed or badly wounded, however, because half of the three-year volunteers of 1861 reenlisted and the terms of the 1862 three-year volunteers did not expire before Appomattox. Among these men, and among most Confederate soldiers, little change in the values of honor and courage they brought into the war is reflected in their letters and diaries. "I do most earnestly hope that I may be enabled to meet my duties like a man when the breath of battle blows around me," wrote a corporal in the 64th Ohio in language that sounds like 1861 but was actually written in 1864 as he returned from his reenlistment furlough. Although he had fought in such bloody battles as Shiloh, Perryville, Stones River, Chickamauga, and Missionary Ridge, he expressed the same sentiments that had animated him three years earlier: "I do hope I may be brave and true for of all names most terrible and to be dreaded is coward." Another reenlisted veteran of many battles, a private in the 2nd Vermont of the Vermont brigade, which suffered more combat deaths than any other brigade in the Union army, wrote after his regiment lost 80 men killed and 254 wounded in the Wilderness that "I am sure if I had acted just as I felt I should have gone in the opposite direction [that is, to the rear] but I wouldn't act the coward. . . . I clenched my musket and pushed ahead determined to die if I must, in my place and like a man."

These were far from isolated examples. If anything, the motivating power of soldiers' ideals of manhood and honor seemed to increase rather than decrease during the last terrible year of the war. A veteran in the 122nd Ohio wrote in 1864 that "I would rather go into fifty battles and run the risk of getting killed than to be . . . a coward in time of battle." The lieutenant colonel commanding the 70th Indiana in Sherman's Atlanta campaign broke down from stress in June 1864 after a month of almost continuous fighting. Although he was still sick and exhausted, he returned to his regiment after a week in the hospital because "those who keep up are full of ugly feelings toward those who fall [behind], intimating in every way possible that it is cowardice that is the cause. . . . By being with the rest [I] can prevent anyone feeling that I lack the pluck to face what others do." And on the eve of marching through South Carolina with Sherman in 1865, a veteran corporal in the 102nd Illinois wrote simply, in language he might have used three years earlier, of "the soldier's person—more valuable to him than all else in the army, save his honor."

Earl J. Hess on the Nature of Bravery[10]

In his 1997 book *The Union Soldier in Battle*, Earl Hess notes, "There was a tenuous point in every soldier's career when he began to realize that battle was not what he expected it to be and that he would have to come to grips with that new reality. How he acted in that moment determined whether he would become a victim of war or a victor over its horrors." He goes on to add that "most soldiers managed to meet this challenge successfully." These statements are at the heart of Hess's argument that Civil War soldiers were able to cope with the stresses of battle. They were not, as Gerald Linderman claimed, driven to a disillusionment that caused them to question or reject their previous system of values. They did, however, have a few things to learn about the nature of courage.

In the passage that follows, Hess describes the soldiers' own definition of courage. Note how he demonstrates that they developed a more sophisticated and practical concept than the brittle one described by Linderman.

Observant soldiers concluded that most warriors were a mixture of good and bad qualities. William A. Ketcham of Indiana believed that 10 percent of the Northern army were "arrant cowards" who had to be bullied and prodded into battle. They were adept at finding ways to get out of combat and always came up with plausible excuses for the absence. Other commentators placed the proportion of these men as high as 25 percent. Ketcham believed that another 10 percent of the Northern army were genuinely courageous, and the remaining 80 percent fell somewhere in the range between cowardice and bravery. Some of the latter tended consistently to one extreme or the other in every engagement; others waffled in their tendencies from one battle to the next. These men remained within the safe margins of acceptability. However, whether they gave consistently good service to the cause or limited their contributions, they did not desert, refuse to perform duty, or stage mutinies. They held on, to a greater or lesser degree, to the role of the soldier and pulled the Northern war effort through to victory.

Soldiers often differentiated between moral and physical courage, believing the former to be inspired by a recognition of the terror and danger of the battlefield. The man of moral courage consciously rose above those fears and performed his duty. The man of physical courage responded only to the nervous stimulus of combat; his bravery was the unthinking action of one who foolishly ignored danger and indulged in the rush of sensation. Perhaps a major reason that so many essentially solid and sincere men waffled in their duties during the war was that they could not consistently balance their moral and their physical courage. At times, one force or the other might be weaker or stronger.

Moral courage was widely recognized as the more reliable form of bravery, because it was based on reflection and higher purpose. Physical courage, by nature, could be fickle. Excitement could lead a man to run away as readily as it could inspire him to fight. William T. Sherman believed that the soldier who had "true courage" was one who possessed "all his faculties and sense[d] perfectly when serious danger is actually present." Thus observers were convinced that moral courage was "a daily necessity," and physical courage was needed "only in emergencies."

The lack of physical courage, and of moral courage as well, was strongly illustrated in the case of a gunner who served with William A. Moore in the 3d New York Light Battery. He had been a professional boxer before the war and was full of enthusiasm for a fight. In fact, he constantly bragged about his willingness to take on any man in the battery. But when he first heard Rebel artillery, "he went into convulsions through fear." Moore called him "the only case of constitutional cowardice" he had encountered during the war. The deflated fighter was assigned as company cook. In his own way, he aided the Union cause without having to deal with battle.

Like the unfortunate New York boxer, many soldiers found that the hardest part of the test was their first battle. Those men with no previous insight into the psychology of the soldier simply took what battle had to offer and either caved in under its pressure or managed to cope. A few, such as Frank Holsinger of Pennsylvania, sensed enough about the environment of battle before their first engagement to debate with their comrades about how they would react to it. Holsinger argued that if he broke and ran at the first shot, he could forget about becoming a useful soldier. If he managed to stand his ground through the initial volleys, he would know that he had passed the test. Holsinger won this contest with his nerves.

Many other new soldiers did not fare as well as Holsinger. The Northern war effort was characterized by several battlefield reverses involving green troops, many of whom not only retreated under fire but also lost their sense of unit cohesion and turned into masses of uncontrolled men of no use to their commanders. In some cases, these masses became infected with fear and turned into mobs. The impact of these events cast a pall over Northern soldiers' sense of pride and confidence. They had to overcome these setbacks, which were not only battlefield defeats but severe tests of civilian morale on the home front as well. . . .

It was hardly surprising that untried soldiers were particularly vulnerable in their first battle. Taken beyond their naïve conceptions of what combat was like, stripped bare of smug patriotism and ideals of glory, many of them reacted to the first shock purely by instinct. Self-survival, that marvelous natural imperative, often moved them. They had no control over their reactions but acted as if in a trance, conscious of their movements but not thinking of them. As Captain James Franklin Fitts of the 114th New York put it, a soldier was "a creature of habit quite as much as of reflection, and what he does in the moment of danger is often the impulse of instinct.". . .

Instinct led George P. Metcalf of the 136th New York to perform some rather jumpy exercises while skirmishing on the wet
morning of July 4 [1863] at Gettysburg. His company received orders to advance. Stiff and chilled from spending the night in a rain-
filled rifle pit, Metcalf crawled out, stood up, and immediately felt a
Rebel bullet whistle by his head. Without "any second thought I
was back in my pit of water." Metcalf looked about and was relieved
to see that everyone else had done the same. Orders were shouted
to try again. The New Yorkers screwed up their courage and gathered their nerves, and they all jumped out at the same time, yelling
like demons to steady themselves. Metcalf found comfort in using
his "trusty old frying-pan and knapsack" as a shield for his face; he
somehow convinced himself that they would "stop any unfriendly
bullet." It was illogical but effective; Metcalf and his comrades advanced as ordered.

A fascinating example of a man unnerved by his first combat
experience and pressed to the hard, unforgiving edge of courage
occurred in the 12th Connecticut Infantry in a small fight on October 27, 1862. Captain John William DeForest [*sic*] noticed that while
advancing across an open field under fire, the bearer of the state
flag suddenly turned around and began moving to the rear. "I never
saw anything done more naturally and promptly. He did not look
wild with fright; he simply looked alarmed and resolved to get out
of danger." DeForest would later realize that this man was not a
coward, but in this battle he was "confounded by the peril of the
moment and thought of nothing but getting away from it." DeForest
set the man straight by rushing to his side, drawing his sword, and
threatening to crack his skull open. Still, the conscientious captain
had to grab the color-bearer and physically turn him around before
the man obeyed "in silence, with a curious dazed expression." Each
time the Rebels loosed a volley of fire at the regiment, the color-
bearer "fell back a pace with a nervous start; but each time I howled
'forward!' in his ear and sent him on again." This man, whom
DeForest refused to identify in his memoirs, went on to become a
reliable soldier in subsequent engagements. . . .

But there were men who did not fare so well under the pressure. Their instinctual reactions led them to act in ways that neu-
tralized their effectiveness on the battlefield. Nerves and reflexive
action led them to "pop off their pieces [guns] long before there
[was] any thing to aim at," particularly if the regiment was facing

combat for the first time. This reaction would have an effect on others, and pretty soon half the regiment was wasting "ammunition, courage and morale." In addition to firing at unseen targets, soldiers sometimes became too nervous or excited to load properly. "They drop their cartridges," observed the surgeon of the 2nd Maryland Infantry. "They load and forget to cap their pieces and get half a dozen rounds into their muskets thinking they have fired them off. Most of them just load and fire without any consciousness of shooting at anything in particular." John Schofield, who served on General Nathaniel Lyon's staff at the battle of Wilson's Creek, saw a blatant example of this tendency at the height of that bitter, terrible engagement. He found a man who was "too brave to think of running away, and yet too much frightened to be able to fight." All the soldier could do was fire his musket as rapidly as possible into the air, doing no harm to the Rebels. Schofield grabbed his arm, shook him, and told him what he was doing. The man "seemed as if aroused from a trance, entirely unconscious of what had happened."

Reflexive action could bring the soldiers to rather odd and unpredictable actions on the battlefield. At Gettysburg, Theodore Dodge of the 119th New York Infantry saw a young man who, although shot in the leg, "sat there loading and firing with as much regularity and coolness as if untouched, now and then shouting to some comrade in front of him to make room for his shot; while some scared booby, with a scratch scarce deep enough to draw the blood, would run bellowing out of range." Even a stalwart officer like John William DeForest temporarily lost control of himself when, during the May 27 assault at Port Hudson, he saw a sergeant faint while helping a wounded man to the rear. DeForest began to faint too but managed to catch himself by taking deep breaths. He thus avoided "such a ridiculous and contemptible experience as swooning on the battlefield."

Fainting and wildly firing a musket into the air were breakdowns of self-control, but they were the result of physiological rather than moral failings. Soldiers could not always control their reactions to the shock of battle. A regiment could be thrown into confusion if the first enemy volley took deadly effect in the ranks; conversely, the men could be buoyed up to steadiness if that first volley sailed harmlessly over their heads. Soldiers often responded to battle without thought. The connection between the sounds of combat and the reactions of soldiers was reduced to its essence for David Hunter Strother, a staff officer at the first battle of Winchester. As the Federal column moved along, Rebel artillery projectiles whistled as they passed overhead. "At every report, the living mass started and quickened its motion as if shocked by electricity."

Of course, this innate reaction could work to the benefit of whichever army took the tactical defensive. Soldiers needed more nerve to attack a position than to defend one, and if the terrain or man-made obstacles offered them a convenient opportunity to break their forward motion and take cover, they usually did so. The 13th Indiana Infantry, for example, launched an attack on Rebel earthworks only to find a gully that ran roughly parallel to the Confederate trench. The men instinctively dove into it for cover. "They knew that in [the] economy of God's provi[de]nce that ditch was put right there for the protection and preservation of the 13th Indiana.". . .

The impulse to dive behind some convenient cover was prompted by nervous reactions to battle; the instinct of self-preservation took over, and nothing the line officers did or said could counter it. As one Federal veteran put it after the war, a "hidden hole" offered the nervous soldier a good solution to the conflict between "the physical fear of going forward and the moral fear of turning back." There was no stigma attached to this tendency; it occurred many times on many battlefields and was widely recognized by both officers and privates, and no one was prepared to criticize the men for this natural act.

The soldier's nervous reaction to battle often continued after the engagement ended. Staff officer Horace Porter found it "curious" that for some time after a battle the men "would start at the slightest sound, and dodge at the flight of a bird or a pebble tossed at them." Less nervous soldiers found great fun in deliberately throwing small objects past the heads of these men to make them wince.

That some men could jest about other soldiers' reflexive response to combat is another indication that individuals went through the process of responding to battle differently. Some adapted at a more accelerated pace than others. They defined themselves as soldiers more rapidly and learned the limits of bravery more easily.

Experience became the best teacher of soldiers. After learning how reflexes and instincts could influence their reactions to battle, they calmed down into a pragmatic acceptance of their new lives as soldiers. One of the most important lessons they learned was that all men had limits. They were not expected to be foolishly brave under fire or to throw their lives away in hopeless attacks. Running away from the battlefield might be acceptable if it was done without panic and was immediately followed by reorganizing the battle line and continuing to fight. If William Ketcham was right, 80 percent of the Union army needed to exercise some degree of judgment about whether they could withstand a particular moment in battle. As long as they had a safety valve, an opportunity to temporarily take themselves out of an unbearable situation, they could return quickly to their duty without endangering the war effort or their images as good soldiers.

Notes

1. On the character and motivation of Vietnam soldiers, see B. G. Burkett and Glenna Whitley's groundbreaking book, *Stolen Valor: How the Vietnam Generation Was Robbed of Its Heroes and Its History* (Dallas: Verity Press, 1988).

2. Gerald F. Linderman, *Embattled Courage: The Experience of Combat in the American Civil War* (New York: Free Press, 1987), 297.

3. Abner R. Small, *The Road to Richmond: The Civil War Memoirs of Maj. Abner R. Small of the 16th Maine Vols., with His Diary as a Prisoner of War*, ed. Harold Adams Small (Berkeley: University of California Press, 1959), 185. © 1939 by The Regents of the University of California. Reprinted by permission of the University of California Press.

4. Thomas F. Galwey, *The Valiant Hours*, ed. W. S. Nye (Harrisburg, PA: Stackpole, 1961), 80–81.

5. John W. De Forest, *A Volunteer's Adventures: A Union Captain's Record of the Civil War*, ed. James H. Croushore (New Haven, CT: Yale University Press, 1946), 59–66. Reprinted by permission of Yale University Press.

6. Rice C. Bull, *Soldiering: The Civil War Diary of Rice C. Bull, 123rd New York Volunteer Infantry*, ed. K. Jack Bauer (San Rafael, CA: Presidio Press, 1977), 115–18. © 1977 by the Presidio Press, Novato, California. Reprinted by permission of the Presidio Press.

7. George H. Allen, *Forty-six Months with the Fourth R.I. Volunteers, in the War of 1861–1865* (Providence, RI: J. A. & R. A. Reid, 1887), 278–79.

8. Linderman, *Embattled Courage*, 156–57. © 1987 by Gerald F. Linderman. Reprinted by permission of the Free Press, a Division of Simon & Schuster.

9. James M. McPherson, *For Cause and Comrades: Why Men Fought in the Civil War* (New York: Oxford University Press, 1977), 81–82. © 1997 by Oxford University Press. Reprinted by permission of Oxford University Press.

CHAPTER FOUR

In the Hospital

*T*he soldier's courage and endurance were tested not only on the field but also in the hospital—if he were unfortunate enough to find himself in one. Midnineteenth-century medical science was spectacularly ill equipped to deal with the ghastly nature and appalling number of wounds that Civil War battles yielded. The impact of .58-caliber lead slugs on human bones left the army surgeons with little recourse but amputation, and those physicians plied their bone saws diligently, raising heaps of severed limbs outside their makeshift hospitals. Supplies of anesthetic often ran out, and amputations were then performed without it. Many soldiers died under the surgeons' well-intentioned but often ineffective ministrations.

Aside from the possibility of facing amputation or other treatment in a field hospital as a result of wounds, the soldier might also find himself in a hospital due to sickness. As with every previous war for which statistics exist, the Civil War saw more soldiers die of disease than as a result of enemy action. Dysentery, malaria, and various "fevers" carried off thousands of men. When disease put a soldier in an army hospital, it took him away from the comforting fellowship of friends in his company, who had probably been the boyhood friends of his hometown as well. Whatever the circumstances that placed him there, a Civil War soldier needed to summon all his reserves of fortitude.

John H. W. Stuckenberg on the Horrors of a Military Field Hospital[1]

John Stuckenberg was simultaneously pastor of two Lutheran churches in Erie, Pennsylvania, when the war broke out. The vast armies that the nation raised at the outset of the conflict and over the next year or two required large numbers of chaplains who were drawn from civilian parishes. Stuckenberg felt called to leave his congregations in northwestern Pennsylvania to minister to the soldiers by becoming chaplain of the 145th Pennsylvania Volunteers. In this post he witnessed scenes that he had never imagined while along the shores of Lake Erie or during his travels to Germany to pursue his theological studies. From the debacle at Fredericksburg in December 1862 to the repulse of Pickett's Charge at Gettysburg the following July, Stuckenberg witnessed some of the most ghastly scenes of carnage in the Civil War. None seemed to leave a more powerful impression on him than his visit to the army hospitals around Gettysburg after the battle was over. Of that visit he left this harrowing account.

What a hospital on or near the field of battle is can only be known by those that have seen one. There were between 2000 and 3000 wounded in our 2nd corps hospital. In 1st Division there were two operating stands, where the Surgeons were constantly consulting about operations and were performing amputations. Heaps of amputated feet and hands, arms and legs were seen lying under the tables and by their sides. Go around among the wounded and you witness the most saddening and sickening sights. Some are writhing with pain, and deeply moaning and groaning and calling for relief which cannot be afforded them. The first forms are horribly disfigured and mutilated. Wounds are found in all parts of the body. Here lies one with his leg shattered, the flesh torn by a shell, nothing but shreds being left. There lies one shot through the abdomen, the intestines protruding—his life cannot be saved, perhaps even opium gives him but little temporary relief. He is but waiting to die. Here lies one with his arm almost severed from his body— waiting for amputation. There lies one young and once handsome shot through the face and head—his eyes swollen shut and covered with a yellow, putrid matter, his hair clotted with blood, his jaws torn, and a bullet hole through each cheek. Some of the wounds are dressed, some not. From some the blood still oozes, in others maggots are perhaps found. Perhaps they are poorly waited on, there not being nurses enough. No physician may have examined their wounds and dressed them. Their physical wants may not have been attended to. They long for home and their friends, but they cannot get to the one, the other cannot come to them. Through neglect, perhaps, they die. They are buried in their clothes, without shroud, without coffin, perhaps without religious services and a board to mark their resting place. The hospital soon becomes foul, especially in summer—the stench sometimes being almost intolerable. Medicines may be scarce, the food unpalatable—perhaps scarce. Near the battle field of Gettysburg many barns for miles were filled with wounded, many of whom had neither surgeons, nor nurses nor food.

Bell I. Wiley on Confederate Care of the Wounded[2]

In this passage, modern historian Bell Wiley describes the miseries of wounded Southern soldiers who suffered "unspeakable tortures of hunger, thirst and pain" and, finally, death at the hands of the inadequate Confederate medical service. Compare this passage to Stuckenberg's firsthand observations of Union hospitals during and after great battles. Note the wider scope of Wiley's discussion, made possible by the fact that as a historian, rather than an eyewitness, he drew on the accounts of many soldiers in many different places to produce this composite of Confederate hospitals.

The machinery for disposing of battle casualties was fairly simple. When a conflict was imminent, buildings or tents near the scene of contemplated action were designated as field hospitals and marked with flags. A small squad of men, preferably convalescents and others not in best fighting trim, was detailed from each company to remove the wounded to the field infirmaries. Each man so detailed was equipped with a knapsack containing dressings, stimulants and tourniquets; when fighting commenced, assistant surgeons, accompanied by the details, moved forward to dispose of the wounded. Assistant surgeons supervised the administration of first aid and told litter bearers which cases required removal to field hospitals. Regimental surgeons remained at the field infirmaries of their respective brigades to attend to the wounded as they were brought in. They operated immediately on the most urgent cases and directed removal in ambulances—which were simply canvas-covered wagons—of those that were to be transferred to interior hospitals. Patients thus removed were sent first to receiving hospitals; from there they were distributed as soon as possible to the general hospitals located in most cities.

Early in the war the custom prevailed of permitting convalescents to go home as soon as they were able to travel, but consequent relapses from hemorrhages and from improper care, plus
increasing reluctance of those on furlough to return to camp, caused
an abatement of this practice after 1863.

The system which Confederate authorities set up for the care
of the wounded was basically sound, but numerous factors hindered
its operation. In the first place commanding generals sometimes
failed to inform hard-pressed medical officers of contemplated campaigns in sufficient time to allow for adequate preparations. Lee's
medical director complained on one occasion to Surgeon General
[Samuel Preston] Moore: "The movements of the army cannot be
anticipated by me for the General commanding never discloses any
of his plans to those around him . . . every thing is done hurriedly
and mysteriously." Even when ample notice was given and advance
preparation carefully made, medical authorities, because of limita-
tions of personnel and essential facilities, were utterly unable to
provide prompt and adequate care for the thousands of men who
were wounded in every major encounter.

This was particularly true of the Confederacy's first great fights.
At Shiloh many wounded lay in the mud of the battlefield all night
under a cold pelting rain, without attention of any sort, even though
infirmary corps[men] moved about as rapidly as possible and doctors labored to the point of collapse. The falling back of the army
necessitated a hurried removal, and shivering, moaning men were
loaded into wagons, many of which were not equipped with springs,
and hauled more than twenty miles over "the roughest and ruttiest
roads in the Southern Confederacy" to Corinth [Mississippi]. Here
hotels, school buildings, churches and private homes were converted
into hospitals, but all these did not provide enough shelter.

For days after the battle groaning men might be seen lying about
the depot waiting transportation to improvised infirmaries at Mem-
phis, Holly Springs and Oxford. Doctors came from far and near
and made their contributions to the pile of amputated limbs that
accumulated in the yard of Corinth's Tishomingo Hotel. . . .

Less than two months after Shiloh the Seven Days' campaign
around Richmond produced a tide of casualties such as the Confederacy had not seen before. Citizens of the capital and of Petersburg took omnibuses and private carriages to the battlefields and
piled the injured into stores, tobacco warehouses, factories, resi-

dences and tents. But even these extraordinary measures fell short of the need. A newspaper appeal, dated three days after fighting ceased, stated that "hundreds and even thousands of . . . soldiers are lying wounded upon the battlefield waiting in extreme agony for some pitying hands to remove them to a place of refuge from the tortures which they endure." The gruesome results of this neglect were vividly suggested by an article on the treatment of flyblow. Other newspaper notices urged citizens to bring ice and food to the hospitals, to tear up old cotton clothes for bandages, and to volunteer their services as nurses and cooks. Not until more than two weeks after the last of the series of battles was the situation brought under control. In the meantime hundreds, if not thousands, of brave men whom timely attention could have saved had endured unspeakable tortures of hunger, thirst and pain, and had finally died. . . .

Many soldiers looked with abhorrence on all hospitals, and there can be no doubt that they were justified. Operations were often rendered excruciatingly painful because of the scarcity of opiates and the dullness of scalpels. Some excellent sets of surgical implements were imported and others were captured, but there was never enough of these to go around; those manufactured in the Confederacy were characterized by Lee's medical director as "entirely useless."

Post-operational care was inadequate. In Richmond, where conditions probably were better than average, the supervisor of hospitals reported on one occasion that 131 medical officers, many of whom were occupied with executive duties, were charged with attending 10,200 patients—a proportion of 1 to 70. Inmates of hospitals complained repeatedly of an insufficiency of nourishment, and reports of medical officers leave little doubt that fare in some institutions was notoriously poor. Clothing and bed covering were frequently inadequate and sanitary conditions often left much to be desired. At the Newsom Hospital in Chattanooga soldiers were given clean garments for the duration of their treatment, but on dismissal they were required to wear the filthy attire which they wore when admitted.

"I beleave the Doctors kills more than they cour," wrote an Alabama private in 1862; "Doctors haint Got half Sence." And a Georgian expressed the opinion that army surgeons were the "most unworthy of all the human famaly." These particular Rebs may have had no other foundation for their statements than the tendency of

soldiers—well or sick—to grouse. But with full allowance for prejudices and overstatement, the conclusion remains inescapable that
much of the suffering endured by the wounded was due to poor
physicians. Examinations required of candidates for surgical appoint-
ments were sometimes no more than farces. One doctor said that
his examining committee was composed of five members of whom
one owed his position to the favor of kinsmen, another had failed to
pass the course at the University of Virginia, and a third was very
drunk.

The practice of appointing surgeons with the understanding
that they were to stand examination at a later time led to endless
procrastination on the part of some who were of doubtful abilities.
The category of doctors known as "contract physicians," who in
times of emergency were called on for a considerable portion of
army practice, apparently had to take no examination at all; these
were, as a rule, utterly undeserving of professional status. Many of
the regular appointees of 1861 were young and inexperienced, a
circumstance deriving largely from the fact that few of the established practitioners sought army positions.

It would be erroneous to infer that the Confederate surgical
corps was made up wholly of "culls," novices and quacks. The high-
ranking officials were as a rule men of unusual talent and attain-
ment; many of the regimental surgeons, and some of the assistant
surgeons, discharged their duties ably and conscientiously insofar
as the nature of available supplies would permit. . . .

Confederate surgeons, good and bad, were handicapped greatly
by the undeveloped state of medical science which characterized
their period. They believed that suppuration, or "laudable pus,"
was an essential feature with the healing process. They probed with
ungloved fingers; they deterred recovery by tampering with wounds;
they worked in soiled uniforms; they used bloodstained bandages;
and they were only partially conscious of the importance of clean
instruments. It is not surprising in view of these and other short-
comings that gangrene played havoc with their patients.

The majority of surgeons seem to have been men of sympathy
and of kindness. Sergeant William P. Chambers recorded in his
diary an instance typical of many. When a doctor named Britts approached Chambers to operate he said: "You were soldier enough
to get shot I reckon you are soldier enough to have the ball cut
out." Chambers remarked that he had no choice in the matter of

receiving the wound, and that he supposed the bullet must be extracted. Britts fumbled about uncertainly and said, "Chambers, I don't like to cut there," but presently he seemed to pull himself together, and with the advice "turn your head away, I don't want you to look at me," he began his unpleasant task. The first stroke of the knife struck the missile. When this proved to be only a part of the bullet Britts swore profusely. Not until after a considerable amount of probing, painful to the patient and grievous to the surgeon, was the remnant brought to the surface.

Mortality from wounds, even from those in arms and legs, was woefully high. Patients who recovered often experienced painful setbacks and distressing complications. Indeed, no phase of Confederate history is so dark and tragic as that which reveals the incomprehensible torture endured by the sick and the wounded. And if glory be measured by suffering, the South's greatest heroes are not those who died at the cannon's mouth on Cemetery Ridge, or in any of the other gallant charges made by soldiers in gray, but rather those who, sorely wounded or desperately ill, lived to experience the unspeakable agony of hospitalization.

Gerald F. Linderman on Dying a Courageous Death[3]

In keeping with his theme of courage, Linderman in this passage argues that Civil War soldiers felt obliged to display valor during their stay in the hospital. He notes that hospital workers sought to encourage the wounded men to overcome their sufferings with calmness and with trust in God. However, Linderman presents this effort—despite the workers' dedication—as an imposition on the soldiers and the men's fortitude as something put on for appearances' sake. Needless to say, the soldiers and their attendants would have had a different view.

Those who reached the military hospital found that though it might offer respite to the body, it seldom permitted any relaxation of the will. Thirty years later Oliver Wendell Holmes, Jr., would tell a Harvard audience that "the book for the army is a war-song, not a hospital-sketch," and in obvious ways hospital and battlefield presented contrasting experiences of war, but there was no dichotomy in expectations of soldier comportment. The battlefield's values extended to the hospital and in ways intensified there. The body's debility and the removal of comrades' support contributed to the necessity of what William Howell Reed, a Sanitary Commission medical worker, called "the harder heroism of the hospital." He and his fellow workers—Sanitary Commission and Christian Commission and nurse volunteers—dedicated themselves to the alleviation of the soldiers' suffering. No one could mistake the selflessness of many of them, for to enter army hospitals was always to risk one's own life against disease and against injurious medical treatment. Louisa May Alcott had worked only a month as a volunteer nurse at Georgetown's Union Hotel Hospital when she contracted typhoid fever. The preferred treatment—massive doses of calomel—resulted in a mercury poisoning that caused the loss of teeth and hair and the slow degeneration of the nervous system. She lived until 1888 but was never again entirely well. Her nursing supervisor, the New England feminist reformer Hannah Ropes, succumbed to typhoid pneumonia after eight months. Walt Whitman visited Washington-area hospitals from late 1861 until June 1862, when his physical collapse brought doctors' warnings that he must not return.

Dedicated as they might be, however, such people took up roles not designed simply to make the wounded more comfortable. The problem confronting them was their inability to aid recovery in any medically significant way. Few of the nurses had received training, and in any case the state of medical science had little to offer. Still ignorant of the relationship between germs and infection, doctors amputated wounded limbs and then administered stimulants in misguided efforts to forestall sepsis. Nurses could wash and feed the wounded, could "clean" wounds, bind them with linen and, as theory held beneficial, keep them moistened with water. In the end, however, medical workers had little choice but to rely on the teaching of Florence Nightingale: Nature was the healer, and the task of the nurse, nature's partner, was to encourage in the wounded soldier a receptivity to nature's actions, a task more moral than medical. Indeed, here some nurses felt themselves better qualified than doctors, who were present "because their work proceeded either from obedience to military duty or a contract for pay." They were thus inferior as healers to the nurse volunteers, who were there out of selfless concern for their patients. "Apothecary and medicine chest might be dispensed with," Hannah Ropes said, "if an equal amount of genuine sympathy could be brought home to our stricken men."

In practice, however, nurses could do little (and doctors little more). Though nineteenth-century Americans were well acquainted with chronic illness and death, especially infant mortality, in ways that must have generated some protective emotional callus, virtual impotence amid so much pain surely distressed medical aides. Their reaction was to encourage the soldiers to live—and especially to die—in harmony with soldierly values, to accept pain and death within the framework of those values. The presence of women, the hospital agent Julia Wheelock Freeman said, brought forth "the better angel" of the soldier's nature. "A kind, cheerful look, a smile of recognition, one word of encouragement, enables him to bear his sufferings more bravely." So vital did that seem to nurses that their desire to encourage the courageous death frequently became the determination to compel it.

The nurses' working proposition was the supremacy of the individual will as an extension of courage: Suffering was a refining and properly subduing influence to be borne cheerfully and quietly. No matter how severe the wound, the soldier possessed the spiritual power to triumph over pain. . . . Reed . . . cited with approval an episode in which a young conscript lay dying of lockjaw; while his body twitched with pain, he had resigned himself to God's will and thus his face bore an expression of serenity. Such cases were the assurance that one could remain in control if one's values were the proper ones.

Pain expressed, however, was weakness revealed. "Our American man," Whitman wrote, ". . . holds himself cool and unquestioned, master above all pains and bloody mutilations." Thus wounds offered opportunities to demonstrate a courage transcending even that of the battlefield. Mary Livermore, a Sanitary Commission organizer and frequent traveler to battle sites and hospitals, thought that "it may be easy to face death on the battle-field, when the pulses are maddened by the superhuman desire for victory. . . . But to lie suffering in a hospital bed for months . . . requires more courage." Hospital courage meant staying calm and not complaining, even to the point of death. "He made no display or talk; he met his fate like a man." The coward, on the other hand, abject and groveling, gave voice to his pain. Soldiers often contrasted their wounded comrades' "stoical bravery" ("A Union soldier, if so severely wounded that he could by no possibility assume a cheerful countenance, would shut his teeth close together and say nothing") with the faintheartedness of the enemy ("a rebel, if he could boast of only a flesh wound, would whine and cry like a sick child").

In their efforts to bolster the impulse to courage, hospital workers were certain that they were successful. Whitman recorded the testimony of a doctor who in six months among the wounded had seen none who had died "with a single tremor of unmanly fear," and the poet's own experience bore out the claim: Not one case of a soldier's dying "with cowardly qualms of terror." He thought that record was "the last-needed proof" of American democracy. Mary Livermore did encounter a dying soldier who told her, "I have lived an awful life, and I'm afraid to die. I shall go to hell." "Stop screaming," she commanded. "Be quiet. . . . If you *must* die, die like a man, and not like a coward." God, she assured him, was willing to pardon him. Later a Methodist minister arrived to urge trust in Christ and to sing hymns. Finally, the soldier said, "It's all right with me, chaplain! I will trust in Christ! God will forgive me! I can die now!" Mary Livermore watched as his face grew rapturous. "I looked at the dying man beside me, and saw, underneath the deepening pallor of death, an almost radiant gleam." It was, she reported, the only case of fear of death that she encountered.

Often hospital workers thought of themselves as observers serving in behalf of soldiers' families. Those at home would want to know about their son's or husband's comportment at the end. Especially were they anxious to learn his last words, that they might reveal an ultimate success in pursuit of courage or godliness. Thus the state of one's courage remained until the end—and especially at the end—a matter of intense concern, both to the soldier and to those who surrounded him.

Earl J. Hess on the Wounded Union Soldier[4]

The suffering of soldiers in the Civil War military hospitals was made more grievous by the fact that they had endured a great deal before they got there. In this vivid and straightforward narrative, Hess marshals a number of firsthand accounts to describe the experience of wounded Union soldiers from the time the firing stopped through their ordeals in the field hospitals. Note that Hess's emphasis here is essentially the same as in his discussions of battle and courage: the experience was terrible beyond what any of the soldiers had imagined, "but many soldiers somehow endured."

When the guns fell silent and the haze of smoke drifted away, the landscape of battle appeared littered with human wreckage. Wounded soldiers quickly passed the first few minutes of their newfound status as casualties. The numbness around their wounds dissipated and was replaced by searing, throbbing pain. Thirst set in quickly as the body strove to replace fluids lost as a result of the trauma. Days might pass before overworked stretcher-bearers made their way to all corners of a far-flung battlefield. The waiting seemed longer as injured men began to wonder whether anyone would ever come to their aid. For the less seriously hurt, there was time to gaze upon letters or photographs from home and think about those who would be most affected by their death. For the badly injured, there was only precious time counting away as blood flowed and life slipped away.

After the Seven Days battles had ended, Captain Edward A. Acton of the 5th New Jersey labored to describe the sounds he had heard during the night following the engagement at White Oak Swamp. "Some of the hundreds of wounded strewn across the field called repeatedly for drink. 'For God's sake bring me some water!' Others screamed for help. 'Doctor! Doctor! Oh! My God where is the Doctor?' Others again were groaning aloud in their anguish and calling piteously upon the name of some friend who could not go to him! And I would hear a boyish voice calling in a sobbing and pleading tone for something or somebody, the sobs choking his utterance, so that at the distance I lay I could not distinguish his wants! Again I would hear weeping voices bewailing their fate and begging for some relief from their sufferings and alas! what was more terrible than all, many were blaspheming and cursing most horribly." Clearly shaken by the experience, Acton added an emotional postscript. "No voice can convey the faintest idea, no pen can describe in any but the most imperfect manner, no tongue, however eloquent, could portray but in the feeblest style, nor could any language, no matter how chaste and powerful, illustrate the terrible fearfulness of those cries of anguish."

Rescue from the field of battle did not mean an end to suffering, despair, and death. Nowhere was the horrible cost of battle more apparent than in the primitive field hospitals hastily established behind the lines. They usually were located in farmhouses, barns, and other outbuildings, where sanitary conditions were poor. In the aftermath of a large engagement, the farmsteads of an entire locality were commandeered for this pathetic work. The amateur-ish Union army was ill prepared to handle large numbers of wounded until late in the conflict. Surgeons were mostly civilian doctors who joined volunteer units or who contracted directly with the army to work at assigned posts, usually large hospital complexes in North-ern or occupied Southern cities. The administration of field medi-cal care was woefully inadequate, as was the general state of medical, especially surgical, knowledge in the 1860s. A regiment could suf-fer hundreds of casualties in a single morning with only a surgeon, an assistant surgeon, and a handful of untrained medical orderlies available to deal with the emergency. The system of field medical care was swamped after every serious engagement, overwhelmed by the enormity of battle.

Rufus Meade of the 5th Connecticut saw a field hospital at its worst following the battle of Peach Tree Creek. He beheld "the suffering and dying conditions of the poor fellows that lay there wounded in every part of the body, some crazy and raving and oth-ers suffering all that mortals can. Doctors were busy cutting off limbs which were piled up in heaps to be carried off and buried, while the stench even then was horrible. Flies were flying around in swarms and maggots were crawling in wounds before the doctors could get time to dress them. . . . Suffice it to say that the 20th of July 1864 was the saddest day I ever saw, I think I never saw half the suffering before in one day."

The conditions in the field hospitals were unavoidably primi-tive. Barns, tents, and living rooms were improvised dressing stations, hardly fit for the surgical procedures needed during the hours immediately following a battle. If a wounded soldier sur-vived the first few days, he could look forward to transportation to base hospitals and general hospitals in Northern-controlled cities. These facilities often were constructed from the ground up and thus were well-planned and adequately equipped with beds, wooden floors, and medical supplies. They also were manned by better nurses—women volunteers from the North, even members of reli-gious orders who were specially trained in medical care. The squa-lor and confusion of the field hospital were replaced by order and cleanliness.

Yet even in these comparative havens, a soldier's wound could cause him much pain and anxiety. Colonel Adoniram Judson Warner of the 39th Pennsylvania Infantry survived his severe wound at

Antietam only to endure many months of painful recovery in Northern hospitals. In January 1863, he received the first of two operations for his wound. The ether dulled his senses and he felt no pain, but the anesthetic produced a whirlwind of horrible imagery while the surgeon cut into his mangled body. "I fancied that I was wafting at an inconceivable velocity over space through regions of every degree of darkness and of light now in one and now in another and whirled round and round at a rate so horrible that I shudder to think of it and still I thought there was no end to this and that these wild pangs that I felt would last forever." Warner experienced in his mind a bewildering contrast between calm and terror. "At one moment all would be light and glorious—the universe radiant all over with rainbow light and then in a moment, as it seemed to me, all was black and dark and the universe seemed filled with all loathsome things—serpents, lizzards . . . crocodiles—monstrous beasts of all shapes mixing their slime in their gnashing for me and sounds that no letters will spell greeted my ears."

Perhaps the worst aspect of this experience was that this initial operation had to be followed by a second one. Warner was so terrified by his drug-induced visions that he initially refused to take ether for his second operation, which was more risky than the first. The surgeon had to give him chloroform, a much milder anesthetic, to ease him into the harsher drug. Fortunately for Warner, it worked. He later admitted that he could not have withstood the second operation without ether, which he credited with saving his life.

Soldiers who received major injuries had to struggle for life no matter what hospital they were treated in. Warner won his battle, and so did another seriously injured man, Ebenezer Hannaford of the 6th Ohio Infantry. Hannaford was hit near the throat during the battle of Stone's River. At first he only wanted to crawl to a safe place on the battlefield to die, but the dull ache in his right shoulder and his breath, which came "with a croup-like sound," did not feel so bad after a time. He managed to make his way to a field hospital, where he received emergency care.

But this was only the beginning of Hannaford's ordeal. Carried to a base hospital at Nashville, where he would spend the next three months, Hannaford discovered the true nature of his sacrifice for the cause. "It was there that Death drew near and bent over my pillow, so close that I could feel his icy breath upon my cheek, while in mute, ghastly silence we looked steadfastly each in the other's face for weeks together." More than a month after the battle, Hannaford nearly died when his wound suddenly began to bleed. "I could feel myself sinking rapidly away; a quiet, painless lethargy was stealing over my brain; fixed upon the wall opposite, my eyes saw objects dim, trembling, spectral; in my ears were strange, unearthly ringings, such as I know not how to liken. Earth was receding—eternity at hand." As the surgeon and a nurse entered his ward, Hannaford invited death and closed his eyes with a tired but calm feeling. The doctor managed to stop the flow of blood, however, and Hannaford slowly regained consciousness. It was a "strange, weird sensation, that vague, dreamy return to consciousness." His first thought was to berate the surgeon for saving him. "Those moments of syncope, when over my soul had rolled the waters of oblivion, I seemed to feel had been a very heaven of delight, and it was a pitiful service to recall me thence to life and suffering again." Yet he was destined to live and recount his story in vivid detail for a popular news magazine later that year.

The doctors who tended soldiers like Warner and Hannaford were warriors too. Their job was to try to save the thousands of wounded men streaming rearward during and after an engagement. They came face-to-face with the direct results of combat and tried desperately to deal with physical trauma much more diverse, more terrible, and more voluminous than anything they had encountered in small-town medical practice. "I have been hard at work today dressing wounds," wrote surgeon Seneca B. Thrall, 13th Iowa, to his wife. "The unutterable horror of war most manifest in a hospital, *two weeks* after a battle, is terrible. It required all my will to enable me to properly dress some of the foul, suppurating, erysipelatous fractured limbs." Most surgeons were incapable of working under these conditions without being moved. Kentucky surgeon Claiborne J. Walton was immersed in blood and suffering following the unsuccessful Union assault at Kennesaw Mountain. The wounded of his regiment were forced to lie in the hot sun between the lines for most of the day, and some were nearly covered with maggots by the time they were retrieved. Many who reached the field hospital alive were hardly recognizable as the healthy young men who had volunteered for military service not so long before. "You may well suppose that their suffering is immense," Walton told his wife. "Such as arms shot off—legs shot off. Eyes shot out— brains shot out. Lungs shot through and in a word *everything* shot to pieces and totally ruined for all after life. The horrors of this war can never be half told. Citizens at home can never know one fourth part of the misery brought about by this terrible rebellion."

Soldiers visiting wounded comrades in field hospitals were exposed to the same sights, sounds, and smells as the surgeon, but they usually had more difficulty accepting them. William Wheeler found a man whose wound had so affected his nervous system that pain "came in great wrenches and spasms that made him gnash his teeth and beat on the bed in agony." Wheeler acknowledged that this gruesome scene made him so ill that he had difficulty walking to the door. Even a hardened campaigner could falter in the face of what a regimental surgeon encountered in numerous cases.

Perhaps the most terrible tragedy of the Civil War was that it took place less than two decades before medicine was revolutionized by a series of major biological and technical advances. The use of antiseptics and sterilization, and the implementation of higher professional standards for doctors and nurses, would have saved thousands of lives. Unfortunately, during the Civil War, wounded men far too often had to rely on chance, their own determination, or the uncertain skills of overworked and undertrained medical personnel to decide their fate. The most remarkable feature of the medical history of the Union army was the large number of soldiers who survived their wounds. The horrors of the battlefield were great, and the horrors of the hospital may have been even greater, but many soldiers somehow endured and returned to the ranks or to civilian life.

Reid Mitchell on the Irony of Hospital Care[5]

In *Civil War Soldiers* (1988), historian Reid Mitchell deals with imagery and symbolism. For example, he sees hospitals as symbols of the kind of nurturing that soldiers had received back home but of which they found precious little in the rough male atmosphere of the army or in grisly scenes of war. The bad news, however, discovered by men unfortunate enough to find themselves in an army hospital was that it offered too little of the care that the sick and wounded sought and needed. In this passage, Mitchell addresses the ravages of sickness and the irony that "the hospital, a symbol of concern and care . . . became a symbol of indifference and dread for many soldiers."

Sickness, sometimes minor, sometimes fatal, plagued the country dwellers North and South as they crowded into military camps. Measles, mumps, and colds were common diseases. Life in the army proved more difficult than anticipated. One Confederate warned his uncle that "the camp life is a hard life to live" and asked him to tell the other male members of the family not to volunteer, "for I Dont think that they could stand it for it is hard to do [.]" Another Georgia soldier wrote from his first camp, "There some dying every day on either side the death bells ringing in my ears constant[.]"

Death by disease was not what men had volunteered for. Disease was a far more impersonal enemy than the savage foe men had gone to war to fight. What made such camp deaths even worse was the increasingly matter-of-fact attitude toward them: they were common, barely worth noting. A North Carolina soldier wrote from his first camp that "ef a man dies there is not much sed about it [.]" Anonymous death was not glorious.

One irony of the Civil War was that the hospital, a symbol of concern and care that even now evokes among the literary-minded memories of Walt Whitman, became a symbol of indifference and dread for many soldiers. A Confederate soldier from Marion, Alabama, wrote home from a hospital in Richmond, "If a man Lives he Lives and if he Dies he Dies. A Dog is thought more of Down in Marion than A Solger is hear." And a Union soldier observed, "I had rather risk a battle than the Hospitals." More so than one's company, the hospital represented military bureaucracy and the dehumanization of the American soldier.

Even at its best, medical practice of the 1860s was faulty and barbaric. Particularly after a battle, when surgeons spent a long night in ill-lit hospital tents amputating the arms and legs of wounded men in an assembly-line procedure, medical care impressed the soldiers not only as dubious and painful, but as dehumanizing. One Confederate visited a military hospital after First Bull Run and saw "piles of arms and legs laying about just as you have seen rags and papers laying about a floor where a little child has been playing." The spectacle of men being reduced to their component parts was not a reassuring one.

During the war, however, medical practice was not at its best. Frequently, soldiers came to feel that their doctors were incompetent and uncaring. Perhaps they judged too harshly the men who worked in such miserable conditions. Nonetheless, the belief that the army or the government could not provide decent medical treatment encouraged the soldiers' sense of neglect.

One Mississippi regiment was cursed with a particularly cowardly surgeon. When the regiment was in battle, he cowered in the rear. A skilled surgeon, his absence from his proper place led to the deaths of injured men. One man underwent a series of agonizing and incompetent operations. "A cannonball took his leg off just above the ankle. A green physician amputated his leg which George stood like a noble boy, as he was, but the wound healing it was found that the bone protruded so our young Surgeon cut it off a second time just below the knee and neglected to secure the arteries properly." As the wound healed, the improperly treated artery burst and the doctor amputated the man's leg once again, this time above the knee. The operation resulted in his death. "Poor George was a good boy and an excellent soldier. He told the boys when shot he was sorry to lose his leg but was grateful his life was spared. And told the Surgeon after the Second amputation he knew he was bound to die and if his leg had been properly taken off at first he would have lived."

H. Hampton of the 58th North Carolina wrote the widow of a comrade that her husband had only been wounded in the hand, and that the real cause of his death was the doctor's neglect; "the doctor was very mean to him and did not treat him right." A federal cavalryman told his wife, "When a person is sick in camp they might as well dig a hole and put him in as to take him to one of the infernal hells called hospitals." One man in his regiment had died neglected, while nearby hospital attendants played euchre. After the war another soldier vividly remembered a one-eyed man in the ambulance corps who neglected the wounded to rob the dead.

One last thing that horrified soldiers when they considered military hospitals was the treatment of the dead. Indeed, the Civil War soldier thought burial of great—perhaps ultimate—significance. The dead were entitled to their due. They deserved not just recognition of their valor and patriotism, but proper treatment of their corpses—a decent burial. The anonymous wounded suffered from neglect in the hospital; so did the anonymous dead. One Union soldier wrote from the hospital, "The way the teamsters who bury them treat the bodies is shameful. I have seen them if the coffins were a little short get into them with their boots on, and trample them in even stepping on their faces."

William W. Bennett on Finding Religion[6]

William Bennett was an army missionary during the war—that is, a free-roving minister of the Gospel who worked in various units rather than being tied to a single regiment as a chaplain. Army missionaries also did not receive salaries from the government like regular chaplains but instead served on a volunteer basis. In the North they were organized and directed by the United States Christian Commission, a nongovernmental, interdenominational religious organization set up to facilitate the spread of the Gospel within the Union armies.

Amid the horrors of Civil War hospitals, the soldiers, hurt, frightened, separated from friends, and staring eternity in the face, turned to God and were sustained. Bennett, who served among the Confederate armies, later wrote a book on what he and his fellow missionaries had observed in ministering to the troops. Many of the men came to have a strong interest in religious matters, but nowhere was such interest more intense than amid the hideous scenes of the hospitals. Here, especially in convalescent wards where the wounded had more time to reflect, the ministers found some of their most eager converts.

How does Bennett's eyewitness testimony of courage and consolation amid the most trying circumstances pertain to the contrasting theories of Linderman and Hess? Which one does it tend to bear out?

"I have been a month," wrote a colporteur [a distributor of religious literature] from Richmond, "laboring in this city, during which time I have distributed 41,000 pages of tracts. I preach almost daily in the hospitals; and a notice of a few minutes will give me a large congregation. Never in my life have I witnessed such solemn attention to the preached word. Oftentimes I meet with soldiers who tell me that they have become Christians since they entered the army, and not unfrequently I am asked by anxious inquirers what they must do to be saved. 'O, how encouraging to a soldier is a word of sympathy,' said one of the sick men to me."

Another [colporteur] from Petersburg writes: "I have been for some weeks devoting my time to the hospitals in this city. The noble men are so fond of having one to talk with them about the Friend of sinners, and the heavenly home, that my heart is made to rejoice with theirs. The other day I was reading a few tracts to a sick soldier, and while reading one on 'The Blood of Christ,' he became so happy that he shouted, 'Glory to God!' Another said, 'When I first came into the hospital I was sad and dissatisfied, but since I have been here I have learned of Jesus and thank God even for tribulations.' "

Rev. J. A. Hughes thus speaks of his labors at Atlanta: "In going among the thousands in the hospitals, I have met with many things to gladden my heart, and to cause me to love the work. I find a number of Christians; some tell me that camp-life has had a very unfavorable influence on their religious character; others say it has been of great service to them, that it has bound them closer to the Savior, made them more acquainted with their own weakness and sins, and afforded them a fine field in which to labor for the souls of their fellow-men.". . .

Rev. Joseph E. Martin, from Chimborazo hospital at Richmond, writes: "We have had lately sixteen conversions. One young man was very anxious to learn to read. I procured him a spelling book, and in a few days he learned so rapidly as to be able to read the Testament. He has since professed religion. A middle-aged man from Georgia has learned to read since he joined the army, and has committed to memory almost all the New Testament [along] with the book of Job."

Another faithful laborer says: ". . . While [I was] passing through a hospital with my tracts, one poor, afflicted soldier wept piteously and said, 'Sir, I cannot read; will you be good enough to read some of those tracts to me?' I read several and among them, 'A Mother's Parting Words to her Soldier boy.' 'Oh,' said he, 'that reminds me so much of my poor old mother, who has faded from earth since I joined the army.' He wept and seemed greatly affected."

Rev. George Pearcy, writing from Lynchburg, Va., says: "I collected from Sunday Schools and individuals above a hundred Testaments, a few Bibles, and some books and tracts—these were placed in three large hospitals for the sick soldiers. There have been as many as 10,000 soldiers in the encampment here, hence it is a most interesting field for usefulness. Many soldiers have the Bible or Testament and love to read it. A good number are members of churches. Far away from home and kindred, they are delighted to receive the visits of a brother Christian, and get something to read. All receive the tracts, and read them with delight. The Lord has blessed the work. He has poured out his Spirit upon many. . . .

"Several have died in the triumphs of faith. It was a great pleasure and privilege to speak to them of the Savior, and witness their trust in him during the trying hour. One who died a week ago, said, in a whisper, a short time before he breathed his last, when the nurse held up the tract, 'Come to Jesus,' 'I can't see.' He was told it was the tract, 'Come to Jesus,' and that Jesus says, 'Him that cometh unto me I will in no wise cast out.' 'Thank the Lord for that,' he replied. 'Have you come to him? and do you find him precious?' 'Precious, thank the Lord.' 'He has promised never to leave nor forsake his people.' 'Thank the Lord for that'; and so he would say of all the promises quoted.". . .

One who had visited the hospitals at Richmond wrote: "The field of labor opened here for the accomplishment of good is beyond measure. An angel might covet it. At three o'clock services were held in the main hall of the hospital. It was a most imposing spectacle to see men in all stages of sickness—some sitting upon their beds, while others were lying down listening to the word of God—many of them probably for the last time. I do not think I ever saw a more attentive audience. They seemed to drink in the Word of Life at every breath."

"Some time since," says Rev. A. E. Dickinson, "it was my pleasure to stand up in the presence of a large company of convalescent soldiers in one of our hospitals to proclaim salvation. During the reading of a portion of Scripture tears began to flow. I then announced that dear old hymn,—'There is a fountain filled with blood,/Drawn from Immanuel's veins,' &c., the reading of which seemed to melt every heart, and the entire audience was in tears before God. Every word in reference to spiritual truth fell with a soft, subduing fervor on their chastened hearts."

Sermons, distribution of religious tracts, and reading lessons were relegated to quiet convalescent hospitals far to the rear of the active campaigning. Among the chaos and pain of the field hospitals after a bloody battle there were usually opportunities only for murmured prayers and a few words of spiritual advice. Yet even there many soldiers found consolation in their Christian faith. In another passage, Bennett writes:

"It was just after a battle, where hundreds of brave men had fallen," writes another chaplain, "and where hundreds more were wounded, that a soldier came to my tent and said: 'Chaplain, one of our boys is badly wounded, and wants to see you right away.' Immediately following the soldier, I was taken to the hospital and led to a bed, where lay a noble young man, pale and blood-stained from a terrible wound above the temple. I saw at a glance that he had just a few hours to live. . . . 'Now, chaplain,' said the dying man, 'I want you to kneel down by me and return thanks to God.' 'For what?' I asked. 'For giving me such a mother. Oh, chaplain, she is a good mother; her teachings comfort and console me now. And, chaplain, thank God that by his grace I am a Christian. Oh, what would I do now if I was not a Christian! I know that my Redeemer liveth. I feel that his finished work has saved me. And, chaplain, thank God for giving me dying grace. He has made my bed feel 'soft as downy pillows are.' Thank him for the promised home in glory. I'll soon be there—there, where there is no more war, nor sorrow, nor desolation, nor death—where I'll see Jesus and be forever with the Lord.' I kneeled by him, and thanked God for the blessings he had bestowed upon him—a good mother, a Christian hope, and dying grace to bear testimony to God's faithfulness. Shortly after the prayer, he said: 'Good-bye, chaplain; if you see mother, tell her it was all well.' "

A young soldier, while dying very happily, broke out in singing the following stanza:

> Great Jehovah, we adore thee,
> God the Father, God the Son,
> God the Spirit, joined in glory
> On the same eternal throne:
> Endless praises
> To Jehovah, three in one.

The chaplain then asked if he had any message to send to his friends. "Yes," said he, "Tell my father that I have tried to eat my meals with thanksgiving. Tell him that I have tried to pray as we used to do at home. Tell him that Christ is now all my hope, all my trust, and that he is precious to my soul. Tell him that I am not afraid to die—all is calm. Tell him that I believe Christ will take me to himself, and to my dear sister who is in heaven." The voice of the dying boy faltered in the intervals between these precious sentences. When the hymn commencing, "Nearer, my God, to thee," was read to him at the end of each stanza he exclaimed, with striking energy, "Oh, Lord Jesus, thou art coming near to me."

This was witnessed by about twenty fellow-soldiers, and the effect upon the feelings of all was very marked. . . . Said another, "I never prayed until last night; but when I saw that man die so happy, I determined to seek religion too!"

Notes

1. John Henry Wilburn Stuckenberg, *I'm Surrounded by Methodists: Diary of John H. W. Stuckenberg, Chaplain of the 145th Pennsylvania Volunteer Infantry*, ed. David T. Hedrick and Gordon Barry Davis Jr. (Gettysburg, PA: Thomas Publications, 1995), 83–84. Reprinted by permission of Special Collections, Musselman Library, Gettysburg College, Gettysburg, Pennsylvania.

2. Bell I. Wiley, *The Life of Johnny Reb: The Common Soldier of the Confederacy* (Baton Rouge: Louisiana State University Press, 1994; orig. pub. Indianapolis: Bobbs-Merrill, 1943), 262–69. © 1978 by Bell I. Wiley. Reprinted by permission of Louisiana State University Press.

3. Gerald F. Linderman, *Embattled Courage: The Experience of Combat in the American Civil War* (New York: Free Press, 1987), 28–31. © 1987 by Gerald F. Linderman. Reprinted by permission of The Free Press, a Division of Simon & Schuster.

4. Earl J. Hess, *The Union Soldier in Battle: Enduring the Ordeal of Combat* (Lawrence: University Press of Kansas, 1997), 32–37. © 1997 by the University Press of Kansas. All rights reserved. Reprinted by permission of the University Press of Kansas.

5. Reid Mitchell, *Civil War Soldiers* (New York: Viking, 1988), 60–62. © 1988 by Reid Mitchell. Reprinted by permission of Viking Penguin, a division of Penguin Putnam.

6. William W. Bennett, *A Narrative of the Great Revival in the Southern Armies during the Late Civil War between the States of the Federal Union* (Philadelphia: Claxton, Remsen, & Haffelfinger, 1877), 78–82, 179–83.

CHAPTER FIVE

In Prison

$\mathcal{P}$ risons represented another test of the Civil War soldier's fortitude, for they were places not only of confinement but also of suffering and, for thousands of men, death. Just as neither side at the beginning of the war was prepared for the size and magnitude that it would quickly attain, so neither side was ready for the large numbers of prisoners of war that it would soon have on its hands. At first, this problem appeared to be a minor one. Most Americans expected the war to be over quickly, certainly within the first year, and thus relatively few prisoners would be taken and held for a relatively short time.

Even as the war moved into its second year with a progression of engagements on a scale never before approached on the American continent, the issue of prisoners of war still did not seem pressing. True, the large battles yielded large numbers of prisoners. Ulysses S. Grant's February 1862 capture of Fort Donelson, Tennessee, sent some 13,000 to 15,000 Confederates into captivity, while the Union surrender of Harpers Ferry, Virginia, in the following autumn made prisoners of about 10,000 bluecoats. Even these numbers of prisoners, and those taken in other battles, did not completely overwhelm the two sides because exchanges and paroles kept the prisoner population low.

A captured soldier given the privilege of parole was allowed to give his word of honor, or "parole," that he would not serve again in his country's military forces until duly exchanged. He would then be released. Paroled prisoners were usually granted a month or so of leave by their own armies and then were required to stay in "parole camps" until officially exchanged. Thus, after its capture at Munfordville, Kentucky, in September 1862, the 67th Indiana Regiment was paroled and subsequently spent several unhappy months in a parole camp near Indianapolis. The Hoosier parolees were bored

and uncomfortable in their rough barracks, but they were still better off there than in a Southern prisoner-of-war camp. After their
exchange, the 67th became part of the army with which Grant captured Vicksburg, Mississippi, the following summer.

This system began to change in 1863, as you will read in some
of the selections below. Briefly, the Union began to enlist black
soldiers. The Confederacy, viewing this move as an atrocity, threatened to enslave captured U.S. soldiers of African descent and hang
their white officers. The threat of retaliation stopped the Rebels
short of that dire step, but they did refuse to exchange captured
black soldiers. The Union, honor-bound to protect every man who
wore its uniform, refused to continue the exchange of white soldiers if blacks were not included, and that the Southerners steadfastly refused to do. To compound the problem, the Confederacy
found it expedient to discharge from parole, without exchange, some
30,000 of its own troops captured and paroled by Grant at Vicksburg
in July 1863. Those illegal soldiers helped the Confederate cause
considerably during the next few months, particularly in gaining a
Rebel victory at the battle of Mansfield, Louisiana, in April 1864,
ironically defeating Union troops, including the duly exchanged
67th Indiana, to whom they had surrendered at Vicksburg nine
months before. This action on the part of the Confederate authorities sounded the death knell of the parole system, which could work
only as long as each side could trust the other to keep its word of
honor. From a modern perspective, it is amazing that the system
held up as long as it did.

Thus, by the end of 1863, both outlets for the Civil War prison
population—exchange and parole—had been closed. Meanwhile,
the intensity of the fighting continued to grow and with it the stream
of newly captured soldiers. Massive overcrowding in prisons North
and South came to account for much of the appalling suffering of
the prisoners of war. And yet, crowding alone cannot be blamed for
all the suffering. Men went hungry in the midst of rich agricultural
districts; they lay exposed to blazing sun and driving rain when abundant wood nearby could have been used to build shelters. Why?
The answers are bound up in cultural and moral issues that lie at
the heart of the war itself—and perhaps in the nature of any war—
and are certain to be controversial.

As you read the following selections, think about these issues.
What factors made the prisoners' lot particularly grievous even in

the early months of the conflict? In what ways did that lot grow worse after the system of exchange and parole broke down? How did the prisoner-of-war experience differ in the North and the South? What does the treatment of prisoners-of-war tell us about the culture of nineteenth-century America and about cultural differences between the Union and the Confederacy?

William B. Hesseltine on the North's "War Psychosis"[1]

One of the first historians to address the issue of prisoner-of-war camps was William Hesseltine, whose 1930 book *Civil War Prisons: A Study in War Psychology* was completed two years earlier as his doctoral dissertation. The 1920s and 1930s were an era that tended to see little value in the war for the Union and emancipation. Fashionable historical theory of the time held that the war was the result either of a blundering generation of politicians who failed to compromise their differences or of the desires of great financial powers in the Northeast to oppress the South or agrarian interests generally. Learned Americans took a condescending view of their grandfathers' sacrifice and considered the war to have been an unnecessary, contrived, almost childish squabble between two sides that were both about equally right and equally wrong. Some historians of that era, such as Claude G. Bowers, even took a strongly pro-Southern view. Hesseltine did not fully follow Bowers's lead. Indeed, by the standards of his day he showed admirable restraint, although he did imply that the testimony of a clergyman "of abolitionist leanings" was for that reason not quite reliable, especially when that clergyman asserted that Southern slaves were "oppressed."

At the heart of Hesseltine's argument was his claim that the exaggerated assertions of enemy wrong-doing in the mistreatment of prisoners were products of "war psychosis," which inevitably makes the foe "appear to be defective in all principles which are held dear" by one's own side. That claim no doubt had some validity, but Hesseltine tended to see the North as being the party guilty of "war psychosis" for its condemnation of Southern practices epitomized at the notorious Andersonville prison. Indeed, one chapter of his book was titled "War Psychosis in the North," but he included no corresponding chapter for the South. For Hesseltine, Northern newspapers were "the fomenters and agents for the dissemination of this psychosis." He even suggests that to at least some degree, the oppression perceived by Union prisoners of war in Confederate POW camps was merely the product of their imaginations under the influence of this "psychosis." Exchanged prisoners' firsthand accounts of ill treatment "tended to make each [future] prisoner feel that he was being oppressed." The dying men at Andersonville apparently only *thought* they were being mistreated.

In reading this selection from Hesseltine's book, consider the nature of his argument. How far does it go toward exonerating the Southern prison system? To what extent does Hesseltine attempt to defend this system by attacking its Northern critics? Does the fact that a warring people comes to despise its foe mean that the foe is innocent of the sort of wrong-doing claimed? Also, observe how Hesseltine uses obviously absurd contemporary reports of Confederate atrocities at First Bull Run to cast doubt on more credible and well-substantiated stories of mistreatment of prisoners in places such as Andersonville.

Apparently an inevitable concomitant of armed warfare is the hatred engendered in the minds of the contestants by the conflict. The spirit of patriotism which inspires men to answer the call of their country in its hour of need breeds within those men the fiercest antagonism toward that country's enemies. Such enmity finds its natural expression not only on the battlefield in the heat of conflict but also in the lives of the soldiers and the sentiment of the community from which they come, both of which have been thrown out of their accustomed peace-time routine by the outbreak of the war. The attachment to an ideal, a cause, or a country, when such attachment calls for the sacrifice of security and life, blinds the person feeling that attachment to whatever of virtue there may be in the opposing ideal, cause, or country. Seemingly, it becomes necessary for the supporters of one cause to identify their entire personality with that cause, to identify their opponents with the opposing cause, and to hate the supporters of the enemy cause with a venom which counterbalances their devotion to their own.

To a people actuated by such a devotion to a cause, it is inevitable that their opponents appear to be defective in all principles which are held dear by that people. The enemy becomes a thing to be hated; he does not share the common virtues, and his peculiarities of speech, race, or culture become significant as points of difference or, better, sins of the greater magnitude. The critical faculties, present to some degree in times of peace, atrophy on the approach of national catastrophe.

With such a state of mind coming as the natural result of the upheaval of the social order which the war produced, it was not difficult for credence to be gained for stories of atrocities committed by one or the other side in the Civil War. Immediately after the battle of Bull Run newspaper correspondents, on or near the field, sent accounts of the battle to their home papers. Throughout the loyal portion of the United States the defeat of the Union armies produced a depression which was fed by the stories of barbarities accompanying the correspondents' accounts. "Most shocking barbarities begin to be reported as practiced by the rebels upon the wounded and prisoners of the Union that fall into their hands. We are told of their slashing the throats of some from ear to ear; of their cutting off the heads of others and kicking them about as footballs; and of their setting up the wounded against trees and firing at them as targets or torturing them with plunges of bayonets into their bodies," commented the editor of an administration journal as he characterized the Confederates as "brutal robbers," "fighting as outlaws of civilization." An illustrated weekly carried a full-page picture of rebels plunging their bayonets into the bodies of wounded soldiers. "The Southern character," remarked the first paper, "is infinitely boastful, vainglorious, full of dash, without endurance, treacherous, cunning, timid, and revengeful."

So far as prisons and prisoners of war were concerned, the attention of Northern newspapers, the fomenters and agents for the dissemination of this psychosis, was first directed toward obtaining an exchange for prisoners held in the Confederate prisons. The position of the government, that exchange would be tantamount to recognition, was characterized as absurd by the newspapers, whether they in general supported or opposed the administration. However, the tendency of some papers to support the administration by saying, "In a war of this kind words are things. If we must address [Jefferson] Davis as president of the Confederacy, we cannot exchange and the prisoners should not wish it," led the papers advocating exchange to advance a humanitarian argument. The sufferings of the prisoners in the South were emphasized, and how prisoners were confined in close rooms, "whose poisoned atmosphere is slowly sapping their strength hour by hour," was often related. The more sensational press gathered stories of bad food, cruel treatment, and utter destitution and predicted in the first months of the war that the Richmond tobacco warehouses would "rank with the British prison ships and the dungeons of the Revolution."

Secretary [of War Edwin M.] Stanton, unwilling to give up the position of the administration in regard to exchanges and unable to resist the tide of opposition to the established policy, as his first official act as head of the war department, determined to send Bishop [Edward Raymond] Ames and Hamilton Fish to Richmond to relieve the prisoners' sufferings. This action had for the moment the desired effect of quieting opposition to the administration although it was believed that Mr. [Alfred] Ely should have been sent. Since there was some doubt that supplies which Ames and Fish might send would be delivered to the prisoners, the opinion was expressed "that the best way to supply the wants of our captive soldiers is to bring them home, even at the cost of releasing as many rebels." With this attitude of mind prevailing, the failure of the commissioners to get admission to Richmond was hailed as an "unexpected and most splendid success," and exchange was promised immediately.

As this mission did not consummate the promised exchange, the organs of public opinion returned to their policy of exciting sympathy for the prisoners. Although it was declared that the treatment of prisoners in the South was not due to vindictive spirit on the part of the Confederate authorities, it was stated that they were unable to control the passions of the "drunken and ignorant hordes" of their army, and it was admitted that they did not possess the means to maintain a war prison. Under such conditions exaggerated accounts of outrages on unarmed prisoners by the brutal keepers were legion.

In July an escaped quartermaster of an Iowa regiment reported to the governor of his state an account of his experiences in Montgomery and Selma, Alabama, and Macon, Georgia, which revealed that not everyone was willing to clear the rebels of vindictive feeling. He said that the two hundred and fifty officers who shared his confinement received less than one-fourth the rations of a private in the United States army "and are subjected to all the hardships and indignities which venomous traitors can heap upon them." The prisoners were confined "in a foul and vermin abounding cotton shed." At Tuscaloosa they were forbidden to leave the crowded room to go to the sinks at a time when diarrhoea was prevalent; at Montgomery the prisoners were destitute of clothing; and at both places the hospitals were denied medicines. Cornbread issued to the prisoners was made of unsifted meal and the meat at Montgomery was spoiled. Men were killed for looking out the window—"prohibiting them the poor privilege of looking at their mother earth."

In the East, public opinion of rebel vindictiveness underwent a modification with the beginning of exchanges under the cartel. "It would not be fair to blame the rebels' vindictive spirit entirely," declared a newspaper correspondent, "but partly from that and partly from a lack of food and medicines" the prisoners were suffering. A surgeon told a newspaper correspondent that in the wounds of many of the men "there were enough maggots to fill a wine glass."

As the vindictive spirit of the Confederates came to be more emphasized, the corollary proposition was developed that prisoners in the Northern prisons were accorded excellent treatment. "How different an example of humanity the North is setting," remarked this correspondent; and his paper, demanding exchange, declared that the rebel prisoners were growing stout. They were fed on capital food, given medicines, and fanned with cool breezes in the summer. Its readers were called upon to "think of the crowded and filthy tobacco warehouses, the brutal keepers, the sanguinary guards, the rotten food, the untended wounds, the unmedicined diseases, the miserable marches through the blazing South!" "What horrors has death on the battlefield to this?" Under such pressure as this, the cartel was negotiated and prisoners began to be exchanged.

Clinching evidence of the vindictiveness of the rebels came as a result of Davis' proclamation against General [John] Pope and his officers. "The rebels won't let the United States think good of them," it was declared. "For a full year they have maintained a systematic bedevilment of Union prisoners and now," although Pope had made no arrests, the rebels, "gloating in cruelty, make haste to oppress." During the period that exchanges were carried on under the cartel the attitude of mind already created by the stories from the Southern prisoners was not allowed to die. Instead, by a process of accretion, there developed a firm belief in the mind of the Northern people that the Confederacy deliberately sought to torture the prisoners who fell into its hands. This development took place despite the fact that both Colonel [Michael] Corcoran and Congressman

Ely published accounts of their prison experiences which contradicted the prevailing beliefs. Mr. Ely's account, published in the spring of 1862 before the formation of the cartel, related his experiences without any manifestation of the cruelty of Southern keepers. He revealed an opposition to the administration's policy of not exchanging prisoners, and, although reciting several murders of prisoners at the windows, insisted that such acts of brutality could not have been known to General [John Henry] Winder or the [Confederate] secretary of war. Ely borrowed money from the prison commissary, received gifts from sympathetic friends, and admired General Winder [commander of Confederate military prisons]. The only moral which he pointed out in his book, *The Journal of Alfred Ely*, was that his insight into Southern character was not worth the "sufferings, privations, indignities and discomforts" which he underwent as a result of the unfortunate curiosity which led him to be a spectator at the battle of Bull Run.

Colonel Corcoran, returning with the first of the prisoners to be exchanged under the cartel, also published an account of his experiences. More critical than the work of his fellow prisoner, *The Captivity of General Corcoran* declared the rebel secretary of war to be "one of those disgraces to mankind with which the world is anything but blessed," but he had no harsh words for General Winder. Although "the Hero of Bull Run," as Corcoran described himself in his book, had suffered indignities unbecoming a hero, his account as a whole did not serve to confirm the stories which were current at the time.

More in accordance with the prevailing sentiment was a book from the pen of a Methodist Protestant minister of abolitionist leanings; James J. Geer, of Cincinnati, in *Beyond the Lines; or, a Yankee Loose in Dixie*, related his experiences in Montgomery, Alabama, and Macon, Georgia. He escaped from the latter prison, was recaptured, and finally exchanged. Through these experiences he developed a decided antipathy toward the aristocracy and the "clay eating" classes of the South. Negroes who helped him in his escape and shared his confinement in various jails were revealed as oppressed and kept in ignorance by their white masters. The tone of the book was bitter and stories of rebel barbarities filled its pages.

The influence of such accounts was widespread and tended to make each prisoner feel that he was being oppressed.

James M. McPherson on the Treatment of Prisoners[2]

A modern scholar who has taken issue with some of the claims of Hesseltine and other more or less pro-Southern historians is James McPherson in his Pulitzer Prize-winning 1988 book, *Battle Cry of Freedom*. McPherson also gives a clear and forceful overview of the Civil War prisoner-of-war problem as a whole. The following passage makes clear the reasons for the large numbers of prisoners who overloaded the systems of both North and South during the final year of the war. Note the ways in which McPherson's fact-based argument differs from that of Hesseltine both in content and in style.

The relatively few prisoners captured in 1861 imposed no great strain on either side. Obsolete forts, converted warehouses, county jails, and other existing buildings proved sufficient to hold prisoners while they awaited the informal exchanges that occasionally took place. Field commanders sometimes paroled captives or worked out local exchanges on the spot after a skirmish. Not wishing the burden of feeding prisoners, the Confederacy pressed for a formal exchange cartel. The Lincoln administration was reluctant to grant the official recognition that such a cartel might imply. After the fighting from Fort Donelson to Seven Days poured thousands of prisoners into inadequate facilities, however, the administration succumbed to growing northern pressure for regularized exchanges. Taking care to negotiate with a belligerent army, not government, the Union army accepted an exchange cartel on July 22, 1862. Specifying a rank weighting whereby a non-commissioned officer was equal to two privates, a lieutenant to four, and so on up to a commanding general who was worth sixty privates, this cartel specified a man-for-man exchange of all prisoners. The excess held by one side or another were to be released on parole (that is, they promised not to take up arms until formally exchanged).

For ten months this arrangement worked well enough to empty the prisons except for captives too sick or wounded to travel. But two matters brought exchanges to a halt during 1863. First was the northern response to the southern threat to reenslave or execute the captured black soldiers and their officers. When the Confederate Congress in May 1863 authorized this policy, which Jefferson Davis had announced four months earlier, the Union War Department suspended the cartel in order to hold southern prisoners as

hostages against fulfillment of the threat. A trickle of informal exchanges continued, but the big battles in the second half of 1863
soon filled makeshift prisons with thousands of men. Grant averted
an even greater problem by paroling the 30,000 Vicksburg captives; [General Nathaniel P.] Banks followed suit with the 7,000
captured at Port Hudson. But the South's handling of these parolees provoked a second and clinching breakdown in exchange negotiations. Alleging technical irregularities in their paroles, the
Confederacy arbitrarily declared many of them exchanged (without any real exchange taking place) and returned them to duty. Grant
was outraged when the Union recaptured some of these men at
Chattanooga.

Attempts to renew the cartel foundered on the southern refusal
to treat freedmen soldiers as prisoners of war or to admit culpability in the case of the Vicksburg parolees. "The enlistment of our
slaves is a barbarity," declared the head of the Confederate Bureau
of War. "No people . . . could tolerate . . . the use of savages [against
them]. . . . We cannot on any principle allow that our property can
acquire adverse rights by virtue of a theft of it." By the end of 1863
the Confederacy expressed a willingness to exchange black captives
whom it considered to have been legally free when they enlisted.
But the South would "die in the last ditch," said the Confederate
exchange commissioner, before "giving up the right to send slaves
back to slavery as property recaptured." Very well, responded Union
Secretary of War Stanton. The 26,000 rebel captives in northern
prisons could stay there. For the Union government to accede to
Confederate conditions would be "a shameful dishonor. . . . When
[the rebels] agree to exchange all alike there will be no difficulty."
After becoming general in chief, Grant confirmed this hard line.
"No distinction whatever will be made in the exchange between
white and colored prisoners," he ordered on April 17, 1864. And
there must be "released to us a sufficient number of officers and
men as were captured and paroled at Vicksburg and Port Hudson.
. . . Non-acquiescence by the Confederate authorities in both or
either of these propositions will be regarded as a refusal on their
part to agree to the further exchange of prisoners." Confederate
authorities did not acquiesce.

The South's actual treatment of black prisoners is hard to as-
certain. Even the number of Negro captives is unknown, for in refusing to acknowledge them as legitimate prisoners the Confederates

kept few records. Many black captives never made it to prison camp. In the spirit of Secretary of War [James A.] Seddon's early directive that "we ought never to be inconvenienced with such prisoners . . . summary execution must therefore be inflicted on those taken," hundreds were massacred at Fort Pillow, Poison Spring, the Crater, and elsewhere. An affidavit by a Union sergeant described what happened after Confederates recaptured Plymouth on the North Carolina coast in April 1864:

> All the negroes found in blue uniform or with any outward marks of a Union soldier upon him was killed—I saw some taken into the woods and hung—Others I saw stripped of all their clothing, and they stood upon the bank of the river with their faces riverwards and then they were shot—Still others were killed by having their brains beaten out by the butt end of the muskets in the hands of the Rebels—
>
> All were not killed the day of the capture—Those that were not, were placed in a room with their officers, they (the Officers) having previously been dragged through the town with ropes around their necks, where they were kept confined until the following morning when the remainder of the black soldiers were killed.

Black prisoners who survived the initial rage of their captors sometimes found themselves returned as slaves to their old masters or, occasionally, sold to a new one. While awaiting this fate they were often placed at hard labor on Confederate fortifications. The *Mobile Advertiser and Register* of October 15, 1864, published a list of 575 black prisoners in that city working as laborers until owners claimed them.

What to do about the murder or enslavement of black captives presented the Union government with a dilemma. At first Lincoln threatened an eye-for-an-eye retaliation. "For every soldier of the United States killed in violation of the laws of war," he ordered on July 30, 1863, "a rebel soldier shall be executed; and for every one enslaved by the enemy or sold into slavery, a rebel soldier shall be placed at hard labor on the public works." But this was easier said than done; as Lincoln himself put it, "the difficulty is not in stating the principle, but in practically applying it." After the Fort Pillow massacre the cabinet spent two meetings trying to determine a response. To execute an equal number of rebel prisoners would punish the innocent for the crimes of the guilty. The government must not undertake such a "barbarous . . . inhuman policy," declared Secretary of the Navy [Gideon] Welles. Lincoln agreed that "blood can not restore blood, and government should not act for revenge." The cabinet decided to retaliate against actual offenders from [Nathan Bedford] Forrest's command, if any were captured, and to warn Richmond that a certain number of southern officers in northern prisons would be set apart as hostages against such occurrences in the future.

But no record exists that either recommendation was carried out. As Lincoln sadly told [black abolitionist] Frederick Douglass, "if once begun, there was no telling where [retaliation] would end." Execution of innocent southern prisoners—or even guilty ones— would produce Confederate retaliation against northern prisoners in a never-ending vicious cycle. In the final analysis, concluded the Union exchange commissioner, these cases "can only be effectually reached by a successful prosecution of the war." After all, "the rebellion exists on a question connected with the right or power of the South to hold the colored race in slavery; and the South will only yield this right under military compulsion." Thus "the loyal people of the United States [must] prosecute this war with all the energy that God has given them."

Union field commanders in South Carolina and Virginia carried out the only official retaliation for southern treatment of black prisoners. When Confederates at Charleston and near Richmond put captured Negroes to work on fortifications under enemy fire in 1864, northern generals promptly placed an equal number of rebel prisoners at work on Union facilities under fire. This ended the Confederate practice. . . .

Although Union threats of retaliation did little to help ex-slaves captured by Confederates, they appear to have forced southern officials to make a distinction between former slaves and free blacks. "The serious consequences," wrote Secretary of War Seddon to South Carolina's governor, "which might ensue from a rigid enforcement of the act of Congress" (which required all captured blacks to be turned over to states for punishment as insurrectionists) compel us "to make a distinction between negroes so taken who can be recognized or identified as slaves and those who were free inhabitants of the Federal States." The South generally treated the latter—along with white officers of black regiments—as prisoners of war. This did not necessarily mean equal treatment. Prison guards singled out black captives for latrine and burial details or other onerous labor. At Libby Prison in Richmond ten white officers and four enlisted men of a black regiment were confined to a small cell next to the kitchen where they subsisted on bread and water and almost suffocated from cooking smoke. "An open tub," wrote another prisoner, "was placed in the room for the reception of their excrement, where it was permitted to remain for days before removal." In South Carolina captured black soldiers from the 54th Massachusetts and other northern units were kept in the Charleston jail rather than in a POW camp.

They probably fared as well in jail—if not better—as their white fellows in war prisons. The principal issue that aroused northern emotions was not the treatment of black prisoners but of all Union prisoners. As the heavy fighting of 1864 piled up captives in jerry-built prisons, grim stories of disease, starvation, and brutality began to filter northward. The camp at Andersonville in southwest Georgia became representative in northern eyes of southern barbarity. Andersonville prison was built in early 1864 to accommodate captives previously held at Belle Isle on the James River near Richmond, because the proximity of Union forces threatened liberation of these prisoners and the overworked transport system of Virginia could barely feed southern citizens and soldiers, let alone Yankees. A stockade camp of sixteen acres designed for 10,000 prisoners, Andersonville soon became overcrowded with captives from [General William Tecumseh] Sherman's army as well as from the eastern theater. It was enlarged to twenty-six acres, in which 33,000 men were packed by August 1864—an average of thirty-four square feet per man—without shade in a Deep South summer and with no shelter except what they could rig from sticks, tent flies, blankets, and odd bits of cloth. (By way of comparison, the Union prison camp at Elmira, New York, generally considered the worst northern prison, provided barracks for the maximum of 9,600 captives living inside a forty-acre enclosure—an average of 180 square feet per man.) During some weeks in the summer of 1864 more than a hundred prisoners died every day in Andersonville. Altogether 13,000 of the 45,000 men imprisoned there died of disease, exposure, or malnutrition.

Andersonville was the most extreme example of what many northerners regarded as a fiendish plot to murder Yankee prisoners. After the war a Union military commission tried and executed its commandant, Henry Wirz, for war crimes—the only such trial to result from the Civil War. Whether Wirz was actually guilty of anything worse than bad temper and inefficiency remains controversial today. . . .

During 1864 a crescendo rose in the northern press demanding retribution against rebel prisoners to coerce better treatment of Union captives. "Retaliation is a terrible thing," conceded the *New York Times*, "but the miseries and pains and the slowly wasting life of our brethren and friends in those horrible prisons is a worse thing. No people or government ought to allow its soldiers to be treated for one day as our men have been treated for the last three years." When a special exchange of sick prisoners in April returned to the North several living skeletons, woodcut copies of their photographs appeared in illustrated papers and produced a tidal wave of rage. What else could one expect of slaveholders "born to tyranny and reared to cruelty?" asked the normally moderate *Times*. The Committee on the Conduct of the War and the U.S. Sanitary Commission each published an account of Confederate prison conditions based on intelligence reports and on interviews with exchanged or escaped prisoners. "The enormity of the crime committed by the rebels," commented Secretary of War Stanton, "cannot but fill with horror the civilized world. . . . There appears to have been a deliberate system of savage and barbarous treatment." An editorial in an Atlanta newspaper during August made its way across the lines and was picked up by the northern press: "During one of the intensely hot days of last week more than 300 sick and wounded Yankees died at Andersonville. We thank heaven for such blessings." This was the sort of thing that convinced otherwise sensible northerners that "Jefferson Davis's policy is to starve and freeze and kill off by inches all the prisoners he dares not butcher outright. . . . We cannot retaliate, it is said; but why can we not?"

The Union War Department did institute a limited retaliation. In May 1864, Stanton reduced prisoner rations to the same level that the Confederate army issued to its own soldiers. In theory this placed rebel prisoners on the same footing as Yankee prisoners in the South, who in theory received the same rations as Confederate soldiers. But in practice few southern soldiers ever got the official rations by 1864—and Union prisoners inevitably got even less—so most rebel captives in the North probably ate better than they had in their own army. Nevertheless, the reduction of prisoner rations was indicative of a hardening northern attitude. Combined with the huge increase in the number of prisoners during 1864, this produced a deterioration of conditions in northern prisons until the suffering, sickness, and death in some of them rivaled that in southern prisons—except Andersonville, which was in a class by itself.

This state of affairs produced enormous pressures for a renewal of exchanges. Many inmates at Andersonville and other southern prisons signed petitions to Lincoln asking for renewal, and the Confederates allowed delegations of prisoners to bear these petitions to Washington. Nothing came of them. . . .

Lincoln could indeed have renewed the exchange if he had been willing to forget about ex-slave soldiers. But he no more wanted to concede this principle than to renounce emancipation as a condition of peace. On August 27, Benjamin Butler, who had been appointed a special exchange agent, made the administration's position clear in a long letter to the Confederate exchange commissioner—a letter that was published widely in the newspapers. The United States government would renew exchanges, said Butler, whenever the Confederacy was ready to exchange all classes of prisoners. "The wrongs, indignities, and privations suffered by our soldiers," wrote Butler, who was a master of rhetoric, "would move me to consent to anything to procure their exchange, except to barter away the honor and faith of the Government of the United States, which has been so solemnly pledged to the colored soldiers in its ranks. Consistently with national faith and justice we cannot relinquish that position."

General Grant had privately enunciated another argument against exchange: it would strengthen enemy armies more than Union armies. "It is hard on our men held in Southern prisons not to exchange them," Grant said in August 1864, "but it is humanity to those left in our ranks to fight our battles." Most exchanged rebels—"hale, hearty, and well-fed" as northerners believed them to be—would "become active soldier[s] against us at once" while "the half-starved, sick, emaciated" Union prisoners could never fight again. "We have got to fight until the military power of the South is exhausted, and if we release or exchange prisoners captured it simply becomes a war of extermination."

A good many historians—especially those of southern birth—have pointed to Grant's remarks as the real reason for the North's refusal to exchange. Concern for the rights of black soldiers, in this view, was just for show. The northern strategy of a war of attrition, therefore, was responsible for the horrors of Andersonville and the suffering of prisoners on both sides. This position is untenable. Grant expressed his opinion more than a year after the exchange cartel had broken down over the Negro prisoner question. And an opinion was precisely what it was; Grant did not *order* exchanges prohibited for purposes of attrition, and the evidence indicates that if the Confederates had conceded on the issue of ex-slaves the exchanges would have resumed. In October 1864, General Lee proposed an informal exchange of prisoners captured in recent fighting on the Richmond-Petersburg front. Grant agreed, on condition that blacks be exchanged "the same as white soldiers." If this had been done, it might have provided a precedent to break the impasse that had by then penned up more than a hundred thousand men in POW camps. But Lee replied that "negroes belonging to our citizens are not considered subjects of exchange and were not included in my proposition." Grant thereupon closed the correspondence with the words that because his "Government is bound to secure to all persons received into her armies the rights due to soldiers," Lee's refusal to grant such rights to former slaves "induces me to decline making the exchanges you ask."

In January 1865 the rebels finally gave in and offered to exchange "all" prisoners. Hoping soon to begin recruiting black soldiers for their own armies, Davis and Lee suddenly found the Yankee policy less barbaric. The cartel began functioning again and several thousand captives a week were exchanged over the next three months, until Appomattox liberated everyone.

Few if any historians would now contend that the Confederacy deliberately mistreated prisoners. Rather, they would concur with contemporary opinions—held by some northerners as well as southerners—that a deficiency of resources and the deterioration of the southern economy were mainly responsible for the sufferings of Union prisoners. The South could not feed its own soldiers and civilians; how could it feed enemy prisoners? The Confederacy could not supply its own troops with enough tents; how could it provide tents for captives? A certain makeshift quality in southern prison administration, a lack of planning and efficiency, also contributed to the plight of prisoners. Because Confederates kept expecting exchanges to be resumed, they made no long-range plans. The matter of shelter at Andersonville affords an example of shortages and lack of foresight. Although the South had plenty of cotton, it did not have the industrial capacity to turn enough of that cotton into tent canvas. The South had plenty of wood to build barracks, but there was a shortage of nails at Andersonville and no one thought to order them far enough in advance. . . .

So the prisoners broiled in the sun and shivered in the rain. Union captives at other enlisted men's prison camps endured a similar lack of shelter—in contrast to northern prisoners, all of which provided barracks except Point Lookout in Maryland, where prisoners lived in tents. During the war numerous southerners criticized their own prisons. . . . A young Georgia woman [wrote] after a visit to Andersonville, "I am afraid God will suffer some terrible retribution to fall upon us for letting such things happen. If the Yankees ever should come to South-West Georgia . . . and see the graves there, God have mercy on the land!"

"And yet, what can we do?" she asked herself. "The Yankees themselves are really more to blame than we, for they won't exchange these prisoners, and our poor, hard-pressed Confederacy has not the means to provide for them, when our own soldiers are starving in the field." This defensive tone became dominant in southern rhetoric after the war.

Warren Lee Goss on Life in Confederate Prisons[3]

Massachusetts soldier Warren Goss had the misfortune to be an eyewitness to many of the appalling scenes that James McPherson describes. It was Goss's lot to make the acquaintance of three of the most infamous of the Confederacy's prisons: Libby, Belle Isle, and Andersonville. Here he describes an old tobacco warehouse in which he was held after his capture during the June 1862 Seven Days battles. He was subsequently moved to Richmond's Libby Prison and then to nearby Belle Isle. Goss found that while most of his captors, both soldiers and civilians, behaved viciously toward their prisoners, some at times were kind and merciful. Meanwhile, Goss discovered to his dismay that in conditions of extreme stress and demoralization even his fellow soldiers could become cruel and uncaring toward one another.

The prison was one of the large tobacco warehouses, three stories high; the rooms were large, poorly ventilated, and disgustingly filthy. The dust and tobacco juice of years had gathered in hillocks and ridges over the floor. These apartments were indescribably foul.

They had been filled with prisoners who had but just been removed to make room for us, and had left behind them all the offal of mortal maladies, weakness, and wounds. There had been no sweeping or cleaning, but into these rooms we were forced, compelled to drink in the suffocating air, the first breath of which caused one to shudder.

The room in which I, with about two hundred of my companions, was placed, was too filthy for description. Here, for five days, almost suffocating from want of air, and crowded for room, I remained, having rations issued to me only twice during the five days, and those poor in quality, and insufficient in quantity for a sick man. So [it was] with all the sick and wounded. No medical attention was given, and the horror of our situation seemed more than could be borne. To such a degree were we crowded, that we were obliged to arrange ourselves in tiers, like pins on paper, when we slept at night. And even with this precaution we were crowded for sleeping-room. Constant interference of some one's feet with another's head or shins caused such continued wrangling as to make night and day more like an abode of fiends than one of human beings.

At last I was taken from this place, and sent to Libby Prison, which has often been described; and yet from the description given, no adequate idea of the sufferings endured can be formed. The filth and heat were greater than even the place I had left. With some five hundred others I was crowded into the garret, next the roof, of the prison. The hot sun, beating down upon the roof, made the filthy garret, crowded with men clamoring for standing-room, suffocating in a degree which one cannot well understand who never experienced it. During the day, in the corners of our garret the dead remained among the living, and from these through all the rooms came the pestilent breath of a charnel-house. The vermin swarmed in every crack and crevice; the floors had not been cleaned for years. To consign men to such quarters was like signing their death warrant. Two men were shot by the rebel guard while trying to get breath at the windows.

The third day of my confinement in this abode of torture, I noticed a young soldier dying: his long, fair hair was matted in the indescribable liquid filth and dirt which clotted and ran over the floor of the prison. He was covered with vermin; the flies had gathered on his wasted hands, on his face, and in the sunken sockets of his eyes. But even in this condition hunger had not left him. The scene seemed to fascinate me, and in spite of the repulsiveness of the picture, I continued to look upon it, though it was much against my will. I saw him try to get to his mouth a dirty piece of bread, which he held in his hand: the effort was in vain; the hand fell nerveless by his side; a convulsive shudder, and he was dead. After he had been dead half an hour, his hand still clasped over the poor dirty piece of bread, a Zouave who had one leg amputated, observing the bread, dragged himself through the filth and dirt, and unclasping the dead man's fingers, took the bread from the rigid hand, and ate it like a famished wolf.

Men lay on the filthy floor unable to help themselves, gasping for breath, while their more healthy companions trod upon and stumbled over them. The common expression used was, "I shall die unless I get fresh air." Every breath they breathed was loaded with the poison of fever and the effluvia of the dead. When rations were issued, two thirds of the very sick got nothing, for the manner of issuing was without order, and the distribution was by a general scramble among those who were the best able to wrangle for it. I was fortunate in getting rations the first day in Libby, but the second and third I got none. Meanwhile, my fever grew worse and worse; oppressed for breath, crowded for room, unable to get into the prison yard to perform the common functions of nature, to which was added the want of medicines and even common food, made my situation so horribly intolerable that I could only hope for relief in death. All this was made worse by the constant wrangling for room, for air, and food. I succeeded in obtaining some pieces of board, by which means I raised myself from the dirty floor and the liquid filth around me.

I had been in Libby about a week, when an officer passed through the rooms, announcing that those who were able to walk could be accommodated with quarters in a healthy location on Belle Island. None of us had heard of Belle Island as a prison at that time, and we were eager to better our condition. Worse it did not seem possible it could be, and we believed there would be some truth even with rebels in dealing with men in our situation. The chance of benefiting myself was irresistible, and so I managed to crawl and stumble down stairs into the streets. The breathing of fresh air once more was refreshing; but, trying to get into line, I stumbled, and fell fainting to the ground. I was carried by some kind people into an

Irishwoman's shop, where I was treated to raspberry wine and baker's bread. She asked me if I thought our army would come into Richmond. I answered her (believing it true), that I thought our army would have Richmond in a week or two. "I hope they will," said she; "for this is a devilish place, and I wish I was in New York." I got into line after being persuaded by the bayonet of the guard, and, being too weak to stand, fell down on the pavement. A rebel guard, addressing me, said, "I guess you'd better not go down there, old hoss; Belle Isle's a right smart hard place, and I reckon you won't any mor'n live to get down thar any way." About the time we commenced our line of march for Belle Isle, it began to rain in torrents, drenching me through. I should never have reached the prison camp alive, had it not been for the kind assistance tendered me by the rebel soldier who had previously addressed me as "old hoss."

We arrived at one of the long bridges which cross the James River between Belle Isle and Richmond; after which I have a confused recollection of falling, succeeded by a blank. I knew no more, until I found myself lying on the damp ground, with no shelter from the driving rain, and hundreds of others around me in the same situation. I have only a confused recollection of what occurred for four or five days after my arrival, when I inquired where I was. I was addressed as "old crazy" by my companions, and told to keep still. I afterwards learned that I had been delirious most of the time for four or five days, during which I had received no medical attention or care except the coldwater cure of nature. . . . It was three weeks before I got a shelter, though there were quite a number of tents on the Island; and the shelter which I became possessed of consisted of an old striped bedtick ripped open, and set upon sticks, in poor imitation of an A tent.

Belle Island is situated on a bend of the James River, about half a mile west of Richmond. The river at this point is very swift of current, and full of fantastic groups of rocks and little islands, covered with luxuriant foliage, among which the water dashes in sparkling foam. Three bridges span the river between the island and the city. The island contains some forty or fifty superficial acres, rises at the lower extremity, towards Richmond, in a gentle, sandy plain, and upon this was situated the prison camp, consisting of about four acres of the lowest land on the James River—almost on a level with the river, and consequently unhealthy. Beyond the prison grounds to the westward the island rises into a precipitous bluff, there crowned by strong earthworks, which commanded the river above. The prison grounds were surrounded by a low board railing, around which guards were stationed at intervals of fifteen paces.

The guard regulations on the island were very strict. The rules established were, that there should be no conversation between the prisoners and the guard, and that no prisoner was to come within three feet of the railing or fence which enclosed the prison. But, in spite of rules and regulations, the irresistible Yankee spirit of trade and dicker perverted even the virtuous grayback guardians of the prison. Trading over the line on the sly was one of the professions, and all became more or less expert at the business. As the guard had orders to shoot or bayonet any one infringing these rules, the business was sometimes risky, especially when a new guard was put on who knew not the ways of those who were before them, when some contrary Secesh [Secessionist, or Rebel] was on duty who did not care to learn, or some confiding individual of the grayback species who had been cheated in a sharp trading speculation.

The common way in opening negotiations for trade with a new or ugly guard was to hold up, at a safe distance, some article of a tempting nature—a jackknife, watch, or a pair of boots—making signs that they were to be purchased cheap, until the virtuous Secesh broke the ice by inquiring the price. A lookout being established to give warning of the approach of the officers of the guard, trade would commence, and spread from guard to guard, and sometimes beyond the guard all along the line. In this manner a whole guard would be seduced from virtue, and put to silence by the fascination of high-top Yankee boots and pinchback watches. The commodities of trade on the Yankee side were articles of clothing which could ill be afforded, bone rings of prison manufacture, watches, chains, and jackknives, the last-named being temptations against which the most obdurate of Johnnies was not proof. Even a commissioned officer would condescend to chaffer and trade for a pair of boots or a jackknife. In return, we were the recipients of hoe-cake, wood to cook with, apples, and sometimes potatoes and tobacco. Occasionally officers from Richmond came into the prison, and traded for clothing, and were not too honest sometimes to walk off without paying for their purchases.

Goss was later exchanged, but became a prisoner again when the Union garrison of Plymouth, North Carolina, surrendered. This time Goss and his fellow prisoners were sent to Andersonville. His account of his arrival and the early days of his imprisonment in that fearsome place shows the callousness of the captors and the vicious disposition of camp commandant Henry Wirz as well as the tendency, which Goss had observed at Libby and Belle Isle, for men in extreme conditions to turn on each other. Yet at the same time, Goss suggests the inner resources by which the prisoners were able to cope and survive even in the squalor of Andersonville.

We arrived at Andersonville about four o'clock P.M., May 1, 1864. It was raining severely when the train reached the place. Even then we did not imagine to what kind of quarters we were to be consigned. The guard answered our interrogations as to where we were going to put up, by ironically pointing out some comfortable looking barracks as our habitations.

Suddenly the whole scene changed! A ferocious, round-shouldered little man, mounted upon a bay mare, surrounded by the guard who were to take the place of those who had accompanied us on the cars, came raving, swearing, and tearing round in a most extravagant manner. So ridiculous appeared to us his gestures, person, and looks, that we burst into a roar of laughter; whereupon he turned upon us, bristling with rage, exclaiming, "By Got! You tam Yankees; you won't laugh ven you gets into the pull pen." It was a gratuitous prophecy, afterwards understood in all its horrors; and the threats of Captain Wirz had too much significance in them to be laughed at. The recollection, even now, of the light manner we received so gross a monster, causes a shudder when I think what action our laugh might have prompted him to. I was selected out on account of my sergeant's uniform, when, asking me if I could write, I was furnished with paper, and told to take the names, regiment, and company of my car load of companions. When it was done, the names of some thirty more were given me, making in all ninety men, which was called "Detachment 21–30." The other prisoners were similarly divided, and placed under non-commissioned officers.

The new guard belonging to the station relieved the old one, and we were marched a short distance, where a curious-looking structure, fifteen feet high, loomed up before us. Sentries were stationed on the top of little platforms, scaffolded up near and at the height of the enclosure. This was the "Stockade," which was to become our future quarters. It was composed of the trunks of pine trees, which were set vertically into a trench, so close as to touch together, forming a close fence. In this manner about fifteen acres were fenced in. As we halted before the headquarters of the prison, waiting, like so many drowning rats, crouching in the rain, the guard, in answer to our questions as to what kind of a place it was inside the stockade, replied, we would find out when we got in there. They said prisoners tried to escape sometimes but the dogs always caught them. Never, to their knowledge, had a man escaped, except one, and he was drowned while trying to swim a pond to get clear of the dogs. This was a crusher to the idea I had formed that the stockade might prove a good place for an escape.

As we waited, the great gates of the prison swung on their ponderous oaken hinges, and we were ushered into what seemed to us Hades itself. Strange, skeleton men, in tattered, faded blue—and not much of blue either, so obscured with dirt were their habiliments—gathered and crowded around us; their faces were so begrimed with pitch-pine smoke and dirt, that for a while we could not discern whether they were negroes or white men. They gathered and crowded around us to ask the news, and inquire from whence we came; and in return we received the information that they had mostly come from Belle Island, when they were sent the 1st of March. The air of the prison seemed putrid; offal and filth covered the ground; and the hearts buoyed with expectation of good quarters, sank within them when they knew that no shelter was furnished beyond what could be constructed of blankets or garments. All my former experience of prison life had not prepared me for such unmitigated misery as met me everywhere. Our poor fellows, who had so confidingly believed in the humanity of rebels, were now depressed by despondency and gloomy forebodings, destined to be more than fulfilled. Of those of our company who that day entered these prison gates, not one third passed beyond them again, except to their pitiful, hastily-made, almost begrudged graves.

The prison at Andersonville was situated on two hill-sides, and through the centre ran a sluggish brook, or branch, as it was commonly termed. There were no signs of vegetation in the pen—it had all been trampled out. Our squads were ordered to take their positions near the hill-side, on the borders, and partially in a murky slough or swamp. This was between the brook, or branch, on the north side, and was used by the prisoners as a "sink," until it had become pestilent with a dreadful stench. Sadly thinking of home, and its dreadful contrast here, that night we lay down in the rain and dirt, on the filthy hill-side, to endeavor to get rest. But when sleep visited us, it was with an accompaniment of horrid dreams and fancies, more than realized in the horrors of the future, and familiar now, more or less, to the whole civilized world. With burdened hearts we realized how hard was our position. The first morning after our arrival about twenty pounds of bacon and a bushel of Indian meal was given me to distribute among ninety men. We had no wood to cook with, when two of my comrades, with myself, succeeded in buying six or seven small pieces for two dollars, and soon got some johnny-cake made. At our coming into the stockade there were about ten thousand prisoners, increased to about twelve thousand by our arrival. The next day three others with myself formed a mess together; and taking two of our blankets, constructed a temporary shelter from sun and rain, and thus settled down, experiencing the common life of hunger and privations of prisoners. We soon became conversant with the ways and means of the prison. There is a certain flexibility of character in men that adapts itself with readiness to their circumstances. This adaptability to inevitable, unalterable fate, against which it is useless to strive, or where it is death to repine, softens much of the sufferings otherwise unendurable in such a life. In no position is this adaptability more fruitful of good results to its possessor than in prison. It enables the luckless prisoner to extract whatever of comfort there may be in the barren species of existence which surrounds him, and mitigates the mental torments and pains endured by those who are suddenly thrown upon their own resources, amid the acutest sufferings which squalid misery can inflict. While some pass their time in useless repinings, others set themselves resolutely at work, like Robinson Crusoe, to develop the resources of their surroundings into all the comforts they can force them to yield.

Originally the interior of the prison had been densely wooded with pitch-pine, in which that country abounds; but at the time of our arrival it had been, with the exception of two trees, entirely cut to supply the want of fuel demanded by the prisoners. The camp at that time was dependent upon the roots and stumps of the trees which had been cut down for fuel. A limited number of those who were among the first arrivals had constructed rude shelters of the branches of trees, thatched with pitch-pine to shed the rain. The common shelter was, however, constructed with blankets, old shirts, &c., while a great number had no shelter at all, or burrowed for the want of one in the ground. An aristocratic shelter, which few could indulge in, was made of two blankets pinned together with wooden pegs, stretched upon a ridgepole running across two uprights stuck into the ground, in imitation of an A tent; or two poles were tied together, with both the ends stuck into the ground, forming a semicircle. Over three of these a blanket was stretched. A hole was then dug two or three feet deep under the space sheltered by the blankets. These, as a rebel surgeon one day remarked, were little better than graves. When there was a sudden shower, as was often the case, these holes would as suddenly fill with water, situated as most of them were on the side hill. All over camp men might be seen crawling out of holes like half-drowned kittens, wet, disconsolate, and crestfallen. Those who could summon the philosophy to laugh at the ludicrous view of their troubles, would find but little comfort in such uncomfortable circumstances. These shelters were, at best, but poor protection against rain or a tropical sun; but, as poor as they were, many who had blankets could not, though surrounded by woods on the exterior of the prison, get the necessary poles or branches to construct them. Under such circumstances the unlucky prisoner burrowed in the earth, or laid exposed to the fury of rain and sun, and often chilly nights and mornings.

The organization in camp for the issue of rations was as follows: The men were divided into squads of ninety, over which one of their own sergeants was placed. Over three nineties was also a chief sergeant, who drew rations for the whole. Every twenty-four hours these sergeants issued rations, which they drew at the gate from the prison authorities. The sergeants of nineties issued to sergeants of thirty or ten to suit convenience, and facilitate the distribution of rations. The rations were brought into camp by mule teams, driven by negroes, or, more commonly, by prisoners paroled and detailed for the purpose. A sergeant of ninety men was entitled to an extra ration for his trouble. I resigned, however, my position as sergeant of ninety before I had held it twenty-four hours, as I had foreseen that the position required a great deal of work, and I did not believe in taking an extra ration, which would not have benefited me. It was a task, however, which many among a multitude of hungry mouths were ready to take upon themselves, and but very few qualified to fill in an honorable, impartial manner. When men are cut down to very low rations, they are not always discriminating in attaching blame to the proper source, which made the place all the more difficult to fill with credit. This I early foresaw and, therefore, left the position to some one anxious to fill it.

During the first month of our imprisonment the rations were better than at any subsequent period, except wood, of which by chance we got none. Yet even at this time the rations were miserably inadequate to anything like a healthy organization. Our rations per day, during the first month, were a little over a pint of Indian meal, partly of cob ground with the meal, which was made into mush, and which we called by the appropriate name of chicken feed. Once in two days we got about a teaspoonful of salt. At first, bacon was issued in small quantities of fifteen to twenty pounds to ninety men, but, after the first of July, this was dropped almost entirely from prison rations. Sometimes, instead of Indian meal, we got rice or beans; but each bean had had an occupant in the shape of a grub or worm. Our modes of cooking were entirely primitive. The meal was stirred into water, making a thick dough; then a little meal was sprinkled on the bottom of a plate or half of a canteen, to keep the dough from sticking. The dough was then placed in a plate or canteen, which was set up at an angle of forty-five degrees, to be cooked before a fire. When the front of the cake was "done brown," the plate was fixed upon a split stick, and held over the coals until it was baked or burned upon the bottom. Our meal was sometimes sifted through a split half of a canteen, in which holes had been punched with a sixpenny nail. But even this coarse sieve left us so little of meal for food, it was gradually abandoned as impracticable. In sheer necessity of hunger, we sacrificed quality to quantity.

William N. Tyler Recalls Providence Spring[4]

The conditions in Andersonville were indeed hideous and drove some soldiers insane. Yet contrary to the claims of at least one modern scholar, many soldiers within the prison maintained not only their sanity but also their religious faith. Or perhaps that faith—or its Object—sustained them. Andersonville prisoner William Tyler later wrote about his experiences in the war's worst prison camp. One problem that the prisoners faced there was the lack of potable water, and thousands of men died from drinking contaminated water. In an account that is corroborated by other chroniclers, Tyler describes what happened.

We had some praying men at Andersonville. They held nightly prayer meetings, and they prayed for water. They prayed like men that meant business, for we were all dying for the want of it. One day after one of these meetings there occurred one of the most fearful rains I ever saw. It washed out the stockade as clean as a hound's tooth. Right between the dead-line and the stockade it washed a ditch about two feet deep and a spring of cold water broke out in a stream large enough to fill a four-inch pipe. The spring is there yet, I am told, and to this day is called Providence spring. It broke out in the very best place it could for our benefit. The stockade protected it on one side from the Rebels, and the dead-line on the other side protected it from the prisoners. The fountain head was thus protected. We had good water from then on.[5]

Reid Mitchell on the "Savage Society"[6]

One of the themes developed by Reid Mitchell in *Civil War Soldiers* (1988) is that the men on each side marched off to war convinced that their foes were barbarians and savages. The thought was a particularly unpleasant one for the soldier who found himself suddenly in the hands of the "savages" as a prisoner of war.

Encounters with the enemy in battle were violent and deadly. Encountering them as captors or prisoners passing to the rear could be pleasant; it gave the soldier a chance to investigate their side or at least to confirm his old prejudices. The most obvious way of coming into contact with the enemy's army and the enemy's society was incarceration as a prisoner of war. The death rate of military prisoners during the Civil War was so high that being in prison was as deadly as being in battle. The enemy authorities controlled one's life far more than they did in battle, far more than one's own military superiors did in camp. The soldier's resistance to their control was rarely bloody and decisive; more likely he resisted much as slaves or industrial workers resisted—day-to-day, in small ways that maintained one's self-respect. In the end, mere survival may have been the greatest resistance of all.

During the war both the Union and Confederate armies took large numbers of prisoners. Some were exchanged; others were incarcerated. Nobody foresaw at the war's beginning that the demand for military prisons would be so great. The North converted military camps, barracks, and forts into prisons. Johnson's Island was perhaps the most well-known Northern prison. The South converted existing buildings into prisons—Libby Prison in Richmond was an old tobacco warehouse—and built makeshift enclosures, such as Andersonville. The demands for supplies and personnel placed upon these prison networks was very great, and while both sides tried to meet them, prisons were hardly the first priority. As the Confederate supply system broke down, its prisoners particularly suffered from lack of food, clothing, and shelter.

Soldiers, finding themselves at the mercy of the enemy, often complained of mistreatment. Food was poor, shelter insufficient, guards brutal. Men who had gone to war convinced of their enemy's barbarism were not surprised to find it exhibited in prison. Confederate Capt. W. P. Harper felt himself abused by the Yankees. When he and his fellow prisoners from the Virginia front passed through Baltimore in November 1863, they were kept overnight in an open yard surrounded by a forty-foot-high wall. Without shelter, the men had to lie out all night on the bricks. Harper could not sleep, and he "caught a dreadful cold." Before the war their jail had been "an old negro traders establishment"—the irony was lost on Captain Harper.

Once confined, prisoners frequently did suffer from abusive treatment, although less as a result of systematic enemy policy than of individual acts of cruelty, overzealousness, or fear. For example, a North Carolina soldier at Point Lookout recorded instances of guards shooting prisoners for "peepin threw the cracks of the plankin" of the fence, for crowding around the gate, and for "jawing" a Yankee sergeant.

This North Carolinian was both amused and disgusted by the black guards placed over them. He claimed a black guard "shot one of our men and kild him for no cause attall"; he also witnessed two black soldiers clowning around until one accidentally shot the other dead. Confederates often regarded the mere existence of black guards as Yankee humiliation and cruelty.

Prisoners commonly claimed that guards who had never actually fought in battle—and were therefore likely cowards and certainly men who could not appreciate the character of the soldiers they guarded—were particularly prone to brutality. One prisoner at Johnson's Island rejoiced when he heard that their guards, who were being sent to the front for the first time, would be relieved by "old soldiers." "From soldiers who fight us in the field, better treatment is expected." His expectations were met. In some ways, actually fighting rebels or Yankees was a prerequisite for respecting them.

Ill-treatment also included poor food. At Point Lookout the prisoners sometimes ate rats to supplement their diet. One Confederate, kept in a prison near Charleston, complained of being fed only one-half pint of soup and one-half pint of mush a day, and of being denied salt. It struck him as a particular sign of pettiness for "a great nation" to refuse its dependents salt. Francis Boyle, a prisoner at Point Lookout and Fort Delaware, advanced an explanation for the short rations there that expressed a common Southern opinion about the North. The insufficiency of food was due less to deliberate cruelty, in his opinion, than it was to Yankee greed and corruption. At Point Lookout the authorities denied the prisoners, first, coffee and sugar, then molasses; at the same time they reduced the meat ration and shrank the size of the bread loaves issued. Upon arrival at Fort Delaware, Boyle estimated the daily ration to be about six ounces of meat and four ounces of bread per man—"and the government no doubt charged full rations—What a harvest for somebody!"

Boyle's confidence in "Yankee cupidity" persuaded him that when the prison sutler was forbidden to sell food to the inmates the restriction would somehow be gotten around. True to his prediction, while the War Department's order was in effect, the sutler began "selling us eatables and other contraband articles and charging us extra prices for the risk!!!!" When another Confederate prisoner learned that his brother had not received several letters in which he asked for various items, he decided that the prison authorities had intercepted the requests so that he would be forced to buy from the sutler.

Soldiers found cupidity and corruption to be general in the enemy prisons. At Johnson's Island, for example, a prisoner tried to bribe a guard in order to escape. "At the time appointed, the sentinel appeared, assisted him over the fence, received the bribe—a gold watch and some three hundred dollars—and delivered him over to the officer of the guard who put him in a cell." The Confederates concluded that the soldier and the officer split the money; it was a typical Yankee trick. On the other hand, a Union captain in prison near Columbia, South Carolina, was highly offended because the rebel authorities traded Confederate dollars for Yankee greenbacks at an exorbitant rate. "The Reb Government has thus ascended to the dignity of money brokers."

Unfortunately, it was not simply the malice of the guards or the policy of the enemy government that made prison life so horrible. Soldiers suffered from the conduct of their fellow prisoners. The Confederacy's Andersonville prison was the most spectacular example of this, but violence and theft by inmates disgraced many Civil War prisoners. Prisoners trying to maintain life and decency might find themselves plagued by thieves. For example, at Belle Island in Virginia some Union prisoners bought a barrel of flour; the next day "a Mob rushed about the camp & upset & stole all the flour in camp."

Benton McAdams on the Union Prison at Rock Island[7]

Several Northern prisons gained unenviable reputations for the high death rates among their inmates and for the misery of those who survived. One such was the prison at Rock Island, Illinois, often referred to as "the Andersonville of the North." The label was unfair, both in comparison with other Northern POW camps and with the real Andersonville. Modern historian Benton McAdams places the mortality rate for Rock Island at about 16 percent, comparable to the other Northern prisons except for Elmira, New York, where mortality was 24 percent. By the same method of estimating, however, the death rate at Andersonville was greater than 30 percent.[8] Still, Rock Island's legacy was sealed when fiction writer Margaret Mitchell made it the scene of the wartime suffering of her character Ashley Wilkes in *Gone With the Wind* (1936).

And there was plenty of suffering at Rock Island, whatever the death rate. In this passage from *Rebels at Rock Island* (2000), McAdams explains the circumstances of that suffering and the main reasons for the camp's 16 percent death rate: a sudden massive influx of prisoners, some of whom were already infected with smallpox; and one of the coldest winters ever experienced in northern Illinois.

On 3 December 1863 [*Rock Island Argus** editor John B.] Danforth reported: "A train of cars containing Rebel prisoners is expected to arrive at our depot between 4.30 and 5.30 this after-

---

*Argus was a Copperhead, or a Northern sympathizer with the Southern cause.—Editor's note

noon. They are probably a portion of the prisoners recently taken at Chattanooga, and others will doubtless follow every few days . . . until the Barracks are full."

Danforth was right. On 24 and 25 November the armies of Ulysses Grant had swept Braxton Bragg's Army of Tennessee from the mountains around Chattanooga in the battles of Lookout Mountain and Missionary Ridge. In the process Grant's men had scooped up more than 6,000 prisoners, 5,000 of whom were on their way to the River Bend [that is, Rock Island]. They went by train, generally passing through Nashville and Louisville, on to Indianapolis, Chicago, and Rock Island.

The train actually arrived about four in the afternoon. On board were 466 men from Lookout Mountain, including James Reeves and most of the 34th Mississippi. The prisoners detrained and the citizens stood around gawking, thanks to Danforth's notice of the arrival time. The guards began the laborious process of searching and registering the Rebels. This entailed calling each man four paces to the front so provost guards could relieve him of contraband. An officer serving as the commissary of prisoners recorded the man's name and assigned him to a barracks. A noncommissioned officer and two privates from the guard were assigned to watch over each company. The prisoners were then marched through the gates into the compound, to officially become Rock Island's first prisoners. Once inside, they remained in ranks while the provost marshal read them the prison regulations. Although not stipulated in the rules, some prisoners mentioned that they were searched a second time. Finally, they were released to their quarters. Rock Island Barracks was in business.

Those first prisoners walked into a facility utterly unprepared for them. When [U.S. Commissary General of Prisoners William] Hoffman notified Commandant [Richard H.] Rush that prisoners were on the way, Rush had replied with one of his frenzied telegrams: "Not ready for any prisoners yet. No quartermasters [on] property. Not half enough garrison, no books, blanks, rolls, etc." A week later, when the prisoners were actually on the cars rolling toward the Island, Rush sent another telegram: "Yours rec'd. Will do what I can for the 5000 prisoners expected. No water yet in prison yard except one well at west end. Steam forcing engine not yet ready. Weather extremely cold. No Rebel clothing, blankets, etc. etc. on hand."

Two days later Richard Henry Rush turned command over to
A. J. Johnson. Hoffman told Johnson [that] prisoners were coming
"as fast as the facilities of the railroad will permit." And that was too
fast. Two days after the first prisoners arrived, another 830 men
came in; on 9 December, another 1,300; on 11 December, 1,000.
Almost all these men were from the battles around Chattanooga.
Danforth reported that the prisoners were "generally healthy, clean
and good-looking men," but [editor of the *Davenport (Iowa) Union*
Myron] Barnes said they were "dirty, ragged, careworn looking
objects of pity." Federal General Alpheus Williams agreed with
Barnes. Williams, stationed in Tullahoma, Tennessee, observed the
endless trains full of Chattanooga prisoners wending their way toward Illinois and commented: "We have had for a week past a continuous run of Reb. Prisoners, long lines of railroad trains crammed
with them. . . . They are a hard-looking lot of men without over-
coats and very short of dirty blankets, marked generally 'U.S.' showing that what they have are taken or stolen from us. . . . But you
should see this 'chivalry' to appreciate it. A more dirty, destitute,
and diabolical lot of humanities cannot be conceived."

The long trip north did nothing for the appearance or health of
the diabolical humanities. Crammed into the cars for days without
adequate food or water, they suffered weather that grew progres-
sively colder as the trains rolled north. Added to this was the
sometimes harsh treatment of the guards. A. J. Cantrell of the
16th Tennessee later remembered that as the train traveled along
the shore of Lake Michigan "the prisoners asked the Federal guards
to open the doors, so they could see the lake. They soon saw enough,
as they were thinly clad, and the cold and icy wind chilled them
quickly; so they begged the guards to shut the doors . . . but this was
refused. The prisoners then resorted to boxing and piling on each
other, like boys, to keep from freezing." Another prisoner, W. C.
Dodson, reported that during the trip to the Island the guards "displayed their bravery by forcing us to lie flat on the bottom of box
cars, threatening to shoot the first man who raised his hand or head."
The conditions in the cars grew so bad that Hoffman berated the
quartermasters: "The fact is that in transferring prisoners of war
from place to place on railroads the arrangements are often so care-
lessly made or so badly carried out that much delay and much embarrassment are experienced." Hoffman demanded better
arrangements. Although his primary motives were keeping to sched-

ules and preventing escapes, he also required that "a vessel of water of proper size be placed in each car."

Such privations were the norm for prisoners going to any prison camp; however, going to Rock Island was the worst trip of all, because it was the longest trip of all. In the winter of 1863 no prison was farther from the front than the Barracks. Indeed James Reeves and his friends passed within miles of both Camp Morton in Indianapolis and Camp Douglas in Chicago. But those camps were crowded and Rock Island empty, and although Hoffman did consider sending newly captured prisoners to Camp Douglas, and Douglas prisoners to Rock Island, in the end he did not do so. Reshuffling prisoners to spare them an extra day on the cars was a nicety that events did not afford.

While he may have maintained his position that the men were good looking, Danforth quickly revised his opinion of their health. He had little choice—the evidence rolled through town daily. On 8 December he noted that the arriving prisoners had had "scarcely anything to eat, from the time they left Louisville, (Tuesday morning) until their arrival at Joliet, Thursday morning." After considering the matter for a few days, J. B. told his readers that the prisoners "have been accustomed to a milder climate than this; they have suffered much in the service of the Rebel government, and . . . then to be taken prisoners and placed in box cars and transported to this northern region . . . without being allowed to leave the car, and without regular supplies of water and food, is as much as a well man could endure. The result is that very many are now on the sick list, and hundreds more will follow."

Once inside the compound, the prisoners faced new problems. They had been on short rations for months, and as one of the guards, F. A. Jennings, observed: "I tell you they pitch into the hard tack. It takes two to make a shadow." In addition to hearty appetites and stolen blankets, the Rebels brought with them a host of ailments, most prominently pneumonia and diarrhea. A few weeks before, these prisoners had battled men in blue uniforms; now they would battle disease. Moreover, the disease had an extremely powerful ally: the weather. The first prisoners who arrived at the Barracks had been lucky. The weather in the River Bend proved mild for a few days in early December 1863, with temperatures as high as 60 degrees. This was merely a lull, however; a record-breaking winter had already begun.

It had actually begun on 29 August. As J. B. reported, "[V]ery thin ice was discovered on some boards near the railroad track." Both of the following nights hard frosts struck the Midwest, doing "immense damage to the growing crops. On all the low lands the corn is killed outright." The frost extended as far south as Louisville, Kentucky. The frost was only a harbinger; a week later a few flakes of snow fell in the River Bend, and on 22 October two inches blanketed the ground. The thermometer plunged, and before December the [Mississippi] river froze at the head of the rapids. . . .

By 18 December ice closed the river completely, and three days later teams pulling sleighs could cross to the Island. On 29 December an historic storm descended on the Midwest. It began with rain, a steady drizzle that continued for 48 hours. Then the thermometer began to fall and the rain changed to snow. The wind turned to the northwest and howled through the Barracks and the city. The snow fell through New Year's; the temperature dropped to twenty degrees below zero. It was unprecedented. *Harper's Weekly* reported, "[T]he Western newspapers come to us full of the most thrilling accounts of the recent great snow storm in the West, which covered an area of three thousand miles, and was of unparalleled severity." Schools in the River Bend closed for two weeks; trains stopped running; for days the high temperature remained far below zero.

Inside the barracks, the temperature was warmer, but not much. The compound sat on the riverbank, exposed to the full effect of screaming winter winds that quite literally whipped through the barracks. In constructing his "mere shanties," Captain [Charles A.] Reynolds had used green lumber, which shrank as time went on. Men huddled around the stoves in vain attempts to keep warm. According to prison diarist William Dillon of the 4th Tennessee, water froze only five feet from the stoves. Frostbitten ears and feet became commonplace. Fortunately, Johnson never rationed coal; the prisoners could burn all they wanted day and night. In fact, when the blizzard made it impossible for him to hire teams to haul coal, Johnson sent troops into town and impressed eleven teams so he could keep his prisoners from freezing. Another problem was a lack of blankets and bedding straw. One of the first inspectors to arrive at the prison echoed Rush's earlier statement: "Blankets and bedding . . . not sufficient—supplies for which requisitions have been made, expected daily." Louisianian J. W. Minnich said that during his entire time on the Island he saw no straw but "only bare bunks, unless someone gathered leaves." Still, being inside was better than being outside, and despite the weather the men had to go out, to use the privies and to collect their rations, a job that could take as long as an hour. Lafayette Rogan of the 34th Mississippi, another prisoner who kept a diary, noted that getting rations "was a cold job . . . some of the detail cried with the pain produced by the cold."

Notes

1. William Best Hesseltine, *Civil War Prisoners: A Study in War Psychology* (New York: Frederick Ungar, 1930), 172–77.

2. James M. McPherson, *Battle Cry of Freedom: The Civil War Era* (New York: Oxford University Press, 1988), 791–802. © 1988 by Oxford University Press. Reprinted by permission of Oxford University Press.

3. Warren Lee Goss, *The Soldier's Story of His Captivity at Andersonville, Belle Isle, and Other Rebel Prisons* (Boston: I. N. Richardson, 1873), 26–34, 71–79.

4. William N. Tyler, *Memoirs of Andersonville* (Bernalillo, NM: Joel Beer & Gwendy MacMaster, 1992), 19–20.

5. This story is corroborated by the William A. Miller Reminiscences, Civil War Miscellaneous Collection, USAMHI. Remarkably, Gerald F. Linderman asserts that at Andersonville, "Religious sensibility seemed almost to disappear . . . and prayer diminished." *Embattled Courage: The Experience of Combat in the American Civil War* (New York: Free Press, 1987), 259.

6. Reid Mitchell, *Civil War Soldiers* (New York: Viking, 1988), 44–50. © 1988 by Reid Mitchell. Reprinted by permission of Viking Penguin, a division of Penguin Putnam.

7. Benton McAdams, *Rebels at Rock Island: The Story of a Civil War Prison* (De Kalb: Northern Illinois University Press, 2000), 34–36, 45–46. © 2000 by Northern Illinois University Press. Reprinted by permission of Northern Illinois University Press.

8. Ibid., xi.

CHAPTER SIX

In Camp and on the March

The soldier's life was not entirely composed of the horrors of battle, hospital, and prison. By far the greatest portion of his time in the army would be occupied in the relatively mundane activities of the camp and the march. There his concerns centered on keeping warm and dry, getting enough food (preferably appetizing food), and communicating with his friends and family back home by sending and receiving letters.

Food was a subject that never seemed to be far from the soldier's thoughts. Active young men could consume a great deal of it, and the Civil War soldiers devoted considerable effort to getting more and better victuals. This effort was especially important for Confederate soldiers, whose government did not do a very good job of feeding them. Ironically, the one area of economic life in which the South excelled was agriculture, and, indeed, foodstuffs remained abundant throughout most of the region right up to the end of the war. That the gray-clad soldiers did not eat better was the result of poor transportation facilities as well as the unwise policies of the Confederate government in fixing prices at which it would purchase foodstuffs rather than buy them on the open market. Since the same government was financing the war largely by printing money, thereby generating massive inflation, the fixed prices were unrealistic. As is the case when the price of any commodity is set below market value, the result was scarcity. The Confederate government generally could not supply its soldiers with full rations even though plenty of food could be found in the South. Typical Confederate rations might include corn pone and bacon, pork, or beef, if available.

By contrast, Northern soldiers were probably the best fed in the history of warfare up to that time. The North had plenty of farms and packinghouses as well as the railroads to carry what it produced. The standard U.S. ration would have been enough to fatten a man except during times of the most vigorous and sustained marching. That Union soldiers did not grow stout was the result of two factors: the exigencies of operations often kept them from receiving their officially allotted rations; and the rations themselves, though plentiful, were of low quality and unappealing. The chief components were salt pork (also known as side meat or sowbelly), and hardtack. The latter was made of flour, water, and salt, cooked and aged to approximately the consistency of armor plate. Soldiers devised various expedients for rendering these items more palatable. A favorite preparation involved pounding the hardtack to crumbs with a rifle butt and then frying it with pork grease. Not surprisingly, bowel complaints were common. As for coffee, the soldiers drank it with sugar at a rate of a quart or more per man per day; they munched it in the bean if they did not have time to build fires and brew it.

Soldiers of both sides added liberally to the monotonous diet provided by their governments. Northern soldiers might make purchases from the sutler, a civilian merchant who had a concession for trade in each regiment, but the men complained that the sutler's goods were inferior and his prices outrageous. Sometimes no sutler was present; sometimes no money was in pocket. Otherwise the chief means of expanding the diet was by foraging. (In peacetime, foraging was known as stealing.) In the enemy's country, it was relatively easy to deal with the moral questions raised by this practice. Lee's hungry troops foraged cheerfully during their June and July 1863 excursion into Pennsylvania, and Union troops did the same in their war-long progress through the South. Officers might approve or not—the soldiers were not to be thwarted. Pigs encountered in the South almost inevitably turned out to be stubborn Rebels steadfastly refusing to take the Oath of Allegiance when called upon to do so by Federal soldiers, who then, of course, could see no choice but to bayonet the defiant porkers.

Such practices were much harder to justify when directed toward one's own people, and yet hunger and a boring diet being what they were, some soldiers did steal from friendly civilians. John G. Given, a twenty-year-old recruit in the 124th Illinois, wrote to his brother from Camp Butler, near Springfield, where that regiment was being organized: "Stealing is the occupation of a great many of the soldiers, and the country within a mile of camp is almost destitute of anything that could be appropriated to the use of the soldiers." The corn in a large field near the camp had, Given vouchsafed, "all been pressed into the service of the U.S. or rather it has been pressed into those who are serving the U.S. for the soldiers have paid so many nocturnal [visits] to it that when the owner goes to husk it he'll find it missing." Given had to confess that he too was guilty, having taken some hay from a nearby field in order to make a bed for himself, and his conscience was not easy about it. "If we were among the secesh I would glory in stealing every thing they had," he explained, "but I don't like to steal from those who are loyal to the Union."[1]

Like Given, many Civil War soldiers had to give thought not only to how they might fill their bellies but also to how they might sleep warm and tolerably dry. The government usually supplied a tent of some sort—the familiar wedge-tent, or the tall, conical Sibley tent, which could accommodate a dozen men and a portable stove. Far more often, however, it was the two-man shelter, the ubiquitous "pup tent." This practical but unbeloved equipment involved two sheets of cotton duck, their edges variously provided with buttons and buttonholes. Each man carried one, and two comrades buttoned these "shelter-halves" together at night to make a tent, rigged up with whatever sticks they could scrounge for tent poles. Sometimes a third man would join them, his shelter-half being buttoned in on one end to provide more cover for what was by then a crowded sleeping space. In any case, the floor of the tent was the bare ground, unless the soldier had a poncho or oilcloth blanket to spread under him. Those who did not, like John Given, helped themselves to some unfortunate farmer's straw or hay.

The quest for better food and shelter, consuming as it might be, nevertheless left soldiers with abundant time on their hands. In this war as in others, the soldier's life consisted of long periods of intense boredom punctuated by brief periods of stark terror. Drill was part of the routine, but even a hard-driving regimental commander rarely drilled his men more than six hours per day. Guarding and maintaining the camp took additional time, but usually the soldiers were left at loose ends for a few hours each day. Some gambled. Cards were the most popular game of chance, but men might bet on anything. Games like checkers or backgammon might or might not be betting matters. Soldiers might also play, though rarely for gambling purposes, mumblety-peg, a contest of accuracy in throwing pocketknives; or "slap-jackets," an absurd game in which two contestants locked left arms and switched each other's backs with their right. Baseball was a new sport that grew rapidly in popularity in the army camps. Its origins are obscure, but it was not invented by Union Gen. Abner Doubleday.

A large segment of the soldiers on both sides—at least as many as indulged in gambling—took part in religious services. Observers would later speak of fervent "revivals" in the camps, but the movement was so widespread as to be almost a single continuous revival, from late 1862 to the end of the war, punctuated by the interruptions caused by combat operations. Preaching services, prayer meetings, and "experience" meetings (in which individuals told of how God had changed their lives) were numerous and well attended.

Another way to beguile the time in camp was reading, and by far the favorite reading material was letters from home. The soldiers' appetite for these was insatiable and universal, and their own correspondence is filled with scoldings and pleadings for friends and family to write longer and more frequent letters. No detail of home life could be too mundane, no excess of wordiness could tire these bored and homesick men, and letters were reread until they fell apart. Many men read the Bible or religious tracts, which were distributed in large numbers by religious organizations with the approval of army authorities. Others read law, literature, or trashy dime novels.

Abner R. Small on Desiccated Vegetables[2]

The 16th Maine's Abner Small often took a wry tone in detailing the habits and conditions of himself and his fellow soldiers during the war. Here he describes one of the few elements of variety in the otherwise monotonous diet of the Union soldier. Basic rations were hardtack and salt pork with beans if the men were lucky. These staples, however, contained little Vitamin C, and soldiers who ate nothing else would become vulnerable to the disease of scurvy. The Union army tried various ways of getting some sort of vegetable ration to the troops as an antiscorbutic, or preventative of scurvy. One solution was a forerunner of the modern army's MREs (meals ready to eat), desiccated vegetables.

Too many beans with salt junk [salt pork] demanded an antiscorbutic, so the government advertised proposals for some kind of vegetable compound in portable form, and it came—tons of it—in sheets liked pressed hops. I suppose it was healthful, for there was variety enough in its composition to satisfy any condition of stomach and bowels. What in Heaven's name it was composed of, none of us ever discovered. It was called simply "desiccated vegetables." Ben once brought in just before dinner a piece with a big horn button on it, and wanted to know "if dat 'ere was celery or cabbage?" I doubt our men have ever forgotten how a cook would break off a piece as large as a boot top, put it in a kettle of water, and stir it with the handle of a hospital broom. When the stuff was fully dissolved, the water would remind one of a dirty brook with all the dead leaves floating around promiscuously. Still, it was a substitute for food. We ate it, and we liked it, too.

Robert H. Strong on Desiccated Vegetables[3]
Union soldier Robert H. Strong also had memories of this strange concoction. Like Small, Strong found it surprisingly good.

At times we drew what was called desiccated vegetables. This was a composition of everything in the vegetable world—peas, beans, cabbage, turnips, carrots, peppers, onions, beets, radishes, parsnips, parsley—with grass to hold it all together. This mixture was dried and pressed into pieces an inch square. One of these pieces, put in water, would swell and swell, then swell some more, until no one man could eat it all. We made soup of it. It doesn't sound very palatable, but after a regular diet of hard tack, a change to vegetable soup was not to be despised.

Bell I. Wiley on Union Rations[4]
At his best when describing the everyday circumstances of the lives of the common soldiers, here Bell Wiley discusses the diet of the Union troops.

The daily allowance for each Union soldier was . . . about one fifth more than that of the British Army, almost twice that of the French, and compared even more favorably with that of the Prussians, Austrians and Russians. It was also more liberal than the official diet of Confederates. The Southerners, after hopefully adopting the old army ration early in the conflict, were forced repeatedly to cut it, while the Federals in August 1861 effected a substantial increase. Surgeon General [William A.] Hammond was on firm ground when he boasted after this augmentation that the men in blue had the most abundant food allowance of any soldiers in the world.

Indeed, Union subsistence authorities were to conclude after long experience that the issue was overly generous to the point of encouraging waste. On their recommendation Congress in June 1864 revoked the increase, but a provision was retained which allowed substitution of fresh or processed vegetables for other items in the ration.

Throughout the conflict, regulations permitted company commanders to sell back to the subsistence department any portion of the authorized ration not used by their men, the money thus obtained to become a part of the company fund. It was the intent of higher authorities that company commanders use the money accumulated for supplying their men with items not obtainable from commissaries and thus add variety to camp fare. But it seems that this wisely conceived aim rarely materialized in actual practice. Some captains did not know about the company fund; others did not want to be bothered with administering it; and still others appropriated it to their own use. One Yank of unusual intelligence and broad experience wrote after the war: "I have yet to learn of the first company whose members ever received any revenue from such a source, although the name of *Company Fund* is a familiar one to every veteran."

The specification of abundant fare by high authorities did not necessarily mean that the rank and file were consistently well fed. Far from it. Reports of officers and comments of soldiers reveal the greatest variation in the quantity of food actually made available to the men who did the shooting. As one lowly consumer aptly put it early in the war: "Some days we live first rate, and the next we dont have half enough."

Almost every regiment suffered occasional periods of hunger, though usually these did not last more than a few days. But the course of the war was marked by a surprising number of what might be called major food crises, when deprivation extended over a considerable period and involved large numbers of men. . . .

Several factors contributed to the food shortages experienced by the men in blue. Fare was often scant in the early part of the war because officers responsible for drawing and issuing rations were not fully acquainted with army procedure. Failure of supply agencies to have the necessary stocks at the right places at the right time also led to instances of want. This appears to have been the situation at Savannah during Sherman's sojourn in that city. An officer of the Inspector General's Department reported in February 1865: "There was an inexcusable neglect or delay in furnishing rations to the army. . . . Up to the time of leaving Savannah the QM [Quartermaster] & Commissary Depts failed most signally to supply this command with necessary subsistence. The men actually suffered.". . .

Shortages were most common during periods of rapid movement and active fighting. When intensive campaigns were in progress, or when the fortunes of war closed channels of supply, as at Chattanooga, reduced fare was unavoidable. But sometimes soldiers brought hunger upon themselves by the improvident practice of consuming several days' rations shortly after their issue.

Yanks frequently attributed their meager fare to corrupt officers, and unquestionably some of those involved in the procurement and distribution of food were dishonest. It is improbable, however, that peculation was nearly so prevalent as the soldiers charged.

Two specific instances clearly demonstrate how selfishness, indifference and lethargy on the part of officers sometimes caused the enlisted men to receive less than their due allowance of food. In the second winter of the war a scurvy threat occurred in the Army of the Cumberland. [General William S.] Rosecrans was perplexed, since the commissary records indicated an issue of 100 barrels of vegetables daily in his command, and he had taken it for granted that this food was being consumed by the soldiers. But on investigation he was shocked to discover "that one fourth in amount of this issue went to the staff officers and their families at Head-Quarters, and that of the remaining three-fourths, the Commissaries of the various Corps, Divisions and Brigades obtained the larger portions, so that the Regimental Commissaries who supplied the wants of the private soldiers were left almost unprovided." Further inquiry by medical authorities "revealed the extraordinary fact that although this very liberal daily distribution was shown by the books

... still the soldiers had not received on an average from the Government more than three rations of vegetables during the twelve months ending on the first of April, 1863."

A similar instance occurred in the latter part of 1864 in the District of West Florida. There an investigation, inspired by appearance of scurvy, revealed that while officers were purchasing fresh vegetables and other choice items liberally for themselves they were not having comparable distribution made to the men. The table of returns for September showed that of 10,658 pounds of potatoes received by the Commissary Department the 250 officers received 1,850 pounds while only 165 pounds were issued to the 3,850 men; of 1,324 gallons of pickles, officers drew 190 gallons and the men 162 gallons; issues from a stock of 14,249 pounds of dried apples were 1,749 to officers and none to the men. The figures on whisky are especially interesting: From a store of 2,345 gallons the officers obtained 434 gallons and the men (who could not purchase commissary liquors as the officers but had to depend on commanders to order its issue as part of the ration) drew only 162 gallons; in other words, officers obtained on the average one and seven-tenths gallons of whisky each during the month, and the men forty-two one-thousandths!

The culpability of these officers was noted in Washington, a high-level staff member writing on a report forwarded from department headquarters: "The officers seem to have been most negligent of their men. . . . They seem to have appropriated the major portion of everything to their own use and let the men get along the best they could." Whether or not these or the officers involved in the Army of the Cumberland affair were disciplined is not known.

The dietary deficiencies suffered by troops in West Florida in 1864 were due to failures of distribution. The same could be said of food shortages in general. Uncle Sam had at his command enough food to provide amply for all who wore the blue. The fact that soldiers were sometimes hungry was due to his inability always to make it available to them when they needed it.

Billy Yank was not solely dependent on Uncle Sam for his subsistence. His army rations were often supplemented by the homefolk. Soldier letters reveal a considerable flow of boxes, packed with all sorts of food, originating in every loyal state and extending to all areas where Federal troops were encamped. The most active channels of home-to-soldier supply were from Northeastern communities to the Army of the Potomac and from the Midwest to troops stationed along the Mississippi River and its tributaries. Rough handling along the way frequently jumbled contents of these shipments, but damaged boxes were better than none at all. Experience led to improvements in packing and recipients became experts at salvage. . . .

The Sanitary Commission and other volunteer organizations also distributed food from time to time. During the scurvy scare in Rosecrans' command early in 1863, the Sanitary Commission made available a vast quantity of vegetables, and in February 1865 Rebecca Usher, representing the Maine State Agency at City Point, Virginia, reported receipt of twenty-eight barrels of vegetables for Maine soldiers. "The soldiers roasted potatoes all day in the ashes in the reading room," she wrote. "The soldiers come in and ask for a potato as if it was an article of the greatest luxury." She also told of giving out mince pies, apples, sauerkraut and other items that must have brought delight to the recipients.

Sutlers also helped relieve the scantiness and monotony of camp fare, but their cakes, pies, butter, cheese, apples and other delicacies were offered at prices which frequently placed them beyond the reach of the common soldier. Yanks often complained that sutlers were never around except for brief intervals following payday.

The food venders most often patronized by the soldiers seem to have been native peddlers who, as season, location and other circumstances permitted, went through the camps selling pies, bread, butter, milk, fruit, vegetables, watermelons and oysters. A Yank wrote from Savannah, Georgia, in January 1865: "The Negroes are selling all the oysters they can get to our men. The soldier takes the tin cup and dips it into the tub or bucket of oysters, fills it full and then drinks the oysters as if he was drinking water." . . .

Yanks occasionally supplemented their fare by eating at Southern tables. Sometimes they were fed without charge and again they dined as paying guests. Negroes, in view of their friendlier attitude toward the invaders, played host far more frequently than whites. The meals served in Negroes' cabins were normally simple, consisting usually of such items as hoecake, corn bread, field peas, sweet potatoes and turnip greens, and now and then a piece of pork. Sometimes the visitors brought with them flour, sugar, meat and other ingredients not easily obtainable by civilians. Whatever the nature of the meal thus obtained, it afforded relief from camp offerings and was consumed with relish.

John C. Reed on the Plague of "Greybacks"[5]

When Civil War soldiers in later years wrote about their wartime experiences, they were generally willing to describe, often with wry humor, many of the mundane aspects of military life that were unpleasant, disgusting, and even humiliating. Here former Confederate officer John Reed writes about the universal problem of "greybacks," or lice.

I will devote a few pages to a feature of the war which, so far as I know, has been overlooked by both northern and southern writers. The subject is usually regarded as disgusting, and so I shall fastidiously abstain from airing the gross and hateful name which it bears.

For several days shortly after we arrived on the lines near Yorktown [Virginia, in the spring of 1862], I had been now and then tormented by an itching. As I had heard that some of the most careless men in the regiment were afflicted with vermin, one day when the itching returned while I was on duty I attempted to recall if I had of late come in close contact with these men, but I could not. At last I retired to an obscure place, and horror of horrors! when I searched, I found. For the time, I felt as if I had been convicted of misbehavior in front of the enemy. I should have died if I had not found comforting sympathy. Jim Burch, a friend of mine in the 15th Georgia, in [Robert A.] Toombs's brigade, told me that his colonel had endured the same affliction for several weeks. As the colonel was the utmost of neatness and cleanliness, very brave, agreeable, and popular, I was somewhat consoled. Everybody was plagued and everybody for a while tried to keep his secret. One morning just after our march to Richmond was ended, Sergeant Harrison, of company K, was sitting on the ground in a field of wheat, the grown but unripe stalks rising above his head. He was busily inspecting his shirt which he held on his knees, and his white back contrasted prettily with the green around him. His back was spotted with welts. He had forgotten the path which ran over the hill behind him, and, as I was passing along it, a member of his company just ahead of me espied him, and cried, "Hallo, Harrison, what luck with your fishing." Harrison tried to conceal himself beneath the wheat, and with bashful shame he said that he had caught nothing. "The devil you haven't, with so many bites," was answered.

We had ample time to study the creatures, and we became so familiar with them that we often compared notes with one another. I have time to tell only of one of their peculiarities which is greatly to their credit. They loved the clean. As soon as one of the mess changed his clothes, they deserted all the others and concentrated on him. At last it became our established custom for the entire mess to put on clean clothes at the same time.

Just after the Wilderness—I think it was the 8th of May, 1864— [James] Longstreet's corps was marching to confront Grant's new position at Spotsylvania C[ourt] H[ouse], and we had just loaded and were expecting to fight immediately, when I heard a member of the company complain of a greyback, as was the jocular name then in vogue, saying, "He is biting me just behind my knapsack. He knows that I cannot stop now to get at him; and this is a most unfair advantage that the cowardly sneak is taking of a brave soldier."

It was some comfort to us to know that the federal soldiers had no immunity from the plague. The greybacks were like the bush-whackers of East Tennessee, who fought both sides during the whole of the war.

At the last I began to see that there is a physiological justification of these parasites. It is, that they make soldiers boil their clothes often; for this is the only deliverance from them.

John D. Billings on the Most Disagreeable Work Detail[6]

During the 1880s, Union veteran John Billings became aware that the generation that had grown up since the conflict knew nothing of the mundane, everyday aspects of Civil War army life. To help remedy that situation, he wrote *Hardtack and Coffee: The Unwritten Story of Army Life*, relating his observations as a member of the 10th Massachusetts Battery.[7] Billings's writing is sprightly and entertaining but conveys the unvarnished and homely reality faced by three million Civil War soldiers.

One of Billings's chapters deals with "Jonahs and Beats," men who were inept, unlucky, or prone to shirking their fair share of fatigue work. The following passage from that chapter deals with one work detail that everybody wanted to avoid.

There was one detail upon which our shirks, beats [deadbeats], and men unskilled in manual labor, such as the handling of the spade and pickaxe, appeared in all the glory of their artful dodging and ignorance. If a man did not take hold of the work lively, whether because he preferred to shirk it or because he did not understand it, the worse for him. The detail in question was one made to administer the last rites to a batch of deceased horses. It happened to the artillery and cavalry to lose a large number of these animals in winter, which owing to the freezing of the ground, could not be buried until the disappearance of the frost in spring; but by that time, through the action of rain and sun and the frequent depredations of dogs, buzzards, and crows, the remains were not always in the most inviting condition for the administrations of the sexton. Then, again, during the summer season, when the army made a halt for rest and recruiting, another sacrifice of glanders-infected and generally used-up horses was made to the god of war. But as they were not always promptly committed to mother earth, either from a desire to show a decent respect for the memory of the deceased or for some other reason best known to the red-tape of military rule, the odors that were wafted from them on the breezes were wont to become far more "spicy" than agreeable, so that a speedy interment was generally ordered by the military Board of Health. As soon as the nature of the business for which such a detail was ordered became generally known, the fun began, for a lively protest was wont to go up from the men against being selected to participate in the impending equine obsequies. Perhaps the first objection heard from a victim who has drawn a prize in the business is that "he was on guard the day before, and is not yet physically competent for such a detail." The sergeant is charged with unfairness, and with having pets that he gives all the "soft jobs" to, etc. But the warrior of the triple *chevron* is inexorable, and his muttering, much injured subordinate finally reports to the corporal in charge of the detail in front of the camp, betraying in his every word and movement a heart-felt desire for his term of service of this cruel war to be over.

Another one who his sergeant has booked for the enterprise has got wind of what is to be done, so that when found he is tucked up in his bunk. He stoutly insists that he is an invalid, and is only waiting for the next sounding of "Sick call" to respond to it. But his attack is so sudden, and his language and lungs so strong for a sick man, that he finds it difficult to establish his claim. He calls on his tentmates to swear that he is telling the truth, but finds them strangely devout and totally ignorant of his ailments. For they are chuckling internally at their own good fortune in not being selected, which, if he proves his case, one of them *may* be; so, unless his plea is a pitiful and deserving one, they keep mum.

A third victim does not claim to have been selected out of turn, but nevertheless alleges that "the deal is unfair, because he was on the last detail but one made for this horse-burying business, and he does not think that he ought to be the chief mourner for his detachment, for a paltry thirteen dollars a month. Besides, there may be others who would *like* to go on this detail." But as he is unable to name or find the man or men having this highly refined ambition he finally goes off grumbling and joins the squad.

A fourth victim is the constitutionally high-tempered and profane man. He finds no fault with the justice of the sergeant in assigning him to a participation in the ceremonies of the hour; but he had got comfortably seated to write a letter when the summons came, and, pausing only long enough to inquire the nature of the detail, he pitches his half-written letter and materials in one direction, his lap-board in another, gets up, kicks over the box or stool on which he was sitting, pulls on his cap with a vehement jerk, and then opens his battery. He directs none of his unmilitary English at the sergeant—that would hardly do; but he lays his furious lash upon the poor innocent back of the government, though just what *branch* of it is responsible he does not pause between his oaths long enough to state. He pursues it with the most terrible of curses uphill, and then with like violent language follows it down. He blank blanks the whole blank blank war, and hopes that the South may win. He wishes that all the blank horses were in blank, and adds by way of self-reproach that it serves any one, who is such a blank blank fool as to enlist, *right* to have this blank, filthy, disgusting work to do. And he leaves the stockade shutting the door behind him "with a wooden damn," as [Oliver Wendell] Holmes [Sr.] says, and goes off to report, making the air blue with his cursing. Let me say for this man, before leaving him, that he is not so hardened and bad at heart as he makes himself appear; and in the shock of battle he would be found standing manfully at his post minus his temper and profanity.

There is one more man whom I will describe here, representing another class than either mentioned, whose unlucky star has fated *him* to take a part in these obsequies; but he is not a shirk nor a beat. He is the *paper-collar young man*, just from the recruiting station, with enamelled long-legged boots and custom-made clothes, who yet looks with some measure of disdain on government clothing, and yet eats in a most gingerly way of the stern, unpoetical government rations. He is an only son, and was a dry-goods clerk in the city at home, where no reasonable want went ungratified; and now, when he is summoned forth to join the burial party, he responds at once. True, his heart and stomach both revolt at the work ahead, but he wants to be—not an angel—but a veteran among veterans, and his pride prevents his entering any remonstrance in the presence of the older soldiers. As he clutches the spade pointed out to him with one hand he shoves the other vacantly to the bottom of his breeches pocket, his mouth drawn down codfish-like at the corners. He attempts to appear indifferent as he approaches the detail, and as they congratulate him on his good-fortune a sickly smile plays over his countenance; but he is Mark Tapley feigning a jollity which he does not feel and which soon subsides into a pale melancholy. His fellow-victims feel their ill-luck made more endurable by seeing him also drafted for the loathsome task; but their glow of satisfaction is only superficial and speedily wanes as the officer of the day, who is to superintend the job, appears and orders them forward.

And now the fitness of the selection becomes apparent as the squad moves off, for a more genuine body of mourners, to the eye, could not have been chosen. Their faces, with, it may be, a hardened or indifferent exception, wear the most solemn of expressions, and their step is as slow as if they were following a muffled drum beating the requiem of a deceased comrade.

Having arrived at the place of sepulture, the first business is to dig a grave close to each body, so that it may be easily rolled in. But if there has been no fun before, it commences when the rolling in begins. The Hardened Exception, who has occupied much of his time while digging in sketching distasteful pictures for the Profane Man to swear at, now makes a change of base, and calls upon the Paper-Collar Young Man to "take hold and help roll in," which the young man reluctantly and gingerly does, but when the noxious gases begin to make their presence manifest, and the hardened wretch hands him an axe to break the legs that would otherwise protrude from the grave, it is the last straw to an already overburdened sentimental soul: his emotions overpower him, and, turning his back on the deceased, he utters something which sounds like "hurrah! Without the h," as Mark Twain puts it, repeating it with increasing emphasis. But he is not to express his enthusiasm on this question alone a great while. There are more sympathizers in the party than he had anticipated, and not recruits either; and in less time than I have taken to relate it more than half the detail, gallantly led off by the officer of the day, are standing about, leaning over at various angles like the tombstones in an old cemetery, disposed of their hardtack and coffee, and looking as if ready to throw up even the contract. The Profane Man is among them, and just as often as he can catch his breath long enough he blank blanks the government and then dives again. The rest of the detail stand not far away holding on to their sides and roaring with laughter. But I must drop the curtain on this picture. It has been said that one touch of nature makes the whole world kin. Be that as it may, certain it is that the officer, the good duty soldier, the recruit, and the beat, after an occasion of this kind, had a common bond of sympathy, which went far towards levelling military distinctions between them.

John W. De Forest on Forced Marches[8]

Marching was a generally unpleasant aspect of life in the infantry. Contrary to civilian images of cheerful soldiers swinging along in step and belting out some jaunty martial song, the reality was a column of grimy, sweat-streaked men shambling along in a haze of heat and humidity. The clouds of choking dust through which the men marched would have made singing impractical, even if their fatigue had not robbed them of all desire to do anything more than put one foot ahead of the other until the trek mercifully ended. Often the process was made even more vexatious when the troops had to halt and stand waiting in ranks while staff officers tried to untangle some military traffic jam. On the subject of forced marches—especially hard ones of special urgency and rapid pace—John De Forest tried to look on the bright side.

But are there no comforts, no pleasures, in forced marching? Just one: stopping it. Yes, compared with the incessant anguish of going, there was a keen luxury in the act of throwing one's self at full length and remaining motionless. It was a beast's heaven, but it was better than a beast's hell—insupportable fatigue and pain. The march done, the fevered feet bare to the evening breeze, the aching limbs outstretched, the head laid on the blanket roll which had been such a burden through the day, the pipe in mouth, nature revived a little and found that life retained some sweetness. Delicious dreams, too—dreams wonderfully distinct and consecutive—made slumber a conscious pleasure All night I was at home surrounded by loving faces; no visions of war or troubles; no calling up of the sufferings of the day, nor anticipation of those of the morrow, nothing but home, peace, and friends. I do not know why this should be, but I have always found it so when quite worn out with fatigue, and I have heard others say that it was their experience.

James I. Robertson Jr. on the Hardships of Soldiering[9]

An accomplished historian who has carried on in the tradition of Bell Wiley, James Robertson produced a modern synthesis of every-day army life in his 1988 book, *Soldiers Blue and Gray*. In this pas-sage, Robertson looks at the kind of difficulties mentioned in the excerpts by Abner Small, John Reed, and John De Forest.

Homesickness, foul weather, filth, lack of privacy, stern disci-pline, and general discomfort all combined in time to produce nega-tive views of soldier life. Happy enlistees who gaily tramped away to be part of a neat little war full of glory soon found themselves part of an environment none of them had ever imagined. Captain Oliver Wendell Holmes, Jr., surmounted the problem confronting all Civil War soldiers. "I started in this thing a boy," he wrote his mother late in the war. "I'm now a man." Achieving that transition involved enduring a host of hardships.

The first rude awakening was weather and how quickly it caused army life to lose its glamour.

Oppressive heat and stifling humidity prevailed during most of the months in the field. Flies and mosquitoes swarmed at every movement. Army camps acquired an overbearing stench because of the lack of attention given to garbage pits and latrine procedures. The drinking water was usually muddy and warm. A surgeon in the 5th New Hampshire arrived at a Virginia camp in 1862 and recoiled at "the barefooted boys, the sallow men, the threadbare officers and seedy generals, the diarrhea and dysentery, the yellow eyes and malarious faces, the beds upon the bare earth on the mud, the mist and the rain." Such sights, he concluded, totally shattered his "pre-conceived ideas of knight-errantry."

When mud was not reducing a camp to the status of a swamp, dust was stifling. A Connecticut soldier observed in the summer of 1864 that taking a stroll around the regimental area was akin to walking in an ash heap, that within minutes "one's mouth will be so full of dust that you do not want your teeth to touch one another." During one severely dry period, a Federal artillerist swore that whenever a grasshopper jumped up, it raised so much dust as to cause the Confederates to report the Union army on the move.

The second shock to most soldiers came with the marches the units had to make. A Civil War army moved by foot. It often journeyed great distances to maneuver into position. Men were walking more at one time than they had ever done previously. The ordeal quickly lost all vacation-like aspects. A soldier in the 83rd Pennsylvania wrote of his first military hike: "After we had gone three or four miles, the men began to throw off blankets, coats and knapsacks, and towards night the road was strewn with them. I saw men fall down who could not rise without help. The rain soaked everything woolen full of water and made our loads almost mule loads. . . . I never was so tired before." A Massachusetts soldier was even more opinionated by late 1863. "Here we are marching from one end of Virginia to the other, wearing ourselves out and yet nothing seems to be accomplished by it. . . . this everlasting advancing and retreating I am sick of. My God! Hasten the end of this accursed war."

Men usually marched four abreast, sometimes in the road and sometimes alongside it. The average speed was about two and a half miles per hour. The manner of march was "route step," which meant "go as you please." However, a Massachusetts soldier pointed out, "the men were generally in step, because it was easier." Wagon trains and artillery traveled the same roads as infantry, and their faster pace forced the marching columns repeatedly to take to the ditches. Moreover, as veterans rapidly learned, marching outside the road raised less choking dust and thereby reduced "trouble and annoyance."

A typical day's march began somewhat awkwardly, a private in the 19th Massachusetts recalled. "The men threw their muskets over their shoulders like men starting out to hunt, regardless of the manual of arms; others were at the right or left shoulder shift, while occasionally a man would carry his musket with the hammer resting on the shoulder. Another who had been slow at preparing came stumbling along, trying to fasten his roundabout [a short jacket] with his musket under his arm and the barrel punching his file leader in the back. So the day's work began."

Being at the head of the column was very much preferred. Frontliners got skirmish and picket-duty first and thus could get a night of uninterrupted sleep. Men in the van also used the road when it was in its best shape. In addition, being the first elements to halt, they got the jump on foraging and gathering firewood for the bivouac. Troops at the end of the line fared miserably. For one thing, as the 22nd Massachusetts once discovered, they had to eat the dust of the whole procession. "The perspiration flowed in streams," the regimental historian wrote; "the dust almost suffocated, and soon . . . one could hardly distinguish an object a dozen yards away. Fine and penetrating, the dust sifted into the eyes, nose and mouth, and soon changed the appearance of the marching column. The expressions of the countenances were certainly very ludicrous and one could scarcely refrain from laughing as the dust-and-sweat-streaked face of some individual would look up with a rueful glance, with such a pleading, beseeching expression, seemingly asking for sympathies which under the circumstances could not be given, so nearly alike was the condition of all."

When there was no dust, there was mud. "We took one step forward and two backward," Private Bissell of Connecticut wrote of one struggling march. A member of the 10th Illinois wrote of a similar trek: "At times it seemed almost as if pandemonium had let loose. Everybody and everything seemed to be out of sorts. The horses and mules were mad, and some of them balky, the drivers were mad, and the soldiers were not in the best of humor . . . I mean by this that bad words were issued."

For at least nine months of the year, heat was another impediment.

Massachusetts soldier Ernest Waitt captured the misery of marching under the summer's fireball: "The sun was now well up and the air intensely hot, causing the perspiration to run out and, running down the face, drip from the nose and chin. The salty liquid got into the eyes, causing them to burn and smart and it ran down from under the cap, through the dust and down the sides of the face which was soon covered with muddy streaks, the result of repeated wipings upon the sleeves of the blouse."

Scarcity of water characterized most marches. After one all-day tramp, a New England soldier confessed: "I never was so thirsty in my life and I hope I never shall be again." Soldiers learned to grab a handful of water from any nearby pond they passed on a march. "How many wiggletails and tadpoles I have drunk will never be known," wrote a Confederate. Gullies where rainwater had collected became veritable oases. When a soldier took a drink from one, a member of the 5th New Jersey swore, "the sand could be felt and almost heard as it rattled down your throat."

Troops marched accordion-style all day as terrain changed elevations or wagons broke down in the road. "We plodded along at various rates of speed," an artilleryman noted, "now a walk, now a trot, then a halt, then a slow, hardly perceptible movement, then a rapid motion, as if we were struck with compunction for having tarried at all, and felt bound to make amends." If the march was strenuous, and a mounted officer was setting the pace in front, shouts would soon arise from the ranks: "Halt! Give us a rest!" or "Give the horse a rest, never mind the men!" The column would wind through woods, across fields, and up and down hills; soon there was the inevitable dribbling to the rear as ne'er-do-wells, skulkers, and men genuinely ill began to drop back. By the time the rear elements finally reached camp, the men in the front lines were already cooking rations or had fallen asleep.

Night marches were especially fatiguing, a New York soldier emphasized. The most difficult part "is usually the frequent halts. The column often goes by jerks, making sometimes only a few yards at a time, halting from five minutes to an hour, and then moving a few yards further to halt in the same manner. This tries the patience more than anything else. The poor men sit down or lay down by the road, and just as they are wandering off into dreams, their ears are rudely stunned by the gruff 'Forward!' and up they scramble, half asleep and half awake." An Arkansas officer noted: "I have seen numbers of men go to sleep marching along the Roads at night and stager off just like a Drunk man."

If the troops were marching through a battle zone, or were on an especially severe jaunt, another negative element appeared. The 128th Illinois' Laforest Dunham wrote home in March 1864: "Let people talk about thare balm of a thousand flower, but we can beat that heare, we have the balm of a thousand mules. The roads ar strewd with dead mules. It beats any thing I ever hurd tell of."

Any long trek sorely taxed the physical condition of most soldiers. Ill-fitting shoes triggered widespread lameness. The feet of a New Jersey sergeant became swollen, blistered, and infected during the several marches attendant to the Fredericksburg campaign. Every time the regiment halted and the sergeant removed his shoes, he found blood and pus acting as glue between sock and skin. When the march resumed, fresh scabs "cut into the raw flesh like a knife."

Justus Silliman of the 17th Connecticut likewise developed foot blisters. On the second day's hike, he stated, "my gait was somewhat like that of a lame duck, but I waddled along at first as fast as the remainder of our crew, but towards noon I brought up the rear." One of the classic quotations by a Civil War soldier was the Rhode Island private who unthinkingly wrote his wife after a painful march: "I'm all right except [for] the doggorned blisters on my feet, and I hope these few lines will find you enjoying the same blessings."

Corporal Cort of the 92nd Illinois observed after one gruelling advance: "Some of the largest and stoutest men were the first to give out while the small ones stuck to it but I find that it is not the phisical strength but the determination that carrys one through a long march." Ted Barclay of the 4th Virginia said the same thing but in a light vein. "Well, here I am at the old camp near Winchester, broken down, halt, lame, blind, crippled, and whatever else you can think of—but I am still kicking."

The fortitude these citizen-soldiers displayed was extraordinary on a regular basis. In January 1863, a Texas officer wrote proudly of his troops: "It appears almost incredible that men could exhibit such reckless indifference, such strength of will and determination . . . The war, however, developed and decided some strange theories as to the amount of physical powers which the human frame contained—powers of enduring fatigue, hunger, thirst, heat and cold—which would scarcely have been believed before, if asserted."

Two or three times a day, Johnny Rebs and Billy Yanks confronted food supplies. What they had to eat prompted the loudest and most widespread complaints by Civil War soldiers. Army rations of that day offered little sustenance, for what the troops received was poor in quality and monotonous; and so often it was in small quantities. Richmond artillerist George Eggleston offered one explanation for scanty issues. "Red tape was supreme, and no sword was permitted to cut it.". . .

The thinking on both sides during the war was that if the government supplied the basic foodstuffs to the men in large enough proportions, the troops would make out satisfactorily. Such thinking worked out fairly well during long encampments, when rations were regular and unencumbered by government bureaucracy. Yet when the armies were on the move, or in battle, food was both scarce and of suspect quality. As an Indiana soldier wrote after the Seven Days' campaign: "Rotten meat, mouldy bread & parched beans for coffee are common occurrences now."

Rations issued to the soldier by commissary departments ranged from mediocre to downright awful. Considering the combination of irregular and unbalanced diets, the ignorance of cooking methods, and a preference of the men for frying everything in a sea of grease, one might wonder how the troops kept their health. The answer, of course, is that many of them did not. That is why rations were the worst problem in keeping an army fully supplied. One Union surgeon reported that he was having difficulty saving men from "death from the frying pan." A member of the 1st North Carolina concluded a description of skimpy rations by stating to his father: "A soldier's life is calculated to ruin a young man for business afterwards."

Preparation of meals went through a trial-and-error period at war's outset. A Pennsylvanian noted that "the company-cook system introduced was found to be a total failure, principally because of the selection for the trying position of the most uncouth and disqualified men in the companies. As a result of dissatisfaction, company cooks were discontinued, and each mess of three or four comrades accepted the raw rations distributed to the companies and did their own cooking in messes." Different tastes, among other factors, eventually led most soldiers to prepare their meals individually. This required no great talent; the average soldier did little more than fry a slab of bacon or salt pork, and boil coffee to accompany the hard bread which completed the normal meal.

"Coffee was the main stay," a private in the 10th Massachusetts stated. "Without it was misery indeed." This "subtle poison," a

Maine soldier added, was "considered as indispensable to him as the air he breathes." Army officials worked hard to insure that if only one commodity of nourishment was issued, it would be coffee. Union surgeon A. C. Swartwelder provided a long discourse on army coffee.

The bean "is furnished to the soldier in the crude state—that is, just from the sack. The first thing, therefore, he has to do is to 'toast' it." Such was done in a camp kettle for 10-15 minutes or longer. The result was often that "instead of 'toasted' coffee, the soldier had charcoal." To reduce the beans to powder, men used rifle butts and flat boulders, or else left it in the kettle and tamped it down with a bayonet or other instrument. . . . The surgeon concluded: "I am thoroughly convinced that a pint of good coffee is a better beverage for the soldier than all the rye, bourbon, brandy. . . . It has no equal as a preparation for a hard day's march, nor any rival as a restorative after one."

Give soldiers five minutes' idle time and most of them would start boiling water for coffee. "Coffee and sugar we kept in a bag mixed together," Alfred Bellard of the 5th New Jersey wrote, "and when we wanted a cup of coffee we put two tablespoons full of the mixture in a pint cup of water and placing the cup on two sticks with some hot coals beneath it let it boil." A normal day's coffee ration was sufficient to make three to four pints.

Confederates rarely had coffee in adequate quantities. The blockade of Southern ports cut off much of this luxury and forced soldiers (as well as civilians) to resort to substitutes brewed from peanuts, potatoes, peas, corn, and rye.

Larry J. Daniel on Traveling with the Army of Tennessee[10]

In *Soldiering in the Army of Tennessee* (1991), historian Larry J. Daniel examines life in the Confederacy's "other army," the hard-luck Army of Tennessee. While Lee's Army of Northern Virginia won dramatic victories in its namesake state, the Army of Tennessee followed less gifted commanders and suffered defeat after defeat at the hands of Union adversaries more formidable than those whom Lee faced. Nonetheless, the Army of Tennessee's soldiers showed great resilience while operating in a far larger theater of war than did Lee's army. In this passage, Daniel talks about the soldiers' lot when the army was on the move.

The troops often traveled by rail, and accidents involving troop trains were not infrequent. About a month before Shiloh, a train carrying three companies of the Seventh Mississippi, bound for Corinth, collided with a lumber train, killing twenty soldiers and injuring a like number. In transporting troops to Kentucky in the summer of 1862, a rail accident occurred between Mobile and Montgomery, killing six and injuring thirty members of the Sixth Tennessee. The Twenty-seventh Tennessee had an accident on a trestle near the Alabama-Georgia line that violently threw off a number of men, killing and injuring several. The Fourth Florida was ordered to join [Gen. Braxton] Bragg at Chattanooga during that time, but there was a derailment between Pollard, Alabama, and Montgomery. The locomotive and a single car were thrown off, causing injury to eight soldiers. Before Chickamauga, a collision occurred with the "down" train three miles north of Marietta, Georgia. The Fiftieth Tennessee reportedly suffered losses of eighteen killed and seventy-five wounded.

Typically, however, the men were involved in grindingly tiresome marches. When the Louisiana Washington Artillery (Fifth Company) went overland from Grand Junction to Corinth in early 1862, one of its number related: "Some of the men did not ride any part of the way, desiring to test themselves, others only occasionally and a few walking but very little." After Shiloh, a Louisiana soldier wrote that he had had his "first experience in real campaign marching and I found it far more heavy and toilsome than I had supposed . . . the order constantly coming in our ears 'close up there—close up' or 'not so fast up front.' " Describing the withdrawal from Corinth, a lieutenant in the Twenty-first Alabama wrote that "the heat was like an oven, and we passed a fine little stream with only a ten minutes' halt." A soldier of the Thirty-eighth Tennessee told of a similar experience: "By 12 M., our men are so exhausted they all begin to fall back and many are compelled to lay down on the roadside. Our ambulances are all crowded with the poor sufferers."

If any journey was viewed pleasantly by the men, it was the trek from Tupelo to Chattanooga in the Summer of 1862. The infantry, some twenty-five thousand troops, went via rail from Tupelo to Mobile, Montgomery, Atlanta, and Chattanooga. The first soldier arrived on July 20, 1862, just six days after departure. Meanwhile, the wagon train, artillery, and cavalry went overland through central Alabama and northern Georgia by the ordinary dirt roads. They were accompanied by the First Louisiana as an infantry escort. The 430-mile trip required twenty-four days of travel.

In dozens of towns the troops were received royally by supportive citizens. One Tennessean humorously recalled that when his regiment, which had been reduced by sickness and casualties, marched through the streets of Mobile, many citizens laughed and asked why it was so small. Came the reply: "At Shiloh an Alabama regiment in front of us stampeded and killed half our number!" In LaGrange, Georgia, there were a "number of ladies looking for the 41st Georgia Regt. they having quite a number of friends and relatives in that Regt." One infantryman noted that all along the track groups of young girls threw Confederate flags, peaches, and apples, and at Marietta there was "an opera troup of young ladies [who] sang finely." In Atlanta hundreds of cheering women stood on the railroad platform with fruits and provisions for the soldiers as the trains rolled in. The overland column received similar treatment, with frequent picnics and dances along the route. A correspondent who accompanied the column reported that at every camp they were visited by civilians, especially women. Robert Bliss, who was with the wagons, remarked: "I call my trip my furlough from Tupelo to Chattanooga."

The letters and diaries written during that time concentrated on two themes—geography and women. Floridian Washington Ives missed the moss on the trees, which disappeared north of Columbus, Georgia. George Winchester believed that Tuscaloosa was "a rather lonely, deserted place, with the relics of former pretension only." S. R. Simpson was impressed with Montgomery, although the crops in the surrounding countryside looked pitiful because of the recent drought. Atlanta, he thought, was "quite a city." Once in Chattanooga, some of the men hiked to the top of Lookout Mountain to enjoy the view. "Saw the names of some friends carved in the rocks," related one of Bragg's soldiers. Outside Chattanooga, the troops labored to get across Walden's Ridge, but one soldier thought the spectacular view was worth the trouble: "From the top of the mountain was one of the greatest views imaginable. Chattanooga lay way off in the distance, the smoke of the houses and manufactories circling up to the skies. The Tennessee River rolled along between the ranges of mountains for miles."

More than the countryside caught the attention of the men. A Texas Ranger, stunned at the poverty he saw in northern Alabama, commented that he had seen "more big, fat, barefooted girls than I ever saw in my whole life." Cannoneer John Magee was thrilled at the "many pretty girls eager to see the cannon," although at Blue Mountain he believed that the women were "not very good looking." Another artilleryman confirmed the festive atmosphere and related that at an Alabama resort called Shelby Springs the men spent several hours "flirting with the girls," many of whom were refugees from New Orleans.

As the army snaked through portions of east Tennessee and Kentucky, however, the troops were dismayed to discover a populace with staunch Union sentiment. "I have not seen a house fit to live in since we left Chattanooga, nor more than two or three honest looking men, the women are still worse, such looking people as you would suppose traitors to be made of," commented artilleryman James Searcy. Witnessed Bolling Hall: "The people here [Cumberland Gap] are very hostile. They all openly confess their love for the Yankees. You find one in twenty who is true to the South." A Tennessean noticed a change in the social atmosphere as soon as he crossed the Cumberland River. "We were received with no demonstrations of joy; on the contrary, the people look sad and down cast, and I feel as if we were truly in the enemy's country," he explained.

The veterans dispensed with many nonessentials on the march resulting in a stripped-down, less polished, but more practical look. Explained a soldier in July 1863: "We got orders yesterday to throw away all our clothing but one suit[.] We aren't allowed to have but one pair of pants and have them on, one pair of drawers, two shirts, and one pair of socks."

In June 1863 English Lieutenant Colonel Fremantle described [St. John R.] Liddell's Arkansas brigade as being adequately clothed "but without any attempt at uniformity in color or cut; but nearly all were in gray or brown coats and felt hats. I was told that even if a regiment was clothed in proper uniform by the government, it would become parti-colored again in a week, as the soldiers preferred wearing the coarse homespun jackets and trousers made by their mothers and sisters at home. . . . Most of the officers were dressed in uniform which is neat and serviceable viz., a bluish gray frock coat of a color similar to Austrian yagers [jaegers, or riflemen]."

Despite wear and tear, clothing supplies appear to have remained adequate throughout the Atlanta Campaign. A Georgian indicated that he had "clothes a plenty," and a Mississippian revealed that he could "draw all kinds of Clothing from the Government." Writing from Atlanta in August 1864, one Southerner admitted that some of the men were "in rags," but he wondered "why they cannot get clothing from home as I do?" Shortages were often the result of the men's carelessness. On the march, veterans were quick to toss away unwanted items. "There is a great many men in so large an army who neglect themselves and throw away their clothing. This necessarily looks shabby," observed a cavalryman. A Georgian remarked that "as to Co. G being naked that is not so all have got clothes that would carry them some threw [away] their clothes but all have got clothes & shoes."

The men could do without excess clothing in summer, but on the march shoes were a necessity. Spot shortages occurred throughout the fall and winter of 1863. A captain in the Twentieth Alabama reported that fifty men in his battalion could not fight at Missionary Ridge because they were shoeless. Even though 4,200 pairs were received at Dalton in January 1864, General Joseph E. Johnston still counted 13,300 shoeless men in the infantry and artillery alone. He added: "The Fifth Regiment [Tennessee?] is unable to drill for want of shoes. The Eighth Regiment will soon be unfit for duty from the same cause; and indeed, when shoes are supplied, the men will be unable to wear them for a long while, such is the horrible condition of their feet from long exposure." Colonel Bolling Hall of the Fifty-ninth Alabama reported that he had 180 men with no shoes and another 150 who wore only pieces of leather that left the foot half exposed. Yet there is evidence to suggest that by the spring of 1864 the problem had been largely resolved. On March 7, for example, [Carter L.] Stevenson's division of 6,631 men present listed only 137 as shoeless, down from 2,284 the previous December.

A common complaint as the army moved toward Atlanta was the lack of opportunity to bathe and change clothing. "At times we are the dirtiest and filthyest looking creatures you ever saw," confessed a lieutenant, while a cannoneer remarked that "I am as dirty as a hog—no clean clothes—all used up." William Stanley admitted to his wife in Alabama: "I have not changed my clothes in nearly five weeks. You may draw an idea what fix my clothes are in." Even on those rare occasions when there were opportunities to wash, there was little soap.

For two weeks in June 1864 it rained almost incessantly, adding to the misery and bogging down both armies. A Georgian wrote his wife on the twenty-first: "I never was in so much rain it rains encisently our clothing & Blankets havent been dry in several days & the roads is all most so we can not travel atal." To a North Carolina lieutenant, the mud was "like batter & from 3 to 12 inches & no chance to shun it." A Mississippian informed his wife that she had "no idea how fast 60,000 or 70,000 men and horses with wagons will work up the mud when it is raining." Attempting to extricate his cannon from the mud during a night march, remarked a member of [Capt. James J.] Cowan's Mississippi Battery, was "all together . . . the worst night march I ever experienced in the army."

Unlike the 1862 march to Kentucky, [John Bell] Hood's 1864 trek to Tennessee was a depressing and sobering affair, creating a mood that was reflected in the letters and diaries. There were no cheering throngs along the route. Indeed, a Texan observed, "All the citizens have run off." On October 18, J. W. Ward of the Twenty-fourth Mississippi thought that he was in Cherokee County, Alabama, but he was uncertain because the soldiers had not "seen any citizens in some time to tell us." All they observed were scenes of destruction and decline. "This country [Tennessee Valley] is level and you can have an open view as far as your eyes will let you see," noted William Berryhill. "But there is little of it in cultivation now. The Yankees have destroyed every thing but the Negro cabins and I do not recollect seeing a dwelling house left standing on the road from Courtland [Alabama] to this place [Tuscumbia]." Captain [David M.] Key saw nothing in the Tennessee Valley "except wrecks of palaces and devastated plantations." The business section of Tuscumbia, he noted, was "burned and all streets looking weather-worn and delapidated." Captain Samuel T. Foster thought that Waynesboro, Tennessee, was "a very nice little town, but nearly ruined by the war," and Washington Ives described the surrounding countryside as "very poor." Captain E. M. Graham of the Twelfth Louisiana thought that Wayne County was a desolate place. "The roads are very rough today this place is quite a wilderness country. The people are all Union, with very few exceptions," he wrote.

Thomas Roane, surgeon of the Fifty-first Tennessee, was impressed with the speed with which the column moved. "We are doing the finest marching I ever saw from 15 to 20 miles a day with ease on rough roads although many of the men are barefoot & their feet raw & blistered," he wrote on October 21, 1864. "We have a large train of Supply Wagons to haul meal & bacon & drive our beeves along ahead of us. We have here [Gadsden] 7000 beef cattle & Eat from 250 to 300 a day. We have also a Pontoon train of 80 boats which are fitted as wagons like the body of a wagon. . . . So you see we are well prepared for traveling."

So long was the march that the troops apathetically gave up on any attempt to second-guess their destination. A participant conceded that he had "no idea where we will go before we are done. If you will notice in my other letters I have ventured several times to say where we are going but have missed so often that I have quit saying what I think." A Texan, writing the same month, remarked that it "has got to be a matter of indifference as to where we are going. There are but few men who make any inquiries or seem to care anything about it."

J. Tracy Power on Religion in the Camps[11]
In his 1998 study of life in the Army of Northern Virginia during the final year of the war, Power includes this discussion of the faith of Confederate soldiers during the eleven-month-long Petersburg siege. As with William Bennett's description of religious interest in Confederate hospitals, much the same went on in the Union camps across the way. Like their Confederate counterparts, during the final year of the war many Union soldiers attended preaching services, prayer meetings, and the like, as religious fervor continued to grow at about equal rates in both the contending armies. The Confederate camps have been more thoroughly chronicled by historians, but the religious faith found in the Union camps was also deep.

In spite of fatigue, illness, and poor, scanty, or expensive rations, most men in the Army of Northern Virginia did their best to adjust to life under siege. Many of them took advantage of their long stay near Petersburg and attended worship services at the city's various churches when possible or participated in services or prayer meetings in camp, often conducted by the town's ministers or by their own chaplains. Some Confederates went into town on Sunday mornings for a service and attended another in the evening in camp or in the trenches. Chaplain John Cowper Granbery, a Methodist minister who had served as chaplain of the 11th Virginia before becoming a missionary to the Third Corps, conducted three services in the corps one Sunday in late June. The first, in a North Carolina brigade, had no sooner begun with hymns and a prayer than the brigade was ordered to move. Unwilling to have his service canceled, Granbery marched a mile and a half with the brigade and resumed worship "so soon as the men were settled in their new position." He then went out to the trenches, where he preached to a Virginia brigade in one division later that morning and a North Carolina brigade in another division in the evening. Granbery's hard work was appreciated by a member of the latter brigade, who approached him after his sermon and gave him "a little bag of coffee, saying he had nothing else to offer and that he wished to give me some proof of his regard for my sermon."

Several high-ranking officers, including the commanding general, also participated in religious services when possible. On 10 July, for example, Lee invited Rev. William H. Platt of St. Paul's Episcopal Church to hold an open-air service at his headquarters. Platt, whose church was one of several that had been forced to suspend services due to the frequent Federal bombardments of the city, preached what James Albright called a "very fine" sermon to an audience of officers, soldiers, and civilians. Albright, an ordnance sergeant in a Virginia artillery battalion, described the service in his diary, recording his impressions of Lee "humbly kneeling on the ground among the sunburnt soldiers of his army, & joining in the impressive ceremony of the day. . . . I shall never forget this sermon, nor the men who participated—so calmly, even within the range of the enemies guns." On the same Sunday morning, unable to attend the service at Lee's headquarters or to go to a church in Petersburg, one Georgian wrote, "Tolerably pleasant Sabbath morning but alas far from home cannot visit any Sabbath School no Church as once was the case but only live as a soldier as has been the case for a long while past."

Many correspondents and diarists, whether or not they attended worship services and prayer meetings, frequently mentioned their faith in God and His master plan for them, for the army, and for the Confederate people. "With brave hearts and trusting in God, we have only to persevere and the time is not far distant when days of fighting will be past and the much longed for peace will dawn upon our suffering land," a North Carolina private wrote in late June. As the siege wore on day after day, and as events in other theaters also seemed to resolve nothing, some Confederates wondered just when that peace might come. Sgt. Calvin Conner, who had "thought Some time ago that the presant campaign would perhaps close the war," now believed that the Northern presidential election of 1864 would play a critical role in determining both the war's duration and its outcome. "If thay Succeed in electing a peace man I do not think the war will Last Long but Should thay elect a war candidate God alone knows when we will have peace," Conner observed, "but we must trust the issue to God alone and he will in his own good time bring it about when he thinks we are prepared for it."

Notes

1. John G. Given to "Dear Brother," M. E. Morris, September 13, 1862, John G. Given Papers, Illinois State Historical Library.

2. Abner R. Small, *The Road to Richmond: The Civil War Memoirs of Maj. Abner R. Small of the 16th Maine Vols., with His Diary as a Prisoner of War*, ed. Harold Adams Small (Berkeley: University of California Press, 1959), 197. © 1939 by The Regents of the University of California. Reprinted by permission of the University of California Press.

3. Robert Hale Strong, *A Yankee Private's Civil War*, ed. Ashley Halsey (Chicago: H. Regnery, 1961), 104–5. © 1961 by Regnery Publishing. All rights reserved. Reprinted by special permission of Regnery Publishing, Washington, DC.

4. Bell I. Wiley, *The Life of Billy Yank: The Common Soldier of the Union* (Baton Rouge: Louisiana State University Press, 1994; orig. pub. Indianapolis: Bobbs-Merrill, 1941), 224–33. © 1978 by Bell I. Wiley. Reprinted by permission of Louisiana State University Press.

5. John C. Reed manuscript, Alabama Department of Archives and History, Montgomery, Alabama, pp. 37–39. Reprinted by permission of the Alabama Department of Archives and History.

6. John D. Billings, *Hardtack and Coffee: The Unwritten Story of Army Life* (Boston: George M. Smith & Co., 1887; reprint, Lincoln: University of Nebraska Press, 1994), 102–7.

7. William L. Shea, "Introduction," in Billings, *Hardtack and Coffee*, 2–3.

8. John W. De Forest, *A Volunteer's Adventures: A Union Captain's Record of the Civil War*, ed. James H. Croushore (New Haven, CT: Yale University Press, 1946), 96–97. Reprinted by permission of Yale University Press.

9. James I. Robertson Jr., *Soldiers Blue and Gray* (Columbia: University of South Carolina Press, 1988), 60–66. Reprinted by permission of the University of South Carolina Press.

10. Larry J. Daniel, *Soldiering in the Army of Tennessee: A Portrait of Life in a Confederate Army* (Chapel Hill: University of North Carolina Press, 1991), 28–36. © 1992 by the University of North Carolina Press. Reprinted by permission of the University of North Carolina Press.

11. J. Tracy Power, *Lee's Miserables: Life in the Army of Northern Virginia from the Wilderness to Appomattox* (Chapel Hill: University of North Carolina Press, 1998), 125–27. © 1998 by the University of North Carolina Press. Reprinted by permission of the University of North Carolina Press.

CHAPTER SEVEN

The Black Soldier

While he endured all of the other aspects of military life—in battle, in the hospital, in prison, in camp, or on the march—the black soldier had the distinction of belonging to the first generation of African Americans accepted into the U.S. Army in large numbers. He also bore the burden of the nation's still-pervasive racial hostility. Black soldiers who were captured by the Confederates were enslaved—if they were not killed out of hand, as many were. Even within the Union army, blacks at first received lower pay than their white comrades and were liable to mistreatment by some of those same comrades until they had proved themselves in combat.

The idea of enlisting blacks to fight under the banner of the Union (in a war that had been sparked by the South's desire to make the future safe for slavery) had occurred to abolitionists from the very outset of hostilities. Many white Unionists, however, especially in the lower North and border states, were not prepared to accept this notion. Racist assumptions were pervasive in many areas, and white citizens and soldiers saw the war as one to keep "the Union as it was and the Constitution as it is." And, they sometimes added, using a racial epithet, to keep the slaves where they were. Not daring to alienate this large segment of the population—and thereby lose the war in a day—President Lincoln held back both from emancipation and from the use of black troops.

By the second year of the war the battle lines had hardened, figuratively as well as literally. In the former sense, Lincoln now had less to fear from the defection of racist Unionist whites (who by now had cast their lot more or less irreversibly with the Union) and less to hope for from the repentance of rebellious Southern whites restoring their allegiance under the influence of conciliatory

policies. Thus, partially to rule out European intervention by emphasizing the war's pre-existing connection with slavery, partially
to enhance the motivation of the North by making the cause a grand
moral crusade, and mostly because it was what he wanted to do
anyway, Lincoln in September 1862 issued a preliminary proclamation of emancipation. It declared that in areas still in rebellion as
of January 1, 1863, all slaves would be forever free. On that date the
president duly issued the Emancipation Proclamation, making good
his threat and adding that blacks would now be received into the
Union armies.

At first the black troops were used for fatigue duties—digging
entrenchments and the like—for three reasons: black laborers had
already been doing such work for both armies; black regiments were
inexperienced and therefore, at first, less valuable in battle; and racial prejudice persisted. Eventually they came into combat situations, and their early fights—Milliken's Bend and Port Hudson,
Louisiana, and Battery Wagner, South Carolina—demonstrated that
they had the courage to face death. As the war progressed, these
and other examples of bravery won them acceptance as full-fledged
combat troops.

The officers of the black Union regiments were white. Only
one black regiment had black officers, and it was a prewar Louisiana militia regiment composed of well-educated freedmen from
New Orleans. Otherwise the government's insistence on white officers sprang primarily from racial prejudice but had the practical
justification that almost all the former slaves were illiterate and therefore unable to do the paper work required of an officer or even of
an orderly sergeant. The white officers of black regiments were
usually of tolerably good quality since they were selected on the
basis of merit from volunteering junior officers and noncommissioned officers of veteran regiments.

Historical interest in the role of black troops in the Civil War
increased during the second half of the twentieth century. Prior to
that time a sort of unspoken sectional modus vivendi had dictated
that the South would accept reunion; and, in exchange, the North
would look the other way in regard to the South's Jim Crow practices and pretend the war had had nothing to do with slavery. That
attitude began to change with the birth and growth of the civil rights
movement during the 1950s, leading to a historical rediscovery of
blacks' roles in the Civil War and the centrality of slavery as the

conflict's cause. Ironically, the participation of black soldiers in World War II helped to spur the growth of the civil rights movement, as young people who had traveled halfway across the world to fight for their country were not inclined to accept the status quo that made them second-class citizens. Thus, black soldiers of the twentieth century, in an indirect way, helped to remind the world of the black soldiers of the previous century.

In reading the following selections, bear in mind both the struggle of blacks for freedom during the Civil War and also the concern of historians such as William Wells Brown that the story of their efforts not be forgotten. This concern helps to explain the strident tone that sometimes appears in these pieces.

William Wells Brown on Raising Black Regiments in the North[1]

The first author to tell the story of black troops in the Civil War was himself a black man. William Wells Brown had a long association with Northern white abolitionists. He learned the printer's trade under the tutelage of Elijah Lovejoy, a white abolitionist editor who was killed in 1837 by a pro-slavery mob that came to break up his printing press—for the second time—in Alton, Illinois. Brown went on to become the first black American to publish a play, "The Black Man,"[2] and the first to publish a novel, *Clotelle, or The President's Daughter. Clotelle*, a story about a mulatto daughter of Thomas Jefferson, which had some basis in fact, was printed in 1853 by a British firm because no American press would touch it. In 1867 he wrote *The Negro in the American Rebellion.*

In the passage that follows, Brown expresses some of his bitterness that the North did not advance more rapidly in matters of racial equality as well as his pride that his fellow blacks, when finally given a chance, had enlisted to fight for their country. While his judgment of Northern whites had a factual basis, it was unfairly harsh, particularly when he said that "any attempt to engraft upon the organic law of the States provisions extending to the colored man political privileges" was doomed to be "overwhelmingly defeated by the people." That statement was proven wrong during the next few years when those same people, through their elected representatives, added the Fourteenth and Fifteenth Amendments to the U.S. Constitution. Still, there can be no denying the fact that considerable racial prejudice existed even north of the Mason-Dixon Line and the Ohio River. In reading the following passage, look for instances of hyperbole by Brown as he states his case in the most extreme terms.

In the struggle between the Federal Government and the rebels, the colored men asked the question, "Why should we fight?" The question was a legitimate one, at least for those residing in the Northern States, and especially in those States where there were any considerable number of colored people. In every State north of Mason and Dixon's Line, except Massachusetts and Rhode Island, which attempted to raise a regiment of colored men, the blacks are disfranchised, excluded from the jury-box, and in most of them from the public schools. The iron hand of prejudice in the Northern States is as circumscribing and unyielding upon him as the manacles that fettered the slave of the South.

Now, these are facts, deny it who will. The negro has little to hope from Northern sympathy or legislation. Any attempt to en-graft upon the organic law of the States provisions extending to the colored man political privileges is overwhelmingly defeated by the people. It makes no difference that here is a pen, and there a voice, raised in his behalf: the general verdict is against him; and its rep-etition in any case where it is demanded shows that it is inexorable. We talk a great deal about the vice of slavery, and the cruelty of denying to our fellow men their personal freedom and a due re-ward of labor; but we are very careful not to concede the corollary, that the sin of withholding that freedom is not vastly greater than withholding the rights to which he who enjoys it is entitled.

When the war broke out, it was the boast of the Administration that the status of the negro was not to be changed in the rebel States. President Lincoln, in his inaugural address, took particular pains to commit himself against any interference with the condition of the blacks.

When the Rebellion commenced, and the call was made upon the country, the colored men were excluded. In some of the West-ern States into which slaves went when escaping from their rebel masters, in the first and second years of the war, the black-laws were enforced to drive them out. . . . With what grace could the authorities in those States ask the negro to fight? Yet they called upon him; and he, forgetting the wrongs of the past, and demand-ing no pledge for better treatment, left family, home, and every-thing dear, enlisted, and went forth to battle.

James M. McPherson on Arming Blacks[3]

In more sober and measured terms, one of the foremost modern historians here presents the basic circumstances of black enlistment and deployment in the Union armies, but the account is all the more powerful for its simple, direct approach. McPherson begins with Lincoln's January 1, 1863, Emancipation Proclamation, which "sanctioned the enlistment of black soldiers and sailors in Union forces."

Here was revolution in earnest. Armed blacks were truly the *bête noire* of southern nightmares. The idea of black soldiers did not, of course, spring full-blown from Lincoln's head at the time of the Emancipation Proclamation. The notion had been around since the beginning of the war, when northern blacks in several cities had volunteered for the Union army. But on the principle that it was "a white man's war," the War Department had refused to accept them. Despite the service of black soldiers in the Revolution and the War of 1812, Negroes had been barred from state militias since 1792 and the regular army had never enrolled black soldiers. The prejudices of the old order died hard. Lincoln had squelched Secretary of War [Simon] Cameron's reference to arming slaves in December 1861, and the administration refused at first to accept the organization of black regiments in Kansas, occupied Louisiana, and the South Carolina sea islands during the summer of 1862.

The Union navy, however, had taken men of all colors and conditions from the outset. Blacks at sea served mainly as firemen, coal heavers, cooks, and stewards. But as early as August 1861 a group of contrabands served as a gun crew on the U.S.S. *Minnesota*. In May 1862 a South Carolina slave, Robert Smalls, commandeered a dispatch boat in Charleston harbor and ran it out to the blockading fleet. Smalls became a pilot in the U.S. navy.

Meanwhile black leaders, abolitionists, and radical Republicans continued to push for enlistment of black soldiers. This would not only help the North win the war, they said; it would also help free the slaves and earn equal rights for the whole race. Frederick Douglass made the point succinctly: "Once let the black man get upon his person the brass letters, U.S.; let him get an eagle on his button, and a musket on his shoulder and bullets in his pocket, and there is no power on earth which can deny that he has earned the right to citizenship."

Helping blacks to earn citizenship was not the main motive for a congressional mandate (in the militia act of July 17, 1862) to enroll Negroes in "any military or naval service for which they may be found competent." Rather, the need for labor battalions to free white soldiers for combat prompted this legislation. The Emancipation Proclamation envisaged a limited role for black soldiers "to garrison forts, positions, stations, and other places" instead of to fight as front-line troops. But reality had a way of surpassing policy. Just as Lincoln, nine days before issuing the preliminary Proclamation, had told a delegation that such an edict would be like the Pope's bull against the comet, so on August 4, three weeks before the War Department authorized enlistment of contrabands as soldiers in occupied South Carolina, he told a delegation that "to arm the negroes would turn 50,000 bayonets against us that were for us." But even as Lincoln uttered these words, a regiment of free Negroes was completing its organization in Louisiana and a regiment of free and contraband blacks was forming in Kansas. Two more Louisiana regiments along with the authorized South Carolina regiment quietly completed their organization during the fall. In October the Kansans saw action in a Missouri skirmish that left ten of them dead—the first black combat casualties of the war.

By the year's end the government was ready to acknowledge the existence of these regiments. It could hardly help but do so, for Massachusetts had gotten into the act. The colonel of the 1st South Carolina Volunteers was the Bay State's Thomas Wentworth Higginson, whose pen was at least as mighty as his sword. After taking part of his regiment on a minor raid along a South Carolina river in January 1863, Higginson wrote an enthusiastic report to the War Department which, as intended, found its way into the newspapers. "Nobody knows anything about these men who has not seen them in battle," wrote Higginson. "No officer in this regiment now doubts that the key to the successful prosecution of the war lies in the unlimited employment of black troops." The *New York Tribune* commented that such reports were such "to shake our inveterate Saxon prejudice against the capacity and courage of negro troops." About the time of Higginson's raid, Governor [John Albion] Andrew of Massachusetts squeezed permission from the War Department to raise a black regiment. Commissioning prominent abolitionists as recruits and officers, Andrew enlisted enough men from northern states for two regiments, the 54th and 55th Massachusetts, the first of which became the most famous black regiment of the war.

The recruitment of black soldiers did not produce an instantaneous change in northern racial attitudes. Indeed, to some degree it intensified the Democratic backlash against emancipation and exacerbated racial tensions in the army. The black regiments reflected the Jim Crow mores of the society that reluctantly accepted them: they were segregated, given less pay than white soldiers, commanded by white officers some of whom regarded their men as "niggers," and intended for use mainly as garrison and labor battalions. One of the first battles these black troops had to fight was for a chance to prove themselves in combat.

Even so, the organization of black regiments marked the transformation of a war to preserve the Union into a revolution to overthrow the old order. Lincoln's conversion from reluctance to enthusiasm about black soldiers signified the progress of this revolution. By March 1863 the president was writing to Andrew Johnson, military governor of Tennessee: "The bare sight of fifty thousand armed, and drilled black soldiers on the banks of the Mississippi, would end the rebellion at once. And who doubts that we can present that sight, if we but take hold in earnest?"

The southern response to emancipation and the enlistment of black troops was ferocious—at least on paper and, regrettably, sometimes in fact as well. Upon learning of the preliminary Emancipation Proclamation, General [P. G. T.] Beauregard called for "execution of abolition prisoners [that is, captured Union soldiers] after 1st of January. . . . Let the execution be with the garrote." Jefferson Davis's message to Congress on January 12, 1863, pronounced the Emancipation Proclamation "the most execrable measure in the history of guilty man." Davis promised to turn over captured Union officers to state governments for punishment as "criminals engaged in inciting servile insurrection." The punishment for this crime, of course, was death.

Sober second thoughts prevented the enforcement of such a policy. But the South did sometimes execute captured black soldiers and their officers. Even before official adoption of black enlistment by the Union government, southerners got wind of the premature efforts along this line in occupied Louisiana and South Carolina. From Confederate army headquarters on August 21, 1862, came a general order that such "crimes and outrages" required "retaliation" in the form of "execution as a felon" of any officer of black troops who was captured. When a rebel commando raid seized four blacks in Union uniforms on a South Carolina island in November, Secretary of War James A. Seddon and President Davis approved their "summary execution" as an "example" to discourage the arming of slaves. A month later, on Christmas Eve, Davis issued a general order requiring all former slaves and their officers captured in arms to be delivered up to state officials for trial. On May 30, 1863, the Confederate Congress sanctioned this policy but stipulated that captured officers were to be tried and punished by military courts rather than by the states.

Though the South did not actually do this, considerable evidence indicates that captured officers were sometimes "dealt with red-handed on the field or immediately thereafter," as Secretary of War Seddon suggested to General Kirby Smith in 1863. Black prisoners of war were sometimes shot "while attempting to escape." A Confederate colonel whose regiment captured a squad of black soldiers in Louisiana reported that when some of them tried to escape, "I then ordered every one shot, and with my Six Shooter I assisted in the execution of the order." A North Carolina soldier wrote to his mother that after a skirmish with a black regiment "several [were] taken prisoner & afterwards either bayoneted or burnt. The men were perfectly exasperated at the idea of negroes opposed to them & rushed at them like so many devils."

Rumors and reports of several such massacres vexed Union authorities through the rest of the war and forced them more than once to threaten retaliation. This was one reason for the hesitation to use black troops in combat, where they ran a heightened risk of capture.

Reid Mitchell on the "Mysterious Race of Grown Up Children"[4]

In his 1993 book, *The Vacant Chair*, Reid Mitchell uses concepts derived from the family to describe relationships among the Union soldiers. In one chapter, Mitchell deals with the Union's black soldiers. In this discussion he draws extensively on the writings of Thomas Wentworth Higginson. A prewar abolitionist, Higginson was given command of one of the first black regiments, the Union's First South Carolina. Although Higginson was an ardent supporter of emancipation and the social equality of blacks, Mitchell nevertheless believes he sees in Higginson racially condescending attitudes. According to Mitchell, Higginson saw the blacks as a childlike people who required paternalistic care. To Mitchell it was somehow inconsistent for officers such as Higginson to think of their black troops (or white ones either) as being in some ways like children while at the same time recognizing their true manhood.

In the passage that follows, Mitchell expands on this idea and argues that other white Northerners shared this belief. As you read, consider in what ways Mitchell's tone might be similar to that of William Wells Brown. And in what ways different? How do both compare with James McPherson? What thoughts and ideas of Higginson's does Mitchell find offensive, and what sorts of ideas on Higginson's part might have been more acceptable to Mitchell?

Like a good father, Higginson wanted his children to grow up—although, like many a good father, he also sometimes wished his children would never change. In December 1862 he confessed that their "childlike confidence" in him and the other white officers made commanding black soldiers easier. "Nevertheless, it is our business to educate them to manhood." A little over a year later, Higginson wrote that "in every way I see the gradual change in them, sometimes with a sigh, as parents watch their children growing up and miss the droll speeches and confiding ignorance of childhood." The soldiers were becoming "more like white men—less naïve and less grotesque." This acculturation was desirable, no doubt, but nonetheless he regretted it. He hoped that "their joyous buoyancy, at least, will hold out while life does."

Now, it must be remembered that Higginson was drawn to the paternal model of authority in any case. If he cast black soldiers as immature, he also tended to cast white soldiers that way. The first time that the First South Carolina served with white regiments, the Sixth Connecticut and the Eighth Maine, Higginson worried that racial violence might occur within the ranks. He expressed his fears by saying, "if the black and white babies do not quarrel and pull hair, we shall do very well." He cheerfully professed to believe that all soldiers must be treated like children. Perhaps this attitude prevented Higginson from recognizing that his delighted anecdotes of childish freedpeople undercut his principal design in writing *Army*

Life in a Black Regiment: generating support among northern white people of political and civil equality for black people.

Colonel Higginson wrote as if most northerners had accepted black manhood, as if the experience of black soldiering, in which he himself had participated, had persuaded white Americans of the justice of black equality. "It was their demeanor under arms," he proclaimed, "that shamed the nation into recognizing them as men." His initial pleasure that the soldiers of the First South Carolina were "as thoroughly black as the most faithful philanthropist could desire," came from his plans for the regiment: it was to demonstrate the capacity of black people for freedom. Black initiative had too often been attributed to mixed ancestry; mulattos had too often been held the leaders of the race. If the war along the coast was to be the proving ground of African Americans, Higginson preferred that the First South Carolina Volunteers' rank and file be "pure African." In 1869, Higginson pointed with pride to the recent political service of former soldiers. He had already said of Prince Rivers that "if there should ever be a black monarchy in South Carolina, he will be its king." After the war, Rivers and two other sergeants participated in the South Carolina Constitutional Convention; he and Sergeant Henry Hayne became state legislators. Higginson quoted with approval General [Rufus] Saxton's characterization of black soldiers: "Intensely human."

At the conclusion of *Army Life in a Black Regiment*, Higginson contradicted himself. After portraying the soldiers that served with him as boys, Higginson next recounted tales of suffering, endurance, and resistance intended to demonstrate the adulthood of the freed people. Before serving with the regiment, the Wilson brothers successfully led their family to the Union lines and freedom even though all of them were wounded by gunfire during the escape. It was the grandmother in the Miller family who conducted her children and grandchildren to safety and freedom; the Miller brothers joined the regiment. Fanny Wright had her baby "shot dead in her arms" as she crossed from the mainland to an army-occupied island. Indeed, Higginson suggested here that the soldiers in the regiment and their families were more adult than the white junior officers.

One of those officers said of Higginson, "he met a slave and made him a man." But Thomas Long, a private in the regiment, explained matters differently in a sermon during the war. "We can remember, when we fust enlisted, it was hardly safe for we to pass by de camps to Beaufort and back, lest we went in a mob and carried sidearms. But we whipped down all that"—the "all that" was the racist violence of white soldiers—"not by going into de white camps for whip um; we didn't tote our bayonets for whip um; but we lived it down by our naturally manhood; and now de white sojers takes us by de hand and say Broder Sojer. Dats what dis regiment did for de Epiopian race." That was one meaning of black military service; Long continued to explain another one. "If we hadn't become sojers, all might have gone back as it was before; our freedom might have slipped through de two houses of Congress and President Linkum's four years might have passed by and notin' been done for us. But now tings can neber go back, because we have showed our energy and our courage and our naturally manhood." Thomas Long and other soldiers in the First South Carolina insisted that they were already men. He explicated the relationship between manhood, soldiering, and the family in ways that would have easily been understood by a northern volunteer—an image of fathers and children, but not one of paternalistic officers and childish soldiers. "Anoder ting is, suppose you had kept your freedom witout enlisting in dis army, your chilen might have grown up free and been well-cultivated so as to be equal to any business, but it would have been always flung in dere faces—'Your father never fought for he own freedom'—and what could dey answer? Neber can say that to dis African race any more." This dignity was the fruit of the "naturally manhood" of these black soldiers.

And this was the dignity that Higginson ultimately expected white Americans to recognize in black ones. Black military service had proved the right of black men to citizenship—its memory must be perpetuated. Nonetheless, even as he attempted to do this, Higginson also perpetuated old racist stereotypes. What image of black Americans that white Americans would take from reading *Army Life in a Black Regiment* depended on which stories struck them the most—or perhaps on which stories confirmed their prejudices. The image of white parents managing black children was so powerful that Higginson could not escape it, either in structuring his book or in structuring his own experience. The model of parental authority made sense of Higginson's role as colonel of a black regiment. He refused to relinquish this model even when attempting to sustain the ideal of black citizenship.

Higginson was not alone in cherishing this model of race relations. Other white officers commanding black soldiers in the United
States Colored Troops shared his understanding. Brigadier General Daniel Ullmann, advising his officers to "*Let the law of kindness
be your guide,*" described black soldiers as "docile, impressionable,
fully imbued with the spirit of subordination (one of the highest
attributes of a soldier), possessed of a deep appreciation of kindly
treatment and of keen perceptions, which enables them quickly to
discover any flaw in the conduct of their superiors." Even Captain
Luis F. Emilio, in his remarkably uncondescending history of the
54th Massachusetts, observed of the soldiers that served with him,
"Passive obedience—a race trait—characterized them." Like Higginson, Emilio evoked the paternalistic model of military authority—but like Higginson he would have it applied to all soldiers. "To
the soldier his true commander is a father; his superiors, elder brothers to be obeyed; the recruits, his younger kinsmen whom he cares
for and supports by example." Chaplain Samuel L. Gardner, who
wrote to protest the mistreatment of black soldiers by their white
officers, explained such abuses were particularly damaging because
the soldiers were "in a state of pupillage." "For my own part, I came
into the service under a deep conviction, as a citizen—to speak of
no higher obligation—of the heavy responsibility our government
assumed in becoming the guardian of these millions of freedmen,
and from a desire to contribute my help as one man, toward the
great work of leading them up from their enforced degradation to
manhood and citizenship, and I recognize the military service, in
its legitimate operation, as an excellent school for this end." But
such views were shared by some black officers as well. B. F. Randolph,
a black chaplain, wanted profanity on the part of white officers to
cease because it was a bad example for black soldiers: "The poor
oppressed negro of this land needs the most wholesome example
set before him to elevate him."

At the same time, Thomas Long and his fellows in the First
South Carolina were not the only black soldiers who preferred to
think of themselves as men already. In the introductory essay of
their collection of documents on "the black military experience,"
Ira Berlin, Joseph P. Reidy, and Leslie S. Rowland discuss "the well-
meaning paternalism of abolitionist officers," arguing that some
black soldiers found it "more distasteful than the simple contempt
of racist commanders." They conclude that "black soldiers resented

being treated like children no less than being treated like slaves." This may be hyperbole, since "being treated like slaves" meant physical abuse. One of the worst riots of black soldiers occurred in Louisiana in December 1863. Outraged by Lt. Col. August W. Benedict's whipping of two drummer boys, many soldiers grabbed their guns, began firing them in the air, and threatened Benedict alone among the white officers—although Colonel Charles W. Drew heard one voice cry out, "Kill all the damned Yankees." Whipping, both here and throughout the war, reminded black soldiers too forcibly of slavery. But they also insisted that they knew officers had been ordered not to strike their men, and they demanded, "We want to be treated as soldiers." Other mutinies conducted by black soldiers also demonstrated that, just as most white soldiers did, black soldiers rejected the notion that their officers always knew best—i.e., they rejected parental authority.

When the rioters of December 1863 justified their actions by claiming that they had been promised they would not be whipped, they understood their military service as ordered by a contract made among equals. Most of the other mutinies also hinged on the perception that the army and the government failed to keep their end of a bargain, the bargain usually being that of equal pay for white and black soldiers. Higginson himself condemned the government for cheating black soldiers, and helped publicize the demand for equal pay. He pitied the leader of the mutiny in the Third South Carolina, Sergeant William Walker, who "was shot, by order of court-martial, for leading his company to stack arms before their captain's tent, on the avowed ground that they were released from duty by the refusal of the Government to fulfill its share of the contract." As commander of the First South Carolina, Higginson worried that the officers might yet have to execute more soldiers "who, like Sergeant Walker, refuse to fulfill their share of a contract where the Government has openly repudiated the other share." During the battle for equal pay, Higginson recognized the contractual understanding that the soldiers of the First South Carolina had of their enlistments; he also believed that it was only "their childlike faith in their officers" that kept them from mutiny.

Although few spoke with Higginson's seeming authority, some white northerners outside of the black regiments shared his perceptions. Mrs. C. E. McKay, who worked in Union hospitals, visited a contraband camp immediately after the war. "Here are now collected five or six hundred of the colored people, just escaped from the 'barbarism of slavery,' " she said—Higginson once called his black soldiers "young barbarians." Mrs. McKay observed that the freed people "being, as one may say, in the infancy of manhood, the Government, like a 'cherishing mother,' is holding them by the hand until they shall be able to go alone."

The familial model of race relations was hardly the only one available to white northerners, not even the only racist model. One guesses that it was a model that particularly attracted those who felt kindly toward African-Americans. While condescending toward those people, it at least asserted mutual bonds between white and black, and encouraged a sense that white people had some sort of responsibility toward black people. Other white Americans would have disagreed. Most anti-black sentiment was much harsher in tone; according to other white Americans, including many northern soldiers, black people were more savage than childish. White people, it was believed, owed black people nothing. And when the government did propose aid to the freed people, it was viewed in much the way Mrs. McKay viewed it as she watched them in the contraband camp—a paternal government holding the hands of black children.

The hierarchal relationship of white people to black people in the Union army reinforced paternalism among northerners as well as reflected it. Segregation structured the military experience so that white soldiers did not develop camaraderie with black soldiers within their messes, companies, and regiments. White men in black regiments were officers commanding their "boys." White and black men were rarely fellow soldiers. They might fight side-by-side in battle but they belonged to different companies—which was to say different families, different communities. Black soldiering could change white men's image of black men, but it created fewer reciprocal bonds than it might have. Despite the paternalistic constructs of men like Higginson, few northerners embraced black men as either "sons" or "brothers." The image of the family remained white only. Perhaps this was one reason, among so many, that during the years of sectional reconciliation, the nation managed to forget the contribution black people made to the salvation of the Union.

There is a famous image of Thomas Wentworth Higginson that dates from the period of reconciliation. Reading "Marse Chan," Higginson wept. Thomas Nelson Page's story is a tale of a black slave's loyalty to his young master, a slaveholder and a Confederate. Higginson's response to the tale seemed odd indeed, for he had a long anti-slavery career and he had denied the existence of affection of slaves for masters. Edmund Wilson argued that the northern approval of Thomas Nelson Page's fiction came from "feelings of guilt" about the war, and suggested that Higginson may have shared these feelings. Perhaps—although Higginson never lost interest in black rights the way so many other white northerners did. Given Higginson's paternalistic ideals, perhaps there is less of a contradiction between his life and the way "Marse Chan" brought tears into his eyes than there initially seems. He wanted his black soldiers to love him the same way.

Joseph T. Glatthaar on the Training of Black Troops[5]

In his 1990 book *Forged in Battle: The Civil War Alliance of Black Soldiers and White Officers*, Joseph Glatthaar included a discussion of the process of training the newly raised black regiments. He argues that the failure or success of black troops was largely dependent on the attitudes and approach to training adopted by their white officers. Like other modern historians, however, Glatthaar is impatient with well-meaning attempts on the part of some white officers to simplify instructions for the new black troops. This he sees as a demeaning suggestion that the blacks were innately inferior. Need this have been true? Or could the officers have been reacting appropriately to the fact that the former slaves had no military experience and no formal education?

In Civil War armies, training and discipline worked hand in hand. Nearly all fighting took place within viewing range, and in the face of such harrowing scenes it required the utmost discipline and control to keep troops at their positions. They fought in compact formations, in part a throwback to the days of inaccurate muskets when bayonet assaults were highly effective, but also because communication within units was difficult and closely packed men improved commanders' ability to maneuver their troops. Amid the clouds of smoke, deafening noise, and ghastly injuries of battle, soldiers had to be able to perform tactical maneuvers on order with speed and precision, and only through constant training did they learn to execute them properly. Such regimentation through both drill and discipline also fostered the concept of teamwork and bonded soldiers to one another, which in turn improved their battlefield performance by reassuring individual soldiers that they could depend on their comrades.

If USCT [United States Colored Troops] officers had one great asset, it was that most of them had previous military experience. Nearly all of it, however, was on the enlisted level. For the bulk of them, service as officers was an entirely new endeavor. In the enlisted ranks they had had an opportunity to observe good and bad officers and had determined certain qualities that were essential for effective command; nevertheless, their perspective was always from the soldier's point of view. Once they sewed officers' insignia on their shoulders, they began to see things differently. A lieutenant described the transition by writing, "I threw off the dare-devil boy and took on the man." Another officer, who had suffered three wounds in a white regiment and seldom saw action in the USCT, also considered the change dramatic: "Scouting and fighting in the ranks had given place, under a commission, to solving problems of organization, care, drill, discipline and education of ignorant men, to be followed later by control and government of hostile communities." Promotion to the officer corps brought with it responsibilities that few of them had ever known before the war. As a lieutenant wrote to his sister, "One little knows the real work to be done in a company until he has tried the Organization of one." Duty as officers was a strange new world where performance was the only standard of evaluation, so a young man who had just earned a promotion to regimental commander commented: "I sometimes have my misgivings when I think that in military affairs success is the only criterion of worth, & mistakes, or failure in any degree is irretrievable condemnation. However, I ask no allowances, the damnation of failure shall be as completely my own, as might be the approbation for any success."

Unlike their counterparts in most units raised early in the war, these officers did not have the luxury of months and months to teach all the duties and tactical formations. It was imperative that they concentrate on essential skills—those that could make the difference between death and survival—and fill in the others at a later date. Even with this approach, they invariably barraged troops with vast quantities of information and duties, and only through repetition and the vigilance of officers were the soldiers able to master everything that was critical for wartime.

With success or failure resting on their shoulders, the white officers tackled the problem of preparing their men for combat. Both officers and enlisted men in the USCT believed that only on the battlefield could they win the respect of white volunteers, and the best means to prepare for that moment was to drill the troops. This enabled the black units to learn the various tactical maneuvers and formations that were essential for combat, and it also imbued soldiers with a sense of confidence in themselves and their comrades that helped them cope with the ordeal of battle. According to the colonel of an excellent black regiment, "I knew that nothing but drill, discipline, and more drill, would fit the regiment for the field in such condition as to give every officer and soldier absolute confidence in the ability of the regiment to take care of itself under any and all circumstances."

Although officers agreed on the importance of training their troops, their views on how that task should be accomplished varied considerably. At the core of the debate were their impressions of the black soldiers. Those who had high regard for blacks treated them like men, developed them as soldiers, and eventually were able to delegate sundry responsibilities to them, whereas those who believed in racial stereotypes, such as that blacks were childlike and ignorant, had limited expectations of their men and received little in return.

All officers had to devote considerable time to the training of their troops, but some who saw in black soldiers tremendous promise went above and beyond that. Rather than attempt to carry responsibility for everything on their shoulders, to oversee all aspects of military duty within their commands, these officers sought black soldiers whom they could train to perform a variety of supervisory functions, as did noncommissioned officers in white units. They worked with these men, taught them tactics, regulations, and in many cases reading and writing, so that they were capable of fulfilling all the duties of noncommissioned officers. Officers placed their confidence in these men, and they in turn felt an obligation to fulfill their roles and assignments satisfactorily.

Commands raised in the North had an immense advantage over units with Southern blacks, because of the reading and writing skills of the men. Civil War armies ran on paperwork, and without literate troops the burden of this labor rested with the officers. It took one officer four days of constant work, from rising in the morning until bedtime, to prepare all the muster rolls and returns of clothing and camp and garrison equipage for his company, and he had to perform this work every three months. Along with the day-to-day paperwork, this was a heavy load. Training an enlisted man to do this work freed an officer to devote more time to the men. Equally important, it spread responsibility for critical jobs to a few black troops and gave everyone a sense of satisfaction that black soldiers were contributing substantially to the development and administration of the unit.

Officers who recognized black soldiers' potential for development frequently adopted a more positive and progressive training program than did their peers. Instead of berating troops and punishing them vigorously for minor errors, they were much more willing to work with the men to overcome difficult aspects of soldiering and to use incentives to promote achievement. While some officers doled out sets of sergeant's and corporal's stripes immediately, others withheld them to award at a later date to men who merited the positions. As a lieutenant announced to his family, "I have the honor and pleasure of appointing my non-commissioned officers and of giving them their stripes. I tell you they feel proud of it." Incentives, these officers learned, spurred efficiency better than any other means of training. At Camp William Penn, a rendezvous site for Northern black units, standing policy was that as men completed guard duty they were to discharge their loads at a target. The best shot won a forty-eight-hour pass, and any soldier whose gun did not discharge because it was dirty had four more hours of guard duty. An even better incentive was the one instituted by Lt. Col. Robert Cowden. Each month his regiment had a drill competition, judged by impartial officers, and the winning company received a rosette that its members wore on the left breast of their dress-parade jacket. Although the award was trifling, it became a badge of honor for the troops, and it brought out the best in the men. Cowden's contest promoted the concept of teamwork and fostered esprit de corps within companies.

On the other hand, many officers had little confidence in the potential development of their black soldiers. With small hope of progress, their entire approach frequently fostered a self-fulfilling prophecy. They treated their men like children, and the troops responded accordingly. Black soldiers in their commands did the work sloppily, failed to listen to instructions, and for the most part made life miserable for their officers. In return, such behavior vindicated the prejudices of these officers, and they began to view their jobs more as those of baby-sitters than of commanders in the U.S. Army. While troops became lethargic, officers grew more and more frustrated until command became a constant chore and at times a hellish experience. Repeated bad performance on review drove one disillusioned captain to complain, "It seems very hard to make anything of these men, I am about discouraged." The difficulty of teaching troops how to fire weapons caused a lieutenant to lose his temper, call one soldier "a wooly headed nincompoop, aim his gun correctly for him again, and tell him if he did not do it right the next time I would kill him." For another officer the frustration became so intense that he was "ready to quit the business of teaching 'Unbleached Americans.' " He then concluded, "I would rather swing a scythe all day than to endeavor to teach a squad of recruits any of the motions of the Manual of arms." Fortunately he remained in the USCT and became a fine officer, but many others found the work intolerable and damaged the morale of the men.

Often these officers had an unenlightened approach to command. There were no incentives or rewards for achievement, just punishment for mistakes. Rather than instruct the men patiently, "They strike the men with their swords and jab and punch them in their side to show them how to drill," complained a private in the 43rd U.S. Colored Infantry. They found noncommissioned officers through trial and error, yet they made little effort to work with their appointees. In one month the 65th U.S. Colored Infantry reduced thirty-two noncommissioned officers to the ranks and filled their slots with new men. Worse conditions, though, prevailed in the 45th U.S. Colored Infantry. In late September 1864, promotions and demotions affected thirty-three soldiers, and twenty-one more within the next six weeks. Matters reached such a point that regimental headquarters had to warn company commanders, "It is detrimental to the good discipline of the service to reduce non com officers with the same facility with which a guard detail is named in a company." He then warned that if other companies did as Company B, it would not be long before every member of that unit at one time held the rank of sergeant or corporal twice! The regimental commander then urged all company commanders "to test the qualities of each man before promotion, that none may be made hastily." Nevertheless, this warning did not prevent officers from awarding fifty-six promotions on a single day in March 1865, with an almost corresponding number of official reductions. Such wholesale replacements created instability within units and wreaked havoc with the morale of the troops.

To help simplify the training of black soldiers, Maj. Gen. Silas Casey, head of the examining board in Washington, D.C., and the author of the infantry tactics manual, prepared a new version specifically for the USCT. Despite Casey's good intentions, the entire notion was absurd and demeaning. Casey's goal was to make infantry tactics as elementary as possible to aid black troops in mastering them. "The tactics are about as simple as they can be made now and require but little intelligence in the individual in the ranks," Casey wrote of his new manual for black troops. "I don't see how they can be simplified more without destroying the efficiency of the system." The problems, however, were numerous. Black and white Union infantrymen were not using the same tactics manual, which could lead to a catastrophe in battle. For another, Casey had the USCT training with a more elementary manual simply because black soldiers, with presumed inferior intelligence, composed those commands. Finally, the entire effort at simplicity for the sake of black soldiers was ridiculous. Through its entire history, the United States Army had never prepared a tactical manual that fulfilled the needs of its enlisted men, because not enough of them were literate in English. According to the best authority, during the forty years before the war, between one-third and one-fourth of enlisted men were incapable of signing their own names on enlistment papers. In addition, during the 1850s a clear majority of the enlisted population were immigrants. Although many of them may have been literate, it was not in English, and in any event, they were not necessarily literate enough to comprehend a tactics manual. Though Casey's simplified version for the USCT merely eliminated a few tactical movements, it was not more readable. Furthermore, Regular Army troops had to depend on their officers to teach them infantry tactics, just as most black and many white soldiers did during the war, so that tactical manuals were in reality issued for officers' use. The officers of the USCT, as Casey well knew, had demonstrated their knowledge of tactics and other subjects, including reading and writing, and were just as capable of mastering either manual and explaining it cogently to their troops as any officers in the service.

There were no shortcuts in drilling the troops. Soldiers learned different tactical formations and maneuvers only through long and arduous hours of practice. "The men are willing and easy to drill," a colonel authoritatively stated to Adjutant General Lorenzo Thomas, "but only constant attendance and indefatigable energy on the part of the officers will make these regiments do Justice to the Uniform they wear." Officers labored with the men on the drill field hour after hour to pound the information into their heads. Yet despite its complex nature, most troops absorbed the training rapidly. Some officers argued that their troops' ability in drill was innate, derived from their love of music and dance, but more accurate was the opinion of a lieutenant who thought black soldiers were successful because they "pay better attention and take more pride in it than white soldiers do."

Instruction for guard duty required personalized attention, which over the course of a few weeks became extremely tedious. Night after night officers had to take a handful of new troops out to serve as pickets and explain their duty. On picket or guard duty, their job was to halt anyone from entering camp except those with the proper password, which changed daily. Because many black soldiers could not read, troops had to memorize the password; and after several hours at their posts, especially at night, some inevitably forgot the key words or phrase and caused a mix-up. Moreover, many troops had difficulty staying awake during those late-night hours, and officers had to check up on them continually to test their vigilance. As with drill, officers met with both failure and success. A captain found one of his sergeants asleep and discharged the soldier's weapon near his head to frighten him into performing his duty. Another officer, however, instructed his men in the art of guard duty, and despite their total lack of experience, "The tour went on more satisfactorily, if any different, than it would have done with the more experienced soldiers." In fact, one lieutenant thought black soldiers were more alert than white troops, because again they took greater pride in their labors. "They are good for pickett," he boasted. "The 'Johnnies' [Confederates] will have to be sharp to surprise them."

William Wells Brown on Black Troops at the Assault on Port Hudson[6]

With feeling, Brown recounts the story of the assault on Port Hudson, Louisiana, one of the first battles in which black troops proved, at great price in bloodshed, their willingness to fight and to fight bravely. There is no mistaking the fact that Brown's emotions were strongly engaged in his story. Contrary to his claim, however, Brig. Gen. William Dwight did not order a renewal of the assault merely for the purpose of killing the black troops under his command. Like many other Civil War officers, Dwight hoped that with a little more effort, success might be achieved. He was wrong, but the efforts of the black troops in these trying circumstances helped show whites that blacks would make good soldiers. It is also important to note that while history remembers primarily the black units in this action because of the remarkable transformation of their members' status from slaves to soldiers, here at Port Hudson, as in the more famous assault at Battery Wagner outside Charleston, South Carolina, white Union troops fought and died alongside their black comrades.

The First Louisiana Regiment, of which Brown writes here, was an unusual one in that it was composed of relatively well-to-do free blacks from New Orleans and was one of the few black regiments to have, for a time, some black officers. Brown correctly points out that the regiment, known as the New Orleans Native Guards in the pre-war Louisiana militia, "promptly offered its services to aid in crushing the Rebellion." He does not mention that it had previously offered its services to the Confederacy, but these had been declined. No blacks in significant numbers or any organized unit of blacks ever actually entered combat on behalf of the Confederacy.

The very atmosphere seemed as if it were from an overheated oven. The laying aside of all unnecessary articles or accoutrements, and the preparation that showed itself on every side, told all present that the conflict was near at hand. Gen. Dwight, whose antecedents with regard to the rights of the negro, and his ability to fight, were not of the most favorable character, was the officer in command over the colored brigade; and busy Rumor, that knows every thing, had whispered it about that the valor of the black man was to be put to the severest test that day.

The black forces consisted of the First Louisiana under Lieut.-Col. Bassett, and the Third Louisiana, under Col. Nelson. The line officers of the Third were white; and the regiment was composed mostly of freedmen [former slaves], many of whose backs still bore the marks of the lash, and the brave, stout hearts beat high at the thought that the hour had come when they were to meet their proud and unfeeling oppressors. The First was the noted regiment called "The Native Guard," which Gen. [Benjamin F.] Butler found when he entered New Orleans, and which so promptly offered its services to aid in crushing the Rebellion. The line-officers of this regiment were all colored, taken from amongst the most wealthy and influential of the free colored people of New Orleans. It was said that not one of them was worth less than twenty-five thousand dollars. The brave, the enthusiastic, and the patriotic, found full scope for the development of their powers in this regiment, of which all were well educated; some were fine scholars. One of the most efficient officers was Capt. André Cailloux, a man whose identity with his race could not be mistaken; for he prided himself on being the blackest man in the Crescent City. Whether in the drawing room or on parade, he was ever the centre of attraction. Finely educated, polished in his manners, a splendid horseman, a good boxer, bold, athletic, and daring, he never lacked admirers. His men were ready at any time to follow him to the cannon's mouth; and he was as ready to lead them. This regiment petitioned their commander to allow them to occupy the post of danger in the battle, and it was granted.

As the moment of attack drew near, the greatest suppressed excitement existed; but all were eager for the fight. Capt. Cailloux walked proudly up and down the line, and smilingly greeted the familiar faces of his company. Officers and privates of the white regiments looked on as they saw these men at the front, and asked each other what they thought would be the result. Would these blacks stand fire? Was not the test by which they were to be tried too severe? Col. Nelson being called to act as brigadier-general, Lieut.-Col. Finnegas took his place. The enemy in his stronghold felt his power, and bade defiance to the expected attack. At last the welcome word was given, and our men started. The enemy opened a blistering fire of shell, canister, grape, and musketry. The first shell thrown by the enemy killed and wounded a number of the blacks; but on they went. "Charge" was the word.

"Charge!" Trump and drum awoke:
Onward the bondmen broke;
Bayonet and sabre-stroke
Vainly opposed their rush.

At every pace, the column was thinned by the falling dead and wounded. The blacks closed up steadily as their comrades fell, and advanced within fifty yards where the rebels were working a masked battery, situated on a bluff where the guns could sweep the whole field over which the troops must charge. This battery was on the left of the charging line. Another battery of three or four guns commanded the front, and six heavy pieces raked the right of the line as it formed and enfiladed its flank and rear as it charged on the bluff. It was ascertained that a bayou ran under the bluff where the guns lay—a bayou deeper than a man could ford. This charge was repulsed with severe loss. Lieut.-Col. Finnegas was then ordered to charge, and in a well-dressed steady line his men went on the double-quick down over the field of death. No matter how gallantly the men behaved, no matter how bravely they were led, it was not in the course of things that this gallant brigade should take these works by charge. Yet charge after charge was ordered and carried out under all these disasters with Spartan firmness. Six charges in all were made. Col. Nelson reported to Gen. Dwight the fearful odds he had to contend with. Says Gen. Dwight, in reply, "Tell Col. Nelson I shall consider that he has accomplished nothing unless he take those guns." Humanity will never forgive Gen. Dwight for this last order; for he certainly saw that he was only throwing away the lives of his men. But what were his men? "Only niggers." Thus the last charge was made under the spur of desperation.

The ground was already strewn with the dead and wounded, and many of the brave officers had fallen early in the engagement. Among them was the gallant and highly cultivated Anselmo. He was a standard-bearer, and hugged the stars and stripes to his heart as he fell forward upon them pierced by five balls. Two corporals near by struggled between themselves as to who should have the honor of again raising those bloodstained emblems to the breeze. Each was eager for the honor; and during the struggle a missile from the enemy wounded one of them, and the other corporal shouldered the dear old flag in triumph, and bore it through the charge in the front of the advancing lines.

"Now," the flag-sergeant cried,
"Though death and hell betide,
Let the whole nation see
If we are fit to be
Free in this land, or bound
Down, like the whining hound—
Bound with red stripes and pain
In our old chains again."
Oh! What a shout there went
From the black regiment!

Dudley Taylor Cornish on the 54th Massachusetts[7]

One of the first and most famous of the Union's black regiments was the 54th Massachusetts, recruited at the urging of Governor John Andrew from both free blacks in the North and newly freed slaves in areas of the South that had come under Union control. The spring and summer of 1863 saw some of the first large-scale heavy fighting—and dying—by black troops at Milliken's Bend and Port Hudson, Louisiana, and at Battery Wagner, near Charleston, South Carolina, where the 54th kept its appointment with glory. In this passage, originally written in *The Sable Arm* (1956), Dudley Cornish, one of the foremost historians of black Civil War soldiers, tells the dramatic story of the 54th.

The regiment's white commander, Robert Gould Shaw, the scion of an upper-class Boston family, was anxious for the regiment to be given "honorable" duty—neither doing the fatigue work that often was the lot of black troops nor carrying out punitive raids against the Southern economy. Rather, Shaw wanted—and got—the chance to prove his men in the heat of battle.

"I know not, Mr. Commander, where, in all human history, to any given thousand men in arms there has been committed a work at once so proud, so precious, so full of hope and glory as the work committed to you." So spoke Governor John Andrew to Colonel Robert Gould Shaw of the 54th Massachusetts Infantry at the regiment's Readville camp. It was May 18 [1863], a fine cloudless day, and Readville was crowded with the friends and relatives of the men who made up the 54th. Fifteen hundred miles to the west, a detachment of the 1st Kansas Colored was fighting desperately near Sherwood, Missouri, to survive a surprise attack by guerrilla forces. At Readville, the 54th formed in line and moved into regimental square. The dignitaries gathered within the square of Negro companies, and the governor presented the colonel with four silken flags: a national emblem, the state colors, a regimental banner of white silk bearing the figure of the Goddess of Liberty, and another bearing a white cross in a field of blue and the Christian motto, *In Hoc Signo Vinces* [by this sign you will conquer]. More than a thousand spectators, white and colored, thronged the parade ground, among them Frederick Douglass, Wendell Phillips, Samuel May, Professor Louis Agassiz, and William Lloyd Garrison. On that same fair day the secretary of war telegraphed Andrew to have the new regiment report to General David Hunter at Hilton Head [South Carolina].

Ten days later, as the battered regiments of the Corps d'Afrique recovered some of their dead and wounded during a few hours of truce before Port Hudson [Louisiana], the 54th moved out of Readville, entrained for Boston, and there formed to march triumphantly through the flag-hung streets. Past Wendell Phillips's house the Negro regiment marched, reviewed by Garrison himself dramatically standing on a balcony, "his hand resting on a bust of John Brown." At the State House the governor and his staff joined the regiment, and they marched together to the Common. There Colonel Shaw led his men in review past the cream of Massachusetts society. After a rest, the regiment moved on again from the Common to Battery Wharf, the band playing John Brown's hymn as the blue ranks marched down State Street "over ground moistened by the blood of Crispus Attucks," a Negro victim of the Boston Massacre, "and over which Anthony Burns and Thomas Sims," Fugitive slaves, "had been carried back to bondage." At Battery Wharf the regiment embarked on the steamer *Demolay*; late in the afternoon the lines were cast off and the 54th moved south into action and immortality. . . .

General Hunter reported to Governor Andrew that the 54th arrived safely at Hilton Head on June 3. He promised the governor that his regiment would "soon be profitably and honorably employed." After a few days at Beaufort the Massachusetts men were ordered south to St. Simon's Island, Georgia, where Colonel Shaw reported to Colonel James Montgomery on June 9. The latter had been making forays along the coast of Georgia and Florida, and he lost no time in introducing the young Massachusetts colonel to amphibious raiding, Western style. On June 10, while the 54th was still pitching tents and settling into its new camp, Montgomery came to the wharf on a little steamer and, without even coming ashore, called out to Shaw:

"How soon can you be ready to start on an expedition?"

"In half an hour," Shaw replied, correctly reading the challenge implicit in Montgomery's question. Eight companies were readied for the raid, two remaining behind as camp guard. After picking up the old *John Adams* with five of Montgomery's companies aboard, the expedition set out, running up the coast to Doboy Sound, where two gunboats joined the party on June 11. The objective was the pretty little town of Darien, Georgia, on the Altamaha River. The gunboats "searched it with their shells," and the troops landed unopposed. The town was deserted. Montgomery gave orders for foraging parties to go to work, and in a short time the men returned burdened with "every species and all sorts and quantities of furniture, trinkets, etc." That was not all. "After the town was pretty thoroughly disembowelled," Shaw reported afterward, Montgomery turned to him with "a sweet smile" on his bearded face, and said in a quiet voice:

"I shall burn this town. . . . We are outlawed," he declared, "and therefore not bound by the rules of regular warfare." And by his express order, Darien was destroyed.

Shaw indignantly wrote Governor Andrew of the affair. He sent a second letter to Hunter's adjutant, Colonel Halpine, trying to find out if Montgomery was under orders to pillage and burn. The Darien expedition was the worst possible beginning for the career of the 54th. The regiment had been promised "honorable" work. The men had come south to fight rebels, not to burn the homes of defenseless civilians. The memory of Darien plagued Shaw for the rest of his short life.

His friends in the North were as shocked and disappointed as the young colonel. Charles Lowell wrote his fiancee, Shaw's sister: "I don't wonder Rob feels badly about this burning and plundering—it is too bad. Instead of improving the negro character and educating him for a civilized independence, we are re-developing all his savage instincts." Not content merely to sympathize, Lowell wrote William Whiting, solicitor of the War Department, arguing strongly against any repetition of the Darien outrage. "If burning and pillaging is to be the work of our black regiments," Lowell warned, "no first-rate officers will be found to accept promotion in them—it is not war, it is piracy more outrageous than that of [Confederate naval officer Raphael] Semmes.". . .

For whatever reasons, the 54th went on no more raids with Montgomery. The regiment settled into easy, pleasant camp life on St. Simon's, the island made famous by Fanny Kemble, whose husband, Pierce Butler, owned a large plantation there. The tropical idyll ended on June 24, when the regiment shipped north to St. Helena, across Port Royal Sound from Hilton Head. Hunter had been relieved, and Brigadier General Quincy A. Gillmore commanded the Department of the South. Preparations were under way for active operations against Charleston. As more and more regiments left St. Helena for Folly Island in the first days of July, Shaw became fearful that his men would have no chance to show what they could do. In July he wrote Brigadier General George C. Strong, who had briefly commanded at St. Helena, expressing his disappointment at being "left behind," especially since he "had been given to understand that we were to have a share in the work of this department." Convinced that his regiment was "capable of better service than mere guerrilla warfare," Shaw told Strong that it was "important that the colored soldiers should be associated as much as possible with the white troops, in order that they may have other witnesses besides their own officers to what they are capable of doing." Shaw's anxiety was eased on July 8 with the arrival of orders to have the regiment ready to move at an hour's notice.

General Gillmore was launching an offensive to seize Morris Island and with it control of the entrance to Charleston Harbor. The 54th was part of Alfred H. Terry's division, which was assigned to make a diversionary demonstration on James Island, west of Morris and due south of Charleston. With Folly Island as a jumping-off place, the main offensive got under way on July 10. The presence of Terry's 4,000 men on James Island made General P. G. T. Beauregard, commanding at Charleston, anxious for the safety of the city. He reduced his force on Morris to concentrate more men and guns on James. Terry's diversion had been more successful than Gillmore had hoped, and all of Morris Island south of Fort Wagner fell into Union hands. An assault on Wagner failed on July 11. The position was too strongly entrenched and heavily gunned.

Beauregard continued to mistake Terry's demonstration for the main Union attack, and in the gray dawn of July 16 he pushed his forces forward to remove what he considered dangerous pressure toward Charleston. So it was that on James Island the men of the 54th had their first taste of battle, of honorable soldier's work. Massachusetts pickets on the right of the Union line caught the brunt of the Confederate attack. If they had broken, the line must have been rolled up, the 10th Connecticut on the left of the 54th cut to pieces, and the rest of Terry's division caught off balance. Under fire for the first time, the companies of the 54th gave ground slowly, fighting desperately. Their action gave the Connecticut troops time to move from their dangerous position and gave the rest of the division time to form in line of battle and brace for the Confederate assault. It never came. The success of the dawn attack had depended on surprise, and the stubborn resistance of the Negro pickets on the Union right had spoiled what might otherwise have been an effective attack. . . .

His demonstration on James Island accomplished, Terry was ordered to evacuate it that night. Through blinding rain and with lightning flashes as their only illumination, the men of the 54th marched painfully back, literally feeling their way through the tangled marshland of James Island until, early in the morning of July 17, they reached a beach across from Folly Island. There, with no rations and little water, they waited through the day for transportation. They were under orders to report to General George Strong on Morris Island without delay. But there were delays. The transport *General Hunter* finally came for them, but there was no wharf, and they spent the entire night shuttling from beach to transport in a leaky longboat, thirty men at a time. It rained all night, and there were still no rations. On the morning of July 18 the *General Hunter* set them ashore on Folly Island, and they marched some six miles across the island and up the beach to Light House Inlet. There the tired and hungry men waited for transport to Morris Island. It was five o'clock in the afternoon before they were carried over.

Colonel Shaw went forward at once to report to General Strong. Fort Wagner had been under bombardment all day and was to be stormed that evening. Strong, undoubtedly thinking of Shaw's letter and his wish for "better service than mere guerrilla warfare," offered the 54th the honor of leading the assault. Shaw might have refused. His men had gone two nights without rest and two days without rations; they had been on the march most of the day. But the young colonel moved fatally and fatalistically. In a sense he could not refuse this supreme chance to prove the valor of his regiment. For two days he had had a presentiment of death; he seems to have moved like a man caught by Destiny. He had to discharge the duty committed to him and his thousand men in arms by Governor Andrew, his state, and the cause of the Union. He sent Adjutant Wilkie James back to bring up the regiment. This was to be their ordeal by fire.

The assault column, commanded by General Truman Seymour, was composed of three brigades, the first and heaviest under General Strong. Seymour afterwards defended the choice of the 54th to lead the first brigade, maintaining that the regiment "was in every respect as efficient as any other body of men, and as it was one of the strongest and best officered, there seemed to be no good reason why it should not be selected for the advance." After the assault columns had been formed, Strong and Shaw spoke briefly to the men of the 54th. Tensely the regiment stood there in the deepening twilight. The western sky was still bright with sunset afterglow, but a heavy sea fog was gathering over the Atlantic. Indistinct in the darkness ahead, the scarred and battered earthworks of Fort Wagner crouched, waiting. Three-quarters of a mile of level sand lay between the 54th and the defiant flag on those earthworks. To the left lay a salt marsh. On the right the long waves rolled in and broke on the hard-packed sand. There was no danger that the men would lose their way this night.

The signal was given.

As cool and straight as on parade at Readville but a little pale, Colonel Shaw threw away his cigar, took position in the center of the head of the column, and called his men to attention. The dark ranks stiffened on the narrow sands. The flags were lifted up into the ocean breeze. The guns growled hungrily in the distance.

"Move in quick time until within a hundred yards of the fort," Shaw told his men, "then, double-quick and charge!"

"Forward!" he commanded, and the 54th Massachusetts Infantry moved up the beach to meet its destiny. Behind came the 6th Connecticut, the 48th New York, the 3rd New Hampshire, the 9th

Maine, and the 76th Pennsylvania. Colonel Haldimand S. Putnam held his second brigade of four regiments in support.

[Fort] Wagner had been under artillery fire most of the day. Now came the Confederates' turn, and as the column moved forward to the attack, "the guns of Wagner, Gregg, Sumter, and also those on James and Sullivan's Islands opened upon it rapidly and simultaneously." The infantrymen in Wagner held their fire. As the 54th reached the narrowest part of the beach only two hundred yards from Wagner—the right flank men were up to their knees in sea water—"the firing from the navy and that of our own mortars and the gun batteries on the extreme left had to be suspended," General Gillmore reported, and "a compact and most destructive musketry fire was instantly delivered from the parapet by the garrison which, up to that moment, had remained safely ensconced in the bomb-proof shelters."

Into the storm of fire the 54th moved, at the double now, past the southeastern salient of the fort, into the deep ditch before it, up and over the curtain [that is, bastion wall], into Wagner itself. For a time the national and state flags waved on the parapet as the men of the regiment died under them. They fought with bayonet and clubbed rifle against artillery and rifle fire and grenades. Connecticut and New York troops clawed their way into the southeastern salient, but in the darkness their efforts were futile. Seymour sent in the supporting brigade, and although the salient was held for nearly three hours, the net result was an increased number of casualties, Colonel Putnam among them. It is more to be wondered that any men should have lived to gain the interior of Wagner than that the assault should have failed.

In military logic there had been some reason for the effort. The day-long artillery and naval bombardment of the fort had seemed effective. But the correct moment for assault probably came and passed in the afternoon. The hours between five and seven gave the Confederates time to brace for the attack. There was no possibility of surprise: preparations for the assault, every movement of Union troops, were observed from Wagner and other Confederate works in the vicinity. It was the kind of operation that can be justified only by success. It had failed. Colonel Shaw and three other officers of the 54th were killed; eleven other officers and 135 men were wounded; nearly a hundred were missing or taken prisoner. From a narrow military point of view the assault was without value. In a broader view, it was a valuable sacrifice.

Hardly another operation of the war received so much publicity or stirred so much comment. Out of it a legend was born. As a result of it Robert Gould Shaw came as close to canonization as a New England Puritan can. It took another New Englander to put it into words. The lines of James Russell Lowell on the Shaw Monument on Boston Common sum up the meaning of the assault of the 54th on Fort Wagner:

> Right in the van on the red rampart's slippery swell
> With heart that beat a charge he fell
> Foeward [*sic*] as fits a man.
> But the high soul burns on to light men's feet
> Where death for noble ends makes dying sweet.

Colonel Shaw and the 54th became symbols of the best that any troops, white or Negro, could do. "That a gentleman should leave a congenial place in the Second Massachusetts," James Ford Rhodes wrote a generation after the war, "and part from brothers in friendship as well as brothers in arms because his antislavery sentiment impelled him to take a stand against the prejudice in the army and in the country against negro soldiers; that he brought his regiment to a fine degree of discipline; that when the supreme moment came his blacks fought as other soldiers have always fought in desperate assaults—all this moved the hearts and swayed the minds of the Northern people to an appreciation of the colored soldier, to a vital recognition of the end which Lincoln strove for and to the purpose of fighting out the war until the negro should be free.". . .

He was buried at the head of his regiment, too; whether by malevolent design is beside the point. The North believed that Shaw was buried by the Confederates, as a gesture of contempt, in a ditch "with his niggers." The news swept across the North, and indignant reaction was swift and sure. Plans were made to attempt to recover his body, but a letter from Colonel Shaw's father to General Gillmore put a stop to the enterprise. "We hold," Francis Shaw wrote Gillmore, "that a soldier's most appropriate burial-place is on the field where he has fallen." Fort Wagner became not only the pinnacle of Colonel Shaw's short life, but also his abiding place for eternity.

After the assault on Fort Wagner on July 18 there was no longer any doubt about using Negro troops to crush the rebellion. In July of 1863, the turning point of the war, there were some thirty Negro regiments being organized or already in the field. By the end of the year the number had doubled, and the work was gathering momentum and even popularity. Joseph Holt, judge advocate general and former secretary of war, wrote Edwin M. Stanton in August of 1863: "The tenacious and brilliant valor displayed by troops of this race at Port Hudson, Milliken's Bend, and Fort Wagner has sufficiently demonstrated to the President and to the country the character of the service of which they are capable. . . . In view of the loyalty of this race," Holt continued, in words which could have been borrowed from Frederick Douglass, "and of the obstinate courage which they have shown themselves to possess, they certainly constitute, at this crisis in our history, a most powerful and reliable arm of the public defense."

Notes

1. William Wells Brown, *The Negro in the American Rebellion* (Boston: A. G. Brown, 1867; reprint, Miami: Mnemosyne Publishing, 1969), 142–46.

2. Eric Walther, *Shattering of the Union: The United States in the 1850s* (tentative title) (Wilmington, DE: Scholarly Resources, forthcoming).

3. James M. McPherson, *Battle Cry of Freedom: The Civil War Era* (New York: Oxford University Press, 1988), 563–67. © 1988 by Oxford University Press. Reprinted by permission of Oxford University Press.

4. Reid Mitchell, *The Vacant Chair: The Northern Soldier Leaves Home* (New York: Oxford University Press, 1993), 62–69. © 1995 by Reid Mitchell. Reprinted by permission of Oxford University Press.

5. Joseph T. Glatthaar, *Forged in Battle: The Civil War Alliance of Black Soldiers and White Officers* (Baton Rouge: Louisiana State University Press, 1990), 99–104.

6. Brown, *The Negro in the American Rebellion*, 167–73.

7. Dudley Taylor Cornish, *The Sable Arm: Black Troops in the Union Army, 1861–1865* (Lawrence: University Press of Kansas, 1987), 147–56. © 1987 by the University Press of Kansas. All rights reserved. Reprinted by permission of the University Press of Kansas.

CHAPTER EIGHT

On the Meaning of the War

During the century or so after the end of the Civil War, when sectional reconciliation seemed to be the top priority, many historians of the conflict tended to shy away from issues of the war's meaning. After all, if it actually had any meaning, then, as Lincoln once said, "Both sides may be, but one side must be, wrong." That would be divisive. So historians detailed camp life, traced campaigns and battles, and praised the soldiers' courage, but they ignored the causes for which the soldiers fought, leaving the conflict to appear, as Shakespeare's MacBeth describes life, "a tale told by an idiot, full of sound and fury, signifying nothing." But, of course, it *did* signify *something*, and the soldiers knew that. Some of them wrote as much during the first decades after the war. And, more recently, several scholars have taken up the question of what the war meant to the soldiers who fought it.

John C. Reed and the Lost Cause of Slavery[1]

Although proponents of the Lost Cause would eventually deny that slavery had ever had anything to do with the Civil War (and indeed some were already doing so), Confederate veteran John Reed thought otherwise. He tried to hold to the South's basic post-Reconstruction formula that Southerners had been braver and more virtuous than Northerners and had unquestionably been justified in going to war, but, paradoxically, that at the same time it was a blessing that the Union had been preserved and slavery abolished. The problem for Reed was that he did not really believe this. In his heart, he believed that the old slaveholding South had been a paradise for slave and master alike.

This idyllic cotton-growing Eden was in large part a figment of Reed's imagination, an old man's misty memory of the home of his youth. Nonetheless, like thousands of other former Confederate soldiers, Reed believed in it and believed it had been ruined by the abolition of slavery. Now every ill of the South was, in his mind, to be explained by emancipation, even to the loss of fruit trees to "a blight never known until of late." "A curse . . . rests on the fields," Reed lamented; everything had changed when slavery died. Here, too, he was dreaming. Many economic and agricultural factors combined to cause the difficulties that the South faced during the late nineteenth century. Meanwhile, in describing what he imagined to be the glories of the slave system, Reed's frankness is shocking. For him, the Civil War had been about slavery, and the tragedy was that slavery had lost.

There are but few in Middle Georgia now alive [in 1888] who will ever taste any blessings of the restored union except in immunity from war. When one looks in the south only at the growth of a few cities, the development here and there of manufactories, the multiplication of railways, the working of coal, iron, marble, and other rich minerals in a few places, and the largely increased cotton crop, he believes that an era of general prosperity has commenced. For the moment he forgets that the South has ever been and still is chiefly an agricultural people, and that her average planters and farmers have been steadily going from bad to worse since 1865. Let us give a brief explanation of this unavoidable decadence. For many years before 1861, slavery had become the favorite property. If a poor young man had laid by a few hundred dollars from his salary as overseer or teacher, or professional earnings, his parents or uncles and aunts influenced him to buy a negro woman with his money; if a trustee or guardian applied to a chancellor or probate judge to direct what he should do with the funds of beneficiaries or wards, he was generally ordered to invest in slaves, and in executing the order he would purchase as many child-bearing women as he could. If the master had no land, his slaves readily found hirers, and they would multiply. But as land was cheap, and an overseer could be had for a song even the slaves of infants were generally kept at home. Planting was almost the only employment of the community.

I wish to call attention to one peculiarity of planting. That is, it needed less annual outlay of money than any large business I can now call to mind. The owner of 750 acres of land, worth $6000.00, 30 slaves averaging $600.00 apiece, worth $18,000.00, and his mules and livestock worth $1000.00, had usually but five considerable items

of expense. If he employed an overseer—to use the current vogue—
he "found" him and his family, and paid him hardly ever more than
$150 a year for his wages; he bought a few sacks of salt to cure his
meat and to feed occasionally to his animals, and some pounds of
iron for his blacksmith shop; (and, as the fourth item) he paid his
family physician for treating the sick slaves—and he bought some
cloth for clothing. These four items would seldom amount to
$500.00; and remember his active capital was $50,000.00. He paid
no wages; he bred his slaves, and all the animals that he needed for
work, food, or pleasure; the clothing and shoes for the negroes they
made themselves; after lavishly feeding his black and white family,
he sold more than enough of meats, grain, and other produce to
pay his annual expense; and the $1,500.00 which he got for his yearly
crop of 30 bales of cotton was almost net pecuniary saving from
planting. This state of things would have in itself alone accounted
for prosperity. But another important peculiarity is yet to be noticed. That is, the increase of the slaves, which I will illustrate from
a case very well known to me.

In 1798 a man gave his niece a negro girl, named in the gift,
Tiller (a corruption of Matilda). In due time the mistress and the
slave became women, when the former married, and took Tiller to
her new home. In a little while Tiller married also. She bore only
four children, each a daughter. The daughters married—all of them
early—and every one was much more prolific than her mother. In
1856, fifty-eight years after the gift was made, the mistress and Tiller
were alive, and the living issue of Tiller numbered more than sixty,
and being—to use a slave-market phrase, very "likely"—they were
over $40,000.00 in value. The mistress—who had long been a
widow—was a very poor manager, and she had lived most of the
last twenty years by going in debt and now and then selling a negro
to pay out. At the date last mentioned she was still owning Tiller,
with about forty of her descendants, and these slaves were worth at
least $30,000.00. I could give many instances of a still more rapid
and large increase, but I select this one to emphasize the fact that
the slave-owner could become rich even when negligent and idle.
This woman never had any other property than Tiller and her descendants, and the increase of her estate was really rapid in spite of
great wastefulness on her part. Emancipation was the end of this.
Now a small farmer who employs but four hands to his two plows,
in wages, fertilizers that have come to general use since the war, the

purchase of meat, corn and other supplies that the slaves used to
produce, must needs lay out annually more than the planter did
who made sixty bales of cotton, as we have described above. If this
farmer gets 16 bales of cotton, at 8 cents, worth $640.00, and this
is rather above than below the average, more than half goes for
expenses.

This is a momentous change. It is so profound and complete
that I find only now and then a man who understands it. Let me try
to make it plainer, by contrasting the old and the new.

In the old days money grew of itself. Now constant watchful-
ness is needed to see that every dollar put out comes back with
addition. Even the small farmer, in order to keep from falling behind, must have a much higher degree of mercantile talent than he
could ever acquire under the former system. Accumulation of property is now possible only by severe and rigorous saving, and the
average planter and farmer knows nothing of that. And so, under
the instantaneous stoppage of the natural growth of wealth and the
instantaneous substitution therefore of a system of making money
by artificial processes only, the South has lost control of her railroads, and her rural population are yearly becoming poorer. The
two leading characteristics of former days which we have tried to
present clearly—namely, first, the very contracted opportunity given
for learning the management of commercial capital in the small
annual expense on the plantation, and second, the resistless temp-
tation to rely solely on the natural increase of the slaves for enrich-
ment—such increases being so constant and energetic as to
counteract and even conceal all common errors of waste and mistakes in expenditure—these two potent factors have given our people
an education utterly unsuited for present needs. Any important effect of the factors just mentioned must now be told.

After the industrious slave was turned into the holiday-taking
freedman, the planters came more and more every year to buy much
of the agricultural produce of which they once made a surplus, from
a people whose labor system had not been disorganized. To use a
current expression, most of them have long had their corn-cribs
and smoke-houses in the North-west [that is, the Midwest]; and
the only reason that the South can hold to the production of cotton
is because it will not grow in a higher latitude. That you have a
neighbor who by reason of his prosperity tempts you, in your straits,

to depend upon him for what you ought to do for yourself, is a disadvantage, and it may keep you poor for all of your life. The natural remedy for the evil we are now considering, is the immigration of industrious and thrifty laborers and small farmers. But such are kept away by the negroes.

And now I must try to particularize the great alteration in southern affairs under the causes which we have enumerated.

Woodstock [Georgia] is thirteen miles from Lexington [Georgia], and the road between the two has been familiar to me from my ninth year. In 1861, on each side, all along this road, there were laughing fields of corn and cotton, high worm [zigzag] fences around even the groves, and comfort, with royal hospitality and cheer, in every dwelling. Whenever one in this community had the need, in an hour he could raise a thousand dollars among his neighbors on his unsecured note or his mere word. Today that road which once seemed to wind about between gardens and parks, traverses a waste of fields, unfenced, worn and reddening, with a soil so evidently barren that I wonder as I look upon it what possible reward can come from its cultivation. The traveler will see only some little sign of prosperity at one or two farms. And so it is with all the surrounding country. . . .

To one who can recall what used to be, the sights everywhere, as he goes [down] a public road, are almost intolerable. The fresh painted mansion and the cluster of cozy cabins for the negroes around it; the variegated gardens; the conical potato banks that never failed; the full corn-crib, and the rudely built barn running over with provender, and stacks of surplus fodder outside; the spacious gin-house, where great garners of wheat were threshed and fanned in summer, and many pickings of cotton ginned in autumn and winter; the packing screw surmounted with its long hanging levers, and often almost concealed entirely to one looking from the road by a huge bulwark of cotton bales, roofed over with riven boards; the pampered brood mares, the blooded horses and sleek mules; the swine fattened from picking up the fallen fruit in summer, ranging the pea fields and afterwards rooting up the large leavings in the sweet potato patches, in autumn, and at last from being penned and surfeited with corn, in early winter; the pastures pleasantly diversified with shade, natural grass and running water; the high worm fences, annually repaired with two courses of rails at the top, those enclosing the pastures and stable yards increased in height by stakes reaching up and supporting riders above; the negroes, whether the children tumbling in the sun, those tending mansion, kitchen, garden and stable, the laborers with plane and chisel, or at forge, or in the fields, all in tidy clothes, smiling by day and dancing and singing by night—thrift, neatness, good fortune, happy content, spoken forth on every side—such an one as we have supposed to be traveling a public road finds that the scene we have just most inadequately described has vanished, and a disgusting ugliness has taken its place.

Fences cannot now be afforded, even for the ample compensation of saving the gleanings of the cultivated fields and the grass of the resting land for the stock of the owner, and so the no-fence law unavoidably comes in by local option. There are no nibbling sheep to keep down the under brush in the little oak woods that is left. The giant trees of the forest that made a background of relieving shade at every horizon—hardly any of them remain, and soon the stunted second growth pines will be the main supply of timber and fuel. The chestnuts, prized by the planter for their easily worked and durable timber, loved and resorted to by the children with their nurses for their fruit, and gazed upon by lovers of trees with admiration of their noble robes—all except a few of the oldest have died from grief, and their grey and fantastic trunks which stand along old hedgerows and in small clumps of woods are to him who knows their former glory horrible skeletons. The paint has worn off of the old dwellings; their porches and some of the chimneys have fallen; the roofs are leaking; and the cabins, the many outhouses, the cribs, the ginhouse, and the packing screw, after having been stripped of their plank and boards, are rotting down. Hardly any new houses are building except log cabins for the white and negro tenants, scattered about over the plantation in what are called "settlements." The seedling peach trees that once covered the small enclosures near every dwelling and also dotted the corners of the fences around all the open land, have given place to a few unhardy grafts which begin to bear a little earlier but cease long before the old ones did. . . . And all the other fruit trees but the volunteer plums die of a blight never known until of late.

And a curse too rests on the fields. The tenants giving rent in kind or money and the laborers who have a share of the crop, dic-

tate the mode of cultivation; they care nothing for horizontal plow-
ing or ditches. . . . As you look at the arable land you see everywhere the rising red of the poor subsoil. The planter makes
cotton—nothing but cotton—far more than was ever made with
his working force before. But he buys his meat, his flour, often
even his meal, and provender for his plow stock, and he buys on
credit at ruinous time price [that is, interest]. If you will but consider, you will understand how the greatly augmented yield of cotton is really no elevation of his condition but a serious depression.
His soil is rapidly exhausting, and he has no reserve of manure, or
of uncleared land. . . . Everywhere looks the desolate scene of bar-
renness. Shabbiness, like a corroding rust, has settled on houses,
gardens, fields, groves—on even the formerly bright and glossy
leaves of the trees. . . .

And the people are changed as much as the face of the country.
The free-holders who made three fourths of the armies of the Confederacy, those who survive, and their children, stagger under debt
constantly growing heavier, are losing their lands and becoming a
wretched tenantry, many of them falling to the condition of laborers. Their supplies are scant almost beyond belief. A great many
are without cows and gardens, and having no milk, vegetables or
fresh meat, they live chiefly upon cornbread, with an occasional
rasher of bacon. A country merchant of my acquaintance, a very
close and accurate observer, told me, in 1887, that numbers of them
buy everything they use but their water, and often have no other
food for themselves and their families but some nickel purchases
which they carry home in sacks or paper bags. A great increase of
the retail trade, mainly to fill the want of necessaries formerly produced, and the consequent acquisition of broad acres by the merchant, and the slightly elevated condition of a few negroes, while
the great mass of them are nearly the whole year round in rags and
the direst penury—these are all the appearance of improvement
that I can detect.

The once well-to-do, with exceptions diminishing in number
all the while, have generally descended to poverty. Their prolonged
wretchedness has been incalculable, and beyond that of any people
ever scourged by war, save when cities have been sacked, or districts wasted by fire and sword and the inhabitants sold into slavery.
Immediately upon emancipation it was developed as to many a

planter that his property remaining was utterly insufficient to pay his indebtment. This was but a trifle to him when his slaves averaged each in value from $500.00 to $1,000.00, but now, in the twinkling of an eye, it had changed into a fell adversary to drive him from home naked into the world, where he could not find a new occupation. The old men were attacked with heart disease, and soon nearly all of them had died. The survivors betook themselves to stay-laws and other legislation, which kept off the creditor a while. During several years, some who had caught the knack of managing freedmen made money while the famine prices of cotton prevailed. But the prices fell steadily; and when they reached present figures— that is, below ten cents a few years ago—there was hardly anybody sure of an income in the region I am describing except the small number who either rented out many acres or while being ostensibly planters were partly landlords and partly merchants of necessaries, reaping a great profit from tenants and laborers in favorable years but losing heavily in the many droughts which seem to have become more frequent than usual of late. . . .

Parents who think of the former comfort sicken with despair as they look forward. I have a friend in one of these counties who understands the deep change in all of its particulars better than any of my acquaintances. I said to him not long ago, "Why does so and so think so little of himself as to get drunk whenever he comes to town? He was very promising just before the war, and for ten years afterwards he kept the good opinion of all the county." My friend replied with feeling, "Why, as you know, he was reared in the good days, and he was bright enough to understand all of their promise. But now, for a long while, he has seen for himself and children no shunning of the destiny which is bringing them to live in a log cabin and on ash cake; and he tries to blind himself to this by intoxication." Yes, the condition almost universal is impoverishment steadily deepening into want. It is endurable by the young because they have known no better, and by the older because it seems preferable to the war, of which, with its sufferings, their remembrance is vivid. . . .

What, if I am thus reminded of our own Lost Cause! There is healing and solace. It is not in craven disparagement, not in ignoble forgetting of that for which we fought. It is in understanding and loving to the full all of its dearness, and, by resigning it, for this life, making it safe and fast forever. The fair old time, fairer under roof, in grove or in field or by stream, in sun or shade, solitary or with my mates—oh, fairer than I can tell!

Larry M. Logue on Confederate Motivation[2]

During the closing months of the war, thousands of men deserted from the Confederate army as they gave up hope of victory. In *To Appomattox and Beyond: The Civil War Soldier in War and Peace* (1996), historian Larry Logue comments on the question of why 160,000 Southern soldiers did not desert, and in so doing makes some observations about what motivated them to stay in the army. In doing so, he bears out what John Reed had written over a century before.

Why did anyone remain in the army under these circumstances [of hardship and impending defeat]? The South had no reenlistment crisis comparable to the Union's in 1864, because in February its Congress simply extended the terms of three-year men. This act surely encouraged more desertions, but a number of soldiers also took part in symbolic "reenlistments" to raise morale (and to earn furloughs). Simple duty and patriotism explain much of soldiers' perseverance: a Confederate general, for example, felt "honor bound to fight to the bitter end, unless authorities should direct otherwise."

Yet there were other motives woven into patriotic sentiments. In a North Carolina study, desertion rates were especially low among merchants, professionals such as physicians and lawyers, and men from slaveholding areas; deserters were likewise uncommon among slaveholders in Alabama and in a regiment from Virginia's "black belt." Men from the Southern gentry undoubtedly fought on because they could not bear the destruction of their society—an ordered society with propertied gentlemen at the top, setting an example of leadership for all white men. Yankees promised to take away their property and their right to lead, and to make blacks equal with whites—a society not worth living in. Other soldiers found their loyalty to state and country mixed with loyalty to comrades. Deserting a doomed cause was one thing, but abandoning comrades, the only people who truly understood what soldiers had

endured, was unthinkable. And so men made agonizing choices between conflicting ways of surviving, conflicting duties, and conflicting loyalties.

James M. McPherson on the Cause of Liberty[3]

James McPherson's 1997 book *For Cause and Comrades: Why
Men Fought in the Civil War* is the foremost study of soldier motivations during that conflict. With a basis in extensive research, McPherson advances a sophisticated explanation of what moved the Civil
War soldiers to fight, showing various factors that drove men into the
armies and into battle. In a chapter entitled "The Cause of Liberty,"
he discusses the significance of the heritage of the American Revolution and the determination of the Civil War generation to preserve for
the next generation the freedom that struggle had bequeathed to them.

The patriotism of Civil War soldiers existed in a specific historical context. Americans of the Civil War generation revered their
Revolutionary forebears. Every schoolboy and schoolgirl knew how
they had fought against the odds to forge a new republic conceived
in liberty. Northerners and Southerners alike believed themselves
custodians of the legacy of 1776. The crisis of 1861 was the great
test of their worthiness of that heritage. On *their* shoulders rode
the fate of the great experiment of republican government launched
in 1776. Both Abraham Lincoln and Jefferson Davis appealed to
this intense consciousness of parallels between 1776 and 1861. That
is why Lincoln began his great evocation of Union war aims with
the words: "Four score and seven years ago our fathers brought
forth . . . a new government, conceived in Liberty and dedicated to
the proposition that all men are created equal." Likewise, Davis
urged his people to "renew such sacrifices as our fathers made to
the holy cause of constitutional liberty."

The profound irony of the Civil War was that, like Davis and
Lincoln, Confederate and Union soldiers interpreted the heritage
of 1776 in opposite ways. Confederates professed to fight for liberty and independence from a tyrannical government; Unionists
said they fought to preserve the nation conceived in liberty from
dismemberment and destruction. These conflicting impulses, which
had propelled many volunteers into the armies at the war's beginning, became more intense as the fighting escalated.

Patriotic holidays had a special tendency to call forth meditations by Confederate soldiers on the legacy for which they fought. "How trifling were the wrongs complained of by our Revolutionary forefathers, compared with ours!" wrote a captain in the 5th Alabama on Washington's Birthday in 1862. "If the mere imposition of a tax could raise such a tumult what should be the result of the terrible system of oppression instituted by the Yankees?" On the Fourth of July that same year a Kentuckian who had cast his lot with the Confederacy reflected upon George Washington, "who set us an example in bursting the bonds of tyranny." On the same date a year later an Alabama corporal who had just been captured at Gettysburg was not disheartened. Soldiers of the Revolution had endured many setbacks, he noted in his diary, and in fighting for "the same principles which fired the hearts of our ancestors in the revolutionary struggle" the Confederacy would ultimately prevail.

This folk memory of snatching victory from the jaws of defeat four score years earlier sustained the morale of Confederate soldiers during times of discouragement. A wealthy South Carolina planter and a North Carolina farmer's son who both served in elite regiments on the Virginia front wrote similar letters to boost spirits at home after a string of Confederate reverses in early 1862. "Times may grow a great deal worse than they now are," wrote the South Carolinian, "and still we can stand it—And even then not go through what our Grandparents went through, when they were struggling for the same thing that we are now fighting for." The North Carolinian told his father that "instead of indulging in feelings of despondency let us compare our situation and cause to those of our illustrious ancestors who achieved the liberties we have ever enjoyed and for which we are now contending." During the retreat from Gettysburg, a captain in the 50th Georgia learned of the surrender of Vicksburg. "What a calamity!" he wrote to his wife. "But let us not despair. . . . Our forefathers were whipped in nearly every battle & yet after seven years of trials & hardships achieved their independence."

The rhetoric of liberty that had permeated the letters of Confederate volunteers in 1861 grew even stronger as the war progressed. A corporal in the 9th Alabama celebrated his twentieth birthday in 1862 by writing proudly in his diary that "I am engaged in the glorious cause of liberty and justice, fighting for all that we of the South hold dear." The lieutenant colonel of the 10th Tennessee declared in May 1862 that "my whole heart is in the cause of the Confederacy, because I believe that the perpetuity of Republican principles on this Continent depends upon our success." A year later he was killed in the battle of Raymond. In a letter to his Unionist father early in 1863, the son of a Baltimore merchant tried to explain why he was fighting for the Confederacy as a private in the 44th Virginia. The war, he wrote, was "a struggle between Liberty on one side, and Tyranny on the other," and he had decided to "espouse the holy cause of Southern freedom"—for which he gave his life three months later at Chancellorsville. . . .

The opposites of independence and liberty were "subjugation" and "slavery." These two words continued to express the fate worse than death that awaited Confederate soldiers if they lost the war. "If we was to lose," a Mississippi private wrote his wife in 1862, "we would be slaves to the Yanks and our children would have a yoke of bondage thrown around there neck." An enlisted man in the 8th Georgia was "ready to fight them 50 years rather than have them subjugate so noble a people as we are." And a Texas cavalryman who rode with [Nathan Bedford] Forrest agreed that the issue was "either subjugation, slavery, confiscation" or "victorious, glorious, and free."

These soldiers were using the word *slavery* in the same way that Americans in 1776 had used it to describe their subordination to Britain. Unlike many slaveholders in the age of Thomas Jefferson, Confederate soldiers from slaveholding families expressed no feelings of embarrassment or inconsistency in fighting for their own liberty while holding other people in slavery. Indeed, white supremacy and the right of property in slaves were at the core of the ideology for which Confederate soldiers fought. "We are fighting for our liberty," wrote a young Kentucky Confederate, "against tyrants of the North . . . who are determined to destroy slavery." A South Carolina planter in the Army of Northern Virginia declared a willingness to give his life "battling for liberty and independence" but was exasperated when his supposedly faithful body servant ran away to the Yankees. "It is very singular and I can't account for it." A captain in the 15th Georgia who owned forty slaves wrote to his wife in 1863 of "the arch of liberty we are trying to build." When she voiced apprehension about the future of slavery, he assured her that if the Confederacy won the war "it is established for centuries.". . .

Before the war many Southern whites had avoided using the words *slaves* and *slavery*, preferring instead *servants* and *Southern institutions*. Some Confederate soldiers kept up this custom even in private letters, referring to "our own social institutions," "the integrity of all our institutions," "the institutions of the whole South" as the cause for which they fought. In June 1863 a lieutenant in the 2nd North Carolina stopped for a meal at the home of a Pennsylvania farmer during the Gettysburg campaign. "They live in real Yankee style wife & daughters . . . doing all the work," he wrote to his mother. "It makes me more than ever devoted to our own Southern institutions."

A lieutenant in the 53rd Georgia, however, indulged in no euphemisms or circumlocutions. "Pennsylvania is the greatest country I ever saw," he wrote to his wife on the eve of the battle of Gettysburg. "If this state was a slave state and I was able to buy land here after the war you might count on living in Pennsylvania." In January 1865 this same officer whipped his body servant for stealing some of the company's meat allotment. "I give him about four hundred lashes. . . . Mollie you better believe I tore his back and legs all to pieces."

Other soldiers were equally plain-spoken. "This country without slave labor would be completely worthless," wrote a lieutenant in the 28th Mississippi in 1863. "We can only live & exist by that species of labor: and hence I am willing to fight to the last." A captain in the 8th Alabama also vowed "to fight forever, rather than submit to freeing negroes among us. . . . [We are fighting for] rights and property bequeathed to us by our ancestors."

Some Confederate soldiers welcomed Lincoln's Emancipation Proclamation for bringing the real issue into the open. "The Proclamation is worth three hundred thousand soldiers to our Government at least," wrote a Kentucky cavalry sergeant who rode with John Hunt Morgan. "It shows exactly what this war was brought about for and the intention of its damnable authors." A captain in the 27th Virginia, a small slaveholder in the Shenandoah Valley, believed that "after Lincoln's proclamation any man that would not fight to the last should be hung as high as Haman."* Several Union soldiers regretted the Proclamation on just these grounds that it

---

*In the biblical book of Esther, Haman was an enemy of the Jews who was hanged for plotting against them.—Editor's note

would make the enemy fight harder. "My hopes (if I had any) of a speedy termination of the war is thereby nocked in [the] head," wrote a New York corporal, "for I know enough of the southern spirit that I think they will fight for the institution of slavery even to extermination."

Confederate prospects for victory appeared brightest during the months after the Emancipation Proclamation, partly because this measure divided the Northern people and intensified a morale crisis in Union armies. Slave prices rose even faster than the rate of inflation during that springtime of Southern hope. A number of soldiers wrote home advising relatives to invest in slaves. "Every species of property is selling now at a very high price—Negroe men for $1500 to 2000, fancy girls & women with one or two children at about the same," wrote a navy captain commanding the CSS *Morgan*. "I will buy five or six more if I can get them right." The famous "boy colonel" of the Confederacy, the planter's son Henry Burgwyn, who became colonel of the 26th North Carolina at the age of twenty-one, urged his father to put every dollar he had into slaves. "I would buy boys & girls from 15 to 20 years old & take care to have a majority of girls," he wrote. "The increase in the number of negroes by this means would repay the difference in the amount of available labor. . . . I would not be surprised to see negroes in 6 mos. after peace worth from 2 to 3000 dollars." Gettysburg cut short his life before he could witness the collapse of his dreams. . . .

These soldiers, of course, belonged to slaveholding families. They tended to emphasize the right of property in slaves as the basis of the liberty for which they fought. This motive, not surprisingly, was much less in evidence among nonslaveholding soldiers. But some of them emphasized a form of property they did own, one that was central to the liberty for which they fought. That property was their white skins, which put them on a plane of civil equality with slaveholders and far above those who did not possess that property. Herrenvolk democracy—the equality of all who belonged to the master race—was a powerful motivator for many Confederate soldiers.

Even though he was tired of the war, wrote a Louisiana artilleryman in 1862, "I never want to see the day when a negro is put on an equality with a white person. There is too many free niggers . . . now to suit me, let alone having four millions." A private in the 38th North Carolina, a yeoman farmer, vowed to show the Yankees "that a white man is better than a nigger.". . . Many Northern soldiers shared the bewilderment of a private in the 25th Wisconsin who wrote home describing a conversation with Confederate prisoners captured in the Atlanta campaign: "Some of the boys asked them what they were fighting for, and they answered, 'You Yanks want us to marry our daughters to the niggers.' "

Such sentiments were not confined to nonslaveholders. Many slaveholding soldiers also fought for white supremacy as well as for the right of property in slaves. An Arkansas captain was enraged by the idea that if the Yankees won, his "sister, wife, and mother are to be given up to the embraces of their present 'dusky male servitors.' " After reading Lincoln's Proclamation of Amnesty and Reconstruction in December 1863, which required Southern acceptance of emancipation as a condition of peace, another Arkansas soldier, a planter, wrote his wife that Lincoln not only wanted to free the slaves but also "declares them entitled to all the rights and privileges as American citizens. So imagine your sweet little girls in the school room with a black wooly headed negro and have to treat them as their equal." Likewise, a Georgia infantry captain wrote to his wife from the trenches on the Chattahoochee in 1864 that if Atlanta and Richmond fell, "the negro who now waits on you will then be as free as you are & as insolent as she is ignorant."

It would be wrong, however, to assume that Confederate soldiers were constantly preoccupied with this matter. In fact, only 20 percent of the sample of 429 Southern soldiers explicitly voiced proslavery convictions in their letters or diaries. As one might expect, a much higher percentage of soldiers from slaveholding families expressed such a purpose: 33 percent, compared with 12 percent. Ironically, the proportion of Union soldiers who wrote about the slavery question was greater. . . . There is a ready explanation for this apparent paradox. Emancipation was a salient issue for Union soldiers because it was controversial. Slavery was less salient for most Confederate soldiers because it was not controversial. They took slavery for granted as one of the Southern "rights" and institutions for which they fought, and did not feel compelled to discuss it. . . .

Confederates who professed to fight for the same goals as their forebears of 1776 would have been surprised by the intense conviction of Northern soldiers that they were upholding the legacy of the Revolution. A sergeant in the 1st Minnesota proudly told his parents that he fought for "the same glorious ensign that floated over [Fort] Ticonderoga, [and] was carried triumphantly through the Revolution." A schoolteacher with several children of his own, who had enlisted in the 20th Connecticut on his thirty-sixth birthday, celebrated his decision to fight for "those institutions which were achieved for us by our glorious revolution . . . in order that they may be perpetuated to those who may come after." An Illinois farm boy whose parents had opposed his enlistment in 1862 asked them tartly a year later: "Should We the youngest and brightest nation of all the earth bow to traters and forsake the graves of our Fathers?" He answered his own question: "No no never never.". . .

The theme of parallel sacrifice with the patriots of 1776 appeared in the letters of many Union soldiers. An officer in the 101st Ohio wrote in December 1862 that "our fathers in coldest winter, half clad marked the road they trod with crimson stream from their bleeding feet that we might enjoy the blessings of a free government," and therefore "our business in being here [is] to lay down our lives if need be for our country's cause." Two weeks later he was killed at Stone's River. A young private in the 2nd Michigan was killed in action less than a year after he had written a letter to his uncle describing the hardships of a soldier's life. But "did the revolutionary patriots in valley forge," he asked rhetorically, "complain [when] they had to march in the snow with there bare feet and to stand the cold twenty degrees below zero without blankets? We will show our fathers and mothers wifes sisters brothers and sweethearts that we are" worthy of that heritage.

Some of those wives, however, told their soldier husbands that they had a greater responsibility to their present families than to the Founding Fathers. A lieutenant in the 41st Ohio received several such letters from his wife complaining about the burdens of raising three children while worrying about his fate. In response, he asked her to "bear your trouble with good cheer. . . . It only gives another trouble on my mind to know that you are so discontented. . . . If you esteem me with a true woman's love you will not ask me to disgrace myself by deserting the flag of our Union.". . . Justifying to his wife a decision to stay in the army instead of seeking a medical discharge after he was wounded, a thirty-three-year-old Minnesota sergeant, also a father of three children, wrote that "my grandfather fought and risked his life to bequeath to his posterity . . . the glorious Institutions" now threatened by "this infernal rebellion. . . . It is not for you and I, or us & our dear little ones, alone, that I was and am willing to risk the fortunes of the battlefield, but also for the sake of the country's millions who are to come after us."

What were those "glorious Institutions"? An officer in the 54th Ohio defined them as "the guaranty of the rights of property, liberty of action, freedom of thought, religion [and] . . . that kind of government that shall assure life liberty & the pursuit of happiness." But a Confederate soldier would have said that he fought for the same things. His Union adversary might have replied, like Lincoln, that secession was "the essence of anarchy," a challenge to constitutional law and order without which liberty becomes license and leads in turn to despotism. The Founding Fathers fought a revolution and adopted a Constitution to achieve *ordered* liberty under the rule of law. Southern states had seceded in response to Lincoln's election by a constitutional majority in a fair vote held under rules accepted by all parties. To permit them to get away with it, said Lincoln, would be to "fly to anarchy or to despotism.". . .

To an Ohio blacksmith, the cause for which he fought as a private in the 70th Ohio was "the cause of the constitution and law. . . . Admit the right of the seceding states to break up the Union at pleasure . . . and how long will it be before the new confederacies created by the first disruption shall be resolved into still smaller fragments and the continent become a vast theater of civil war, military license, anarchy, and despotism? Better settle it at what cost and settle it forever."

Earl J. Hess on the Ideology of Northern Soldiers[4]

In *Liberty, Virtue, and Progress* (1997), historian Earl Hess deals with the motivations of Northern soldiers and civilians during the Civil War. He too discusses the idea of liberty as it applied to the Union soldiers' concept of the meaning of the war. In the passage that follows, he looks especially at how Northerners used their belief in freedom and the virtue of the Union cause to sustain them through times of great bloodshed.

When Northerners asserted ideology as the motive and aim of their war, they made a conscious effort to defy the experience of battle and all it implied about subordinating ideas to emotions and physical safety. By sustaining the war effort, they continued to hold the idea of liberty as a viable model of government. They believed that support for the Northern form of governance was support for freedom.

"Better lose a million men in battle than allow the government to be overthrown," wrote army officer and future president James Garfield. Adin Ballou, an obscure private in the 10th Maine Infantry, echoed Garfield's sentiments. Ruminating on battle and "suspicious [*sic*] that Death is creeping behind me with his fatal dart," Ballou assured his wife that he knew "how American Civilization now leans upon the triumph of the Government and how great a debt we owe to those who went before us through the blood and suffering of the Revolution; and I am willing [*sic*] perfectly willing to lay down all my joys in this life to help maintain this Government."

Although much of this rhetoric appeared before the soldier experienced battle, it continued even after he fought and suffered. Before his first engagement, Dietrich Smith of Illinois had often written of his willingness to die for the cause. Suffering a shoulder wound at Shiloh, he did not lose his enthusiasm for the values he believed his nation embodied. Even as the wound continued to discharge bone fragments, he repeated his willingness to return to duty.

The inevitable suffering severely tested motives, and many Northerners were able to affirm their convictions only after wracking doubts. The experience of war had the power to turn an individual in on himself, and to drive his thoughts inward and away from contemplation of the larger good. The suffering had the power to make Northerners self-centered and obsessed with their emotional and physical pain, forgetting the goals that could benefit the nation as well as themselves.

Ebenezer Hannaford of Ohio left an amazing description of his wound and near death at Stone's River. He was unique only in his ability to write engrossingly about it, for his experience represented that of thousands of his less-articulate comrades. Severely wounded in the neck, Hannaford found his thoughts absorbed by the physical effects of the wound. Nothing seemed to concern him but the pain. Not until he found a relatively quiet, safe place to hide from the bullets, where he believed he would die, did he have an opportunity to ponder the meaning of his sacrifice. "Thank God, death did not seem so dreadful," he reasoned, "now that it was come. And then the sacrifice was not all in vain, falling thus in God's own holy cause of Freedom."

Sent to a Nashville hospital, Hannaford faced many months of uncertain recovery. It was a horrible time during which he became obsessed with the thought of dying. On two occasions Hannaford's neck wound hemorrhaged, and he nearly lost his life. The end result of this slow agony became palpable to him in the hospital rooms. "It was there that Death drew near and bent over my pillow, so close that I could feel his icy breath upon my cheek, while in mute, ghastly silence we looked steadfastly each in the other's face for weeks together." Indeed, Hannaford felt such peaceful release ("a quiet, painless lethargy was stealing over my brain") that on one occasion when his wound bled profusely, splattering the nearby wall with red patches, he felt angry at the doctor for stopping the flow of blood and bringing him back to consciousness. "Those moments of syncope, when over my soul had rolled the waters of oblivion, I seemed to feel had been a very heaven of delight, and it was a pitiful service to recall me thence to life and suffering again."

Hannaford spent over a year in hospitals before his neck had healed enough that he was able to return home. For months on end, his wound drew his thoughts away from the war and into himself. It was not until his fellow patients, engaged in a songfest to pass away the time, happened to sing "The Battle Cry of Freedom" that his consciousness recalled the larger meanings of the war. No other song of the North better expressed the basic motive for fighting. [See epigraph preceding Acknowledgments.] For Hannaford, its sentiments justified the long months of agony. The song "thrilled me inexpressibly," he recalled later. "The early days of the war; the grand uprising of the loyal North; the wild burning enthusiasm of those [Fort] Sumter times . . . the grand infinitude of principle—of Right, and Truth, and Justice—that was underlying the whole fierce struggle, and had made our Cause one that it was, oh! how noble a thing to have fought and suffered for, and, if need be, yet to die for!"

Notes

1. John C. Reed manuscript, Alabama Department of Archives and History, Montgomery, Alabama. Reprinted by permission of the Alabama Department of Archives and History. Reed's long paragraphs have been divided for the reader.

2. Larry M. Logue, *To Appomattox and Beyond: The Civil War Soldier in War and Peace* (Chicago: Ivan R. Dee, 1996), 80–81. © 1996 by Larry M. Logue. Reprinted by permission of Ivan R. Dee, Publisher.

3. James M. McPherson, *For Cause and Comrades: Why Men Fought in the Civil War* (New York: Oxford University Press, 1997), 104–12. © 1997 by Oxford University Press. Reprinted by permission of Oxford University Press.

4. Earl J. Hess, *Liberty, Virtue, and Progress: Northerners and Their War for the Union* (New York: Fordham University Press, 1997), 33–35. Reprinted by permission of Fordham University Press.

ISBN 0-8420-2930-3

90000 >

9 780842 029308